Austria Made in Hollywood

Maria von Trapp, watching the final scene of *The Sound of Music* for the first time as "her" family escaped into Switzerland, exclaimed, "Don't they know geography in Hollywood? Salzburg does not border on Switzerland!" Had she thought about the beginning of the film, which transports viewers to "Salzburg, Austria in the last Golden Days of the Thirties," when the country was in fact suffering from extreme political and social unrest, she might have asked, "Don't they know history either?" In *The Sound of Music* as well as in Hollywood's many other "Austria" films, the projections on the screen resemble reflections in a funhouse mirror. Elements of a "real" place with a "real" history inhabited by "real" people can be found in the fractured distortions, which have both drawn from and contributed to the general public's perceptions of the country and its citizens.

Austria Made in Hollywood focuses on films set in an identifiable Austria, examining them through the lenses of the historical contexts on both sides of the Atlantic and the prism of the ever-changing domestic film industry. The study chronicles the protean screen images of Austria and Austrians that set them apart both from European projections of Austria and from Hollywood incarnations of other European nations and nationals. It explores explicit and implicit cultural commentaries on domestic and foreign issues inserted in the Austrian stories while considering the many, sometimes conflicting forces that shaped the films.

Screen Cultures: German Film and the Visual

Series Editors
Gerd Gemünden (*Dartmouth College*)
Johannes von Moltke (*University of Michigan*)

Also in this series

Screening War, edited by Paul Cooke and Marc Silberman (2010)

A New History of German Cinema, edited by
Jennifer M. Kapczynski and Michael D. Richardson (2012)

The Counter-Cinema of the Berlin School, by Marco Abel (2013)

Generic Histories of German Cinema, edited by Jaimey Fisher (2013)

*The Autobiographical Turn in Germanophone
Documentary and Experimental Film*, edited by
Robin Curtis and Angelica Fenner (2014)

DEFA after East Germany, edited by
Brigitta B. Wagner (2014)

Last Features, by Reinhild Steingröver (2014)

The Nazi Past in Contemporary German Film, by Axel Bangert (2014)

Continuity and Crisis in German Cinema, 1928–1936, edited by
Barbara Hales, Mihaela Petrescu, and Valerie Weinstein (2016)

Forgotten Dreams, by Laurie Ruth Johnson (2016)

Montage as Perceptual Experience, by Mario Slugan (2017)

Film and Fashion amidst the Ruins of Berlin,
by Mila Ganeva (2018)

Gender and Sexuality in East German Film, edited by
Kyle Frackman and Faye Stewart (2018)

Celluloid Revolt: German Screen Cultures and the Long 1968,
edited by Christina Gerhardt and Marco Abel (2019)

*Moving Images on the Margin: Experimental Film in Late Socialist
East Germany*, by Seth Howes (2019)

The Films of Konrad Wolf: Archive of the Revolution,
by Larson Powell (2020)

Austria Made in Hollywood

Jacqueline Vansant

Rochester, New York

Copyright © 2023 Jacqueline Vansant

All Rights Reserved. Except as permitted under current legislation, no part of this work may be photocopied, stored in a retrieval system, published, performed in public, adapted, broadcast, transmitted, recorded, or reproduced in any form or by any means, without the prior permission of the copyright owner.

First published 2019 by Camden House
Reprinted in paperback 2023

Camden House is an imprint of Boydell & Brewer Inc.
668 Mt. Hope Avenue, Rochester, NY 14620, USA
and of Boydell & Brewer Limited
PO Box 9, Woodbridge, Suffolk IP12 3DF, UK
www.boydellandbrewer.com

Paperback ISBN-13: 978-1-64014-158-2
Hardcover ISBN-13: 978-1-57113-945-0

Library of Congress Cataloging-in-Publication Data

CIP data is available from the Library of Congress.

Contents

List of Illustrations	vii
Acknowledgments	ix
Introduction	1
1: Erich Stroheim, His Austria(ns), and Their US Contexts	23
2: Cross-Cultural Encounters of the Intimate Kind: Hollywood's Americans in Love with Austria(ns), 1932–60	39
3: The Empire Strikes Back: Imperial Austria Fights Nazis, 1938–41	69
4: Reflections and Refractions of the Anschluss on the Hollywood Screen, 1941–42	95
5: Confronting and Escaping History: *The Cardinal* (1963) and *The Sound of Music* (1965)	113
Conclusion: Hollywood's Austria—Its Past, Present, Future	131
Appendix: Hollywood Films Set in Austria	137
Notes	141
Bibliography	167
Index	191

Illustrations

I.1.	A square in "Old-Vienna" at the World's Columbian Exposition, Chicago, 1893	8
I.2.	Concert program of the Austrian Infantry Band at the World's Columbian Exposition, Chicago, 1893	9
1.1.	Drunken fathers arranging their children's marriage at a brothel in *The Wedding March*	29
2.1.	Jenny Kent and Count Franz von Degenthal in the nursery of the Degenthal family castle on the day of its auction in *Evenings for Sale*	43
2.2.	Ballroom flashback in *Champagne Waltz*	51
2.3.	Suggested advertisement from the pressbook for *The Emperor Waltz*	56
3.1.	Adolf Hitler giving a speech on the balcony of the Imperial Palace, Vienna, March 1938	76
3.2.	Emperor Franz Josef and Johann Strauss Jr. on the balcony at Schönbrunn in *The Great Waltz*	76

Acknowledgments

WHEN I GAVE THE TALK "Maria von Trapp meets Harry Lime" at the conference "Austria: A Small State in the Shadow of a Superpower" in November 1994, I had no intention of writing a book. However, the seeds for this project were sown after Ursula Prutsch asked me to contribute to the collection *Das ist Österreich: Innen- und Außensichten* (1997). While working on the article, I discovered a treasure trove of Austria films made in Hollywood studios. One thing led to another, and I have worked periodically on this book for more than two decades. Exploring the many versions of Hollywood's Austria has been fun, informative, eye-opening, amusing, at times disconcerting, and above all intriguing. For her invitation, which set the wheels for this project in motion, I thank Ursula.

Along the way I have had generous financial support from a variety of institutions, beginning with my home institution the University of Michigan-Dearborn and our mother ship the University of Michigan-Ann Arbor. The funds supported two trips to the Harry Ransom Humanities Research Center at The University of Texas at Austin, (1994–95), numerous trips to film archives in California, a trip to the Library of Congress (2005), one to the British Film Museum (2007), and a trip to the University of Syracuse (2010). In 2003, I received a Dorot Fellowship from the Harry Ransom Humanities Research Center at The University of Texas at Austin, where I studied the Ernst Lehmann collection and his work on *The Sound of Music*. In summer 2004 I was awarded a research grant for German exile studies from the Leon Feuchtwanger Archives at the University of Southern California, where I was able to examine the Marta Mierendorff papers. In summer 2007 I participated in the NEH Summer Seminar entitled "German Exile Community in California" hosted at Stanford University, where I presented some preliminary findings. There I received valuable feedback from the director Russell Berman and the participants. I am particularly grateful to James (Chip) Parsons, who offered his musical expertise as we watched *Florian*. In winter 2011 I was awarded a Botstiber Grant, which freed me from teaching and administrative duties and allowed me to visit the Margaret Herrick Library and complete substantial parts of the manuscript. Under the auspices of a Fulbright Grant in 2016 I taught a course at the University of Vienna entitled "Austria: Made in Hollywood," where I profited from my students' many insights.

Researching and writing this book led me to expand my scholarly horizons. Not only was I compelled to study film in greater depth, but I also ventured into the field of American studies. Along the way I received help and encouragement from archivists, scholars, friends, and acquaintances on both sides of the Atlantic. Let me first thank those in Austria who offered their expertise. Elisabeth Streit at the Filmmuseum in Vienna pointed me to important resources on numerous occasions. Her most impressive coup was when she located a version of the silent film *Love Me and the World is Mine* at the Danish Film Institute. My Danophile friend Gabriele Kolar then translated its intertitles for me. During her tenure at the Filmarchiv, Karin Moser repeatedly pointed out valuable resources and made my visits fruitful with her knowledge of Erich von Stroheim and Hollywood's Austria. A recent evening in Vienna with Elisabeth and Karin was a welcome reminder of the many friendships that have grown out of professional activities. After many exchanges and stimulating conversations, Cornelia Szabó-Knotik, Professor at the University of Music and Performing Arts in Vienna, and I collaborated on the talk "Moving Images: Changing Perspectives, A Transatlantic Interdisciplinary Look at Billy Wilder's *The Emperor Waltz* (1948)," which we gave at the Austrian Academy of Sciences in 2016. Her musical expertise and her Austrian eye provided me with fresh perspectives on the film. After giving a talk at the Amerika Haus in 2016, Wolfgang and Hilde Odelga, who worked on many Hollywood movies filmed in Austria, graciously invited me to meet with them and offered fascinating background information on several of the films. Alf-Tobias Zahn's thoughts on Hollywood's Austria and on my earlier publication on *The Sound of Music* led me to revisit and revise some of my claims.

The assistance of archivists and film scholars at the various institutions in the United States has also been invaluable. Early on in my research in film, Ned Comstock, Senior Library Assistant at the University of Southern California made me aware of valuable bibliographic resources. He also helped me from afar with information on *Florian* and *The Red Danube*. Mark Quigley, Manager of the Research and Study Center at the UCLA Film and Television Archive, made most pleasant my visits to the archive, where I viewed several of Hollywood's Austria films. Since my first visit to the Margaret Herrick Library in 2001, I have found working there to be like a dream. From the security guard at the entrance, to those taking my identification at the top of the stairs, to those working in Special Collections, to the knowledgeable research librarians, everyone is most welcoming and helpful.

Over these many years I have profited from the feedback and support of many friends and colleagues. Diane Shooman, who has provided helpful feedback on my writing since dissertation days in the Nationalbibliothek in the 1980s, guided me through a crucial impasse and made completion a reality. I am deeply indebted to Helga Schreckenberger, who read my many talks on Hollywood's Austria films, commented on multiple versions of the book, and even watched *Florian* with me. Lora Lempert, Pat Smith, Maureen Linker, Carolyn Kraus, Georgina Hickey, and Pam Aronson, past and present members of the UM-Dearborn Academic Women's Writing Group, have read and commented on many versions of the book's chapters. Their feedback, good humor, and encouragement have been essential to the completion of this project. Special thanks also go to two historian colleagues at Dearborn, Pam Pennock and Georgina Hickey, for their help in the field of American Studies. The research librarian at the University of Michigan-Dearborn, Teague Orblych, was always ready to help me in my search for arcane references. His tragic death in 2018 is a great loss. Mila Ganeva, Barbara Mennel, Liz Mittman, Ruth Sanders, and Heidi Schlipphacke graciously read various incarnations of my book proposal and gave me useful feedback. Pieter Judson encouraged me to submit an article on *Florian* to the *Journal of Austrian History*. His comments and those of the anonymous readers sharpened my thinking on the film. Gwynedd Cannon's advice as a film archivist and her encouragement have been most welcome. Conversations with Johannes von Moltke helped me sharpen my thinking about Hollywood's Austria. When I ran into trouble capturing screen shots from films to include in the volume, Alfonso Sintjago, the Director of the Media Lab at UM-Dearborn, was very gracious with his time and knowledge.

The people who helped me organize two events related to the project also deserve mention. I had the pleasure of co-organizing the symposium "Imaginiertes Österreich: Imagining Austria," with Helga Embacher. Held in Vienna in November 2000 and sponsored by the Internationales Forschungsinstitut Kulturwissenschaften, it impressed upon me the interest in the topic on that side of the Atlantic. Curating the film series "Habsburgs Go Hollywood" on the invitation of Martin Rauchbauer at the Austrian Forum in New York in November 2008 assured me of interest on this side.

Over the years, I have presented my work at the yearly conferences of the German Studies Association, the Modern Language Association, and the Austrian Studies Association. Colleagues have invited me to give talks at the universities of Vienna, Salzburg, Innsbruck, and Munich, as well as Miami University of Ohio, Bowling Green State University, Michigan State University, University of Michigan-Ann Arbor, and at Dearborn. The questions and comments of students and colleagues always pushed my work a bit further.

Despite all the help I received over the years, there are many reasons why this project has taken me so long. Escaping the cold to Los Angeles, where I spent many a spring break working in the film archives, was certainly one reason. Another is Barbara Zeisl-Schönberg, who has hosted me for many wonderful dinners, when I have been in Los Angeles. Not only do we share an admiration for Billy Wilder and a love of Austrian literature, but Barbara makes the only Sachertorte I find delicious.

I also want to offer special thanks to several non-academics in my life. My aunt and uncle, Ann and Frank Morelli, who are no longer with us, hosted me on many of my California trips. I never tired of visiting them. Joyce Wilbur, who has read my scribblings since high school days, commented on an earlier version of my manuscript. I am sure she will agree that my writing has improved since "The Secret Corn." Although he has never read anything I have written, my brother, Jim Vansant, provided needed humor over afternoon coffee during many a study break. On numerous visits, my mother, Eleanor Vansant, was a second set of ears, as I transcribed parts of the films. Ron Garrett, my partner in life for more than four decades, has patiently climbed over the mountains of library books I have had checked out for the past two decades. He has read and reread the manuscript, catching typos and misspellings, and has offered helpful suggestions on how to make the book more readable. His sense of irony, his warm laugh, his wanderlust, and his love sustain me.

To paraphrase Billy Joel, the mistakes in the book are the only things I can truly call my own.

Introduction

MARIA VON TRAPP, watching the final scene of *The Sound of Music* for the first time as her screen family escaped into Switzerland, allegedly exclaimed, "Don't they know geography in Hollywood? Salzburg does not border on Switzerland!"[1] Had she thought about the beginning of the film, which transports viewers to "Salzburg, Austria, in the last Golden Days of the Thirties," when the country was in fact suffering from extreme political and social unrest, von Trapp might have wondered, "Don't they know history either?" In *The Sound of Music* as well as in Hollywood's many other Austria films, the projections on the screen resemble reflections in a funhouse mirror. Elements of a "real" place with a "real" history inhabited by "real" people can be found in the fractured distortions that have both been drawn from and contributed to the general public's perceptions of the country and its citizens. Many Americans who have seen *The Sound of Music*, for example, are convinced that "Edelweiss" is the Austrian national anthem and that Austrians were overwhelmingly anti-Nazi.

Hollywood studios have produced over fifty Austria films since 1923, when Erich von Stroheim introduced Vienna to movie-goers with *Merry-Go-Round*. This diverse group consists of examples from almost every imaginable fictional genre: dramas, melodramas, farces, comedies, costume dramas, biographical pictures, and musicals, as well as operettas. The sources are just as varied: short stories, novels and novellas, plays, musicals, and operettas have all been turned into Hollywood's Austria. Hollywood studios have also recycled Austrian stories in remakes of foreign and domestic films. Both major and minor studios have set films in Austria and produced extravagant A-productions and obvious B-fillers. Critical and financial successes as well as flops and financial disasters number among the films. Despite the variety, these films easily fall into two categories: (1) films that take place in an Austria or Austria-Hungary identifiable through landmarks, historical personalities, or events; and (2) films where the Austrian locale is merely signified by a label or signaled through dialogue or stock footage, and which could easily have been set elsewhere without impacting on the story.[2]

This book focuses on films with plots in an identifiable Austria and examines them through the magnifying lenses of the historical contexts on both sides of the Atlantic and the prism of the ever-changing domestic film industry. By chronicling the protean screen images of Austria and

Austrians that set them apart both from European projections of Austria and from Hollywood incarnations of other European nations and nationals and considering the many, sometimes conflicting forces that have shaped the films, this book explores explicit and implicit cultural commentaries on domestic and foreign issues inserted in the Austrian stories.

Hollywood's Europe

Hollywood films featuring a European backdrop have a long history. With the transition from shorter to longer narrative films in the 1910s, the domestic film industry began to make movies that transported American audiences to distant worlds. Even when screen cities such as Vienna, London, Paris, Heidelberg, and Monte Carlo were constructed on the studios' back lots and forays into rural Europe were actually filmed in California, viewers could still imagine they were partaking in a bit of foreign culture. Moreover, filmmakers could project desires and actions onto foreign nationals that state censorship boards might have deemed inappropriate for Americans. In *Movie-Made America*, Robert Sklar explains how Hollywood used "Europeans" to present continental or sophisticated stories, after American filmmakers jumped into the void left when World War I crippled the European film industry. According to Sklar, "American moviemakers were thus given a free hand to perpetuate their own versions of the character of European nationalities." He maintains that the celluloid Europeans in the films in the late teens and twenties "were more sensual, decadent, emotional, sinful than Americans, and also more calculating, rational and willful. They dared what the innocent American flirts in a DeMille movie would never dare—to be direct and clear in their intentions, to express themselves emotionally, to seek fulfillment of their desires. They were charming, fascinating, beguiling, dangerous and possibly evil."[3] These homegrown "European" stories reflected domestic shifts in taste and attitudes toward sex and allowed a heterogeneous public to derive different messages from the same stories. They also served as alternatives for later competition with foreign-made imports that the industry sought hard to block.[4]

The American film industry quickly came to associate particular stories with specific countries and their nationals. Plots were drawn from a variety of sources that combined fact and fiction. Popular tales based on the country's history and literature or stories of famous and infamous personalities made their way into films. Familiarity with the country or lack thereof influenced its screen popularity; at the same time, perceived differences based on objective knowledge, prejudices, and clichés about the country shaped images and narratives set there. For example, France's association with the drama of the French Revolution, its draw as an arts and culinary center, and its place as a travel destination from the Grand

Tours of the seventeenth century to recent times have made it a longtime cinema favorite.[5] By the same token, countries' political relations with the United States and American public sentiment also had an impact on Hollywood's portrayals of them. For example, the ups and downs of US-Soviet relations have been a constant subtext in Hollywood's representations of Russia and the Soviet Union from its first appearance on screen.[6] America's anti-Bolshevism allowed for blatant distortions and negative portrayals. In the case of Germany, both external political factors and internal pressures have shaped the changing images of that country in Hollywood. From the teens to the present, the dramatic and cataclysmic historical events of the twentieth century associated with Germany have contributed to that country's images on screen.[7] The extremely negative portrayals of Germans during World War I gave way to more sympathetic portrayals in the twenties and thirties due to the presence of a large ethnic German population in the United States and a change of attitude among the general American populace toward Germans and Germany.[8] This, however, changed with the US involvement in World War II and later revelations of the genocide carried out under the National Socialists.

In his essay "National Types as Hollywood Presents Them," Siegfried Kracauer distinguishes between portraits and projections in films, arguing that the objective factor dominates in portraits and the subjective factor in projections. As in the screen projections of France, Germany, and the Soviet Union, it is this combination of objective and subjective factors that leads to Hollywood's presentations of Austria resembling distorted reflections in a funhouse mirror.

Austria—Off and On Screen

Austria's political and cultural history sets it apart from other European nations, opening up the possibility for different screen incarnations. Austria-Hungary's multi-ethnic fabric (Germans, Hungarians, Slovenians, Bosnians, Croats, Czechs, Slovaks, and Romanians, among others), the long reign of Emperor Franz Josef from 1848 to 1916, the empire's political conservatism and repression, its contributions to art, literature, music, and science (particularly in the first decades of the twentieth century), and its tradition of intolerance and anti-Semitism distinguish it from other European countries. Unlike the French Revolution, Austria's revolutionary movements of 1848 did not reach the same level of violence; unlike the Russian Revolution, the shift from monarchy to republic in 1918 was relatively bloodless. In contrast to Russia's ruling Romanovs, the Habsburgs were not executed, but were given the choice of exile or abdication. The country's post–World War II history also sets it apart from the rest of Europe. When the end of World War I brought about the dissolution of the monarchy into nation-states tied to ethnicity, Austria, which was ethnically predominantly German, was prohibited from joining with Germany. Faced with almost insurmountable economic and political challenges and left without a clear sense of national identity, the fledgling Republic of Austria was short-lived. In March 1933 the Parliament was dissolved and an Austro-fascist corporate state (Ständestaat) was installed. Five years later, the country was incorporated into the German Reich. Like Germany and Berlin, Austria and Vienna were divided into four zones after the defeat of the Nazi regime and the end of World War II in May 1945. However, unlike Germany, the country gained its independence in 1955, with the signing of the State Treaty, and became a neutral country. Also, unlike Germany, one of the founding myths of the Second Republic was the illegitimate claim that the country was Hitler's first victim.

With the dissolution of the empire, Austria lost its geopolitical prestige, but it gained in screen cachet internationally. Austria's imperial heritage and cultural history as well as Vienna's international, mythic reputation as the capital of music, gaiety, and hedonistic pleasures made its way onto movie screens around the world.[9] In *Die Welt des Filmes* (The World of Film) published around 1930, C. Zell and S. Walter Fischer imply that Vienna's screen popularity had been longstanding and ongoing. "Film studios around the world have been inspired by Viennese culture, art, and literature, and today Vienna is still extremely popular as a film setting."[10] According to Zell and Fischer, scores of films shown around the world perpetuated a mythic Vienna. "The old 'imperial' city has been immortalized in hundreds of films—the never-failing joie de vivre, the charm of its inhabitants, the beauty of its unique surroundings have found favor in the entire world. Vienna has become fashionable in the international film world and will hopefully remain so for a good long time."[11] While Zell and Fischer discuss the city's popularity on the world's screens in general terms, Siegfried Kracauer traces the genealogy of German-made Vienna films back to Ludwig Berger's *Ein Walzertraum* (Waltz Dream, 1925), which was in turn based on the operetta by Oscar Straus. Kracauer maintains that the film "established that enchanted Vienna which was to haunt the screen from then on." Kracauer also enumerates the characteristics of the "retrospective utopia" first found in Berger's film and in later escapist Viennese films; this utopia included "gentle archdukes, tender flirtations, baroque décors, Biedermeier rooms, people singing and drinking in a suburban garden restaurant, Johann Strauss, Schubert and the venerable old Emperor."[12] Kracauer's description of Berger's cinematic Vienna appears quite similar to Hollywood's Vienna. Austrian aristocrats, including Emperor Franz Josef, appear in countless Hollywood films; fictitious musicians as well as actual composers abound.

Some would argue that the consistency of themes and images across international boundaries can be attributed to the number of Austrians involved in film industries in Europe and the United States. Indeed, numerous scholars have maintained that celluloid Vienna and by extension Austria was popular on the international screen in part because of the diaspora of Austrians working in the film industry.[13] Whether they were early émigrés who had worked their way up the industry ladder, like Viennese-born directors Erich von Stroheim and Josef von Sternberg, had been actively recruited by Hollywood studios, or were refugees, many Europeans in their capacities as directors, producers, actors, script writers, composers, cameramen, set designers, and technical advisors have had an undeniable impact on Hollywood's Austria.[14] Successful European filmmakers lured to Hollywood in the twenties who made Austria films include the German directors Ernst Lubitsch, Paul L. Stein and E. A. Dupont, the Scandinavians Mauritz Stiller and Victor Seastrom (Victor Sjöström), and the Hungarian Michael Curtiz (Mihály Kertéz).[15] William Dieterle (Wilhelm Dieterle), another German director of Hollywood's Austria, was originally brought over after the introduction of sound to work on remakes of German films and German-language versions of Hollywood productions. Hitler's rise to power in 1933 and the resulting state-sanctioned anti-Semitism led to the flight to the USA of many working in film industries in Europe, many of whom later contributed to Austria's image on the Hollywood screen, such as Billy Wilder, Walter Reisch, and Max Ophuls (Max Ophüls). While the participation of Europeans in the creation of Hollywood's Austria endowed films with an air of authenticity and a sometimes hybrid character, the American contexts proved equally important in the many shapes that Austria assumed and roles "Austrians" played on screen.

Major differences exist between Hollywood's Austria and Austrian stories manufactured in other countries.[16] The differences are striking, particularly in those instances when Austrians have contributed extensively to Hollywood's Austria. In a comparison of Willi Forst's Austrian-made *Maskarade* (1934) and Metro-Goldwyn-Mayer (MGM)'s Hollywood remake *Escapade* (1935), the film historian Jan-Christopher Horak provides a pertinent example. He identifies particular aesthetic features that endow *Escapade* with a decidedly American flavor. Though the American movie reproduces the Austrian film almost scene for scene and the Austrian émigré Walter Reisch wrote the screenplay for both versions, Horak pinpoints how viewer expectations resulted in stark differences: "Where Europeans grant the public an ironic distance, the plot motivates the protagonists, and the actors are allowed to show strength as well as complexity, Americans want to see a clear differentiation between the characters and experience an acting tour de force that serves to promote identification."[17] Although the German-born actress Luise Rainer, who played the female lead, had acted on stage and film in Germany and Austria, her performance in *Escapade* was shaped by the cultural context.

Horak suggests that Rainer's flamboyant rendering of Leopoldine Dur suited American audiences in contrast to the more restrained acting of Paula Wessely.

Horak views American puritanism as equally important in the transfer and transformation of the Austrian story from the European to the American screen: "The fundamentally different points of departure in both films are related to the moral beliefs of the respective cultures or that of their producers. While Forst cultivated a romantic pessimism and moral ambiguity that reflects the zeitgeist of the last days of the Austrian monarchy, MGM constructs a film with every trace of anything morally objectionable removed from it, because in the world of the studio boss Louis B. Mayer the hero and the heroine must above all reflect the puritan moral beliefs of Americans."[18] Despite the Austrian source and Austrian involvement, differing industry practices and divergent mores as well as audience expectations shaped the film in a uniquely American fashion.

The importance of cultural contexts has often been disregarded in publications on émigré filmmakers. Indeed, focusing solely on the involvement of filmmakers from Austria or those familiar with the Habsburg capital and mythic elements of Vienna does not allow for a nuanced consideration of the industrial and cultural contexts. Frieda Grafe provides such an example in her essay "Wiener Beiträge zu einer wahren Geschichte des Kinos" (Viennese Contributions to a True History of Film). Noting the desperate situation of the film industry in post–World War I Austria, Grafe argues that authentic Viennese films were created outside of the country, and she enumerates the contributions that Austrians, Hungarians, and Germans made to these films both in Europe and in Hollywood. She maintains, "the film centers from other countries profited from the love of art, the frivolousness, the inordinate love of pleasure of the Viennese savoir-vivre." She goes on to claim that "Vienna was a dream reservoir," which "also overflowed with talent."[19] Her explorations of Europeans producing Austrian films in Hollywood focus largely on their biographies, and her descriptions of the films rarely extend beyond a perfunctory discussion of the clichés and stereotypes of the Viennese presented in them. Much like others who have written on Erich von Stroheim, she highlights how Stroheim's adopted persona and his directorial ambitions coincided. "By slipping on the uniform he turns himself into the leading man. With this act, the rejected, illegitimate son uses his own trade to appropriate that which had been denied him."[20] Stroheim's on-and-off-screen performances of his persona as a Catholic Austrian noble who served Emperor Franz Josef can be better understood through the lens of the American contexts. When Grafe turns to one of Josef von Sternberg's Vienna films, *The Case of Lena Smith*, she does not look beyond the filmmaker's biography and consequently misses the ways in which multiple factors made an impact on its creation. For example, she sees Schnitzler solely as the inspiration for his melodrama.[21] However, the archives tell a different story. The film began as a piece set in an immigrant community in New York, where a young unmarried mother from Poland who works as a prostitute struggles and reforms in order to regain custody of her son. The original screenplay by Samuel Ornitz, one of the Hollywood Ten, was much in keeping with Sternberg's earlier movies set in outsider milieus in the United States.[22] Grafe mentions Max Ophuls, who was known for his Vienna films *Liebelei*, *Letter from an Unknown Woman*, and *La Ronde*. The context of the only Vienna film he directed in Hollywood is also important. The impetus for *Letter from an Unknown Woman* came from William Dozier, who co-owned Ramparts Production with Joan Fontaine, the film's leading actress. Having read the novella in college, he had long wanted to bring it to the screen.[23]

Before Austria ever appeared on screen, Americans associated a variety of characteristics with the country and its citizenry. By the end of the nineteenth century Vienna had become linked in the minds of many to classical music. Moreover, the widely popular Viennese operetta influenced musical tastes in the early part of the twentieth century and implanted images and scenarios that were coupled in the minds of many with the central European capital.[24] The millions who attended the 1893 World's Columbian Exhibition in Chicago could visit a street in "Old Vienna," where buildings harkening back to a previous century were reproduced, or visitors could attend a concert of Austrian music under the baton of the famous composer and bandleader Carl Michael Ziehrer.

A cursory perusal of *New York Times* articles from the last years of the nineteenth and the beginning of the twentieth centuries provides a window into some of the associations that Americans attached to Austria and Austrians. Around the turn of the century, an ambivalent fascination with Austria's royalty was evident. The fates of the Habsburgs and Americans marrying titled Austrians made their way into numerous news and fictionalized reports.[25] In the early 1900s, Emperor Franz Josef was viewed in numerous articles in a surprisingly sympathetic light. This and the general impression of the Austrian aristocracy darkened with the outbreak of World War I. Travel articles from the prewar period and the early postwar period promulgated the myth of Vienna as gay or a one-time gay capital.[26] Reviews of performances of Arthur Schnitzler's works in the city peppered the paper.[27]

The many, varied notions in circulation that made their way into Hollywood's earliest Austria films were easily adaptable for different messages and would be reshaped in the years to follow. When Austria was introduced to the Hollywood screen in the twenties, it was part of the industry's shift to more "sophisticated" material. Whether in dramas, comedies, or melodramas, pre- and postwar Viennese settings invited the possibility of presenting stories that dealt more openly with love,

Figure I.1. A square in "Old-Vienna" at the World's Columbian Exposition, Chicago, 1893. Reproduced with permission of the Österreichische Nationalbibliothek.

marriage, marital infidelity, and sexuality than the usual sentimental fare.[28] Inserted into these films was often a criticism of the Austrian aristocracy and the rigid class system. *Merry-Go-Round* (1923), *The Blue Danube* (1928), and *The Wedding March* (1928) present cross-class romances in an intractable monarchy. In all three, the upper-class male protagonists are initially interested in women reminiscent of the Austrian writer Arthur Schnitzler's sweet young things (süße Mädel), purely for a dalliance. Although the men are ultimately truly moved by love, the hierarchical system appears stronger than the individuals. In *Merry-Go-Round* it is the prerogative of the Habsburg monarch to determine when and whom his aristocratic subjects marry. In *The Blue Danube*, the lovers, an impoverished aristocrat and the lowly daughter of an innkeeper, are pulled apart by the jealousy and greed of those around them. In *The Wedding March*, money wins out over love. Only when the monarchy is dissolved and the mismatched spouse dies, as in *Merry-Go-Round* and *The Blue Danube*, does love across class lines stand a chance.

By contrast, in both the drama *Love Me and the World Is Mine* (1928) and the comedy *His Glorious Night* (1929) the couples are able to determine their own fates. *Love Me and the World Is Mine* is a variation on

FRIDAY, AUGUST 18th, 1893.

GRAND FESTIVAL ◬◬◬ CONCERT

GIVEN BY THE

HOCH- UND DEUTSCHMEISTER KAPELLE,

(Imperial Austrian Infantry Band)

Under the Leadership of Court Music-Director C. M. ZIEHRER.

PROGRAMME.

1. "Austrian National Anthem"
2. "Viennese Citizens", Waltz — C. M. Ziehrer
3. "Austrian Jubilee", Overture — Em. Bach
4. "Hail Habsburg", March — Kral
5. "Slavonic Dances" — Dworak
6. "Pages of Vienna", Waltz — C. M. Ziehrer

—30 MINUTES INTERMISSION.—

7. "Franz Schubert Overture" — Fr. v. Suppé
8. "Viennese Girls", Waltz — C. M. Ziehrer
9. "Hungarian Dances" — J. Brahms
10. "Lovesong" from "Jonathan" — C. Milloecker
    Cornet Solo by Mr. FRANZ HELL.
11. "The Magic Flute", Overture — v. Mozart
12. "The Dream of an Austrian Soldier of the Reserve", Military Musical Painting — C. M. Ziehrer

—25 MINUTES INTERMISSION.—

13. "My Austria", March — Fr. v. Suppé
14. "Tyrolean Song" — Absenger
    Executed on two Cornets by Messrs. HELL and STRIBERNY.
15. "The blue Danube", Waltz — Joh. Strauss
16. "Radetzki March" — Joh. Strauss

Figure I.2. Concert program of the Austrian Infantry Band at the World's Columbian Exposition, Chicago, 1893. Reproduced with permission of the William L. Clements Library, University of Michigan-Ann Arbor.

the theme of love between a sweet young thing and an officer. Hannerl, the female protagonist, must choose between a comfortable life with a kind and wealthy older man, who adores her, and the love of an officer, who initially saw the relationship as one of many. Here, the outbreak of World War I rather than its end resolves the love triangle. On Hannerl's wedding day, as much as she respects her intended, she realizes that she must follow her heart and runs after the train carrying the young officer off to war. The comedy *His Glorious Night* presents yet another version of a cross-class romance, but with a twist. It humorously attacks snobbery and America's fascination with royalty. Based on Ferenc Molnár's play *Olympia* (1928), the roles are reversed when the aristocratic female protagonist falls in love with a Hungarian officer she feels is beneath her socially and not worth sacrificing her position at court. However, after the "lowly" Hungarian "compromises" her and starts to leave her, she begs forgiveness, and the couple is united in a happy end. At the same time, the film criticizes European snobbery and questions continental morality; it makes fun of America's fascination with European aristocracy by inserting two Americans not in the original play. The wealthy American Mrs. Collingswood, hoping to "bag" her daughter a title, tries to ingratiate herself with Europe's high society. The younger Collingswood is embarrassed by her mother, but at the same time fascinated by the Hungarian officer. However, when she witnesses the nighttime tryst between him and Olympia, the young woman expresses her distaste for loose Europeans morals. While this might have been intended as a condemnation of such behavior, it could also have been a cynical ploy to satisfy censors.

Although it includes an unhappy cross-class relationship and is critical of the reactionary society, *The Case of Lena Smith* (1929) also stands apart from the other early films set before World War I. Rather than a drama about a star-crossed love affair, this film focuses on motherly love. Moreover, Vienna may have been chosen in order to avoid domestic censorship. The original scenario takes place in a section of New York nicknamed "Mixed Pickles" because of its immigrant mixture: Lena Smith, the female protagonist, is an unmarried Polish prostitute with a child.[29] After her son is taken from her, she turns into a model citizen, marrying and earning an "honest" living as a laundrywoman. She even does her best to make friends with the neighbors, who ultimately help her to get back her child. In the film, both the place and nationality of the main character are changed; however, a mother's love is still the focus. In the film, Lena Smith is a Hungarian peasant, who ventures to Vienna where she meets and marries an Austrian officer, who abandons her. Lena works for her officious father-in-law, who is unaware of the marriage and has Lena's son taken away from her when he discovers his existence. After escaping a work farm, she kidnaps her son, returns to Hungary, and marries an earlier admirer for her son's sake, only to have him march off to war and certain death in summer 1914.

Two other cross-class romances from the twenties set primarily during World War I focus on the bravery of the female protagonists and the strength of their love. At the same time, the films depict the depravity of the Russian enemies, which was in line with US distaste for the new regime in Moscow after 1917. Both *Hotel Imperial* (1927) and *The Woman Disputed* (1929) are set against the backdrop of the Austrian-Hungarian forces fighting with the Russians on the eastern front. In *Hotel Imperial* a maid in a hotel in a border town saves an Austrian officer caught behind enemy lines. When the town is recaptured by the Austrians, the maid is publicly thanked for her help and reunited with her officer-love interest. In its story of a woman's bravery, *The Woman Disputed* shows how easily friends can become enemies, while it chides "upright" citizens for their disdain of a former prostitute. The story begins shortly before World War I in Lemberg (now L'viv, Ukraine) when two friends—a Russian and an Austrian—help "reform" Mary Ann Wagner, a prostitute. Given a chance, Mary Ann becomes a model citizen and dear to both friends. The war and the love between the Austrian officer and Mary Ann turn friends into enemies. When the Russian army takes command of the city, the former Russian friend forces Mary Ann to become his lover in exchange for prisoners condemned to death. Only when one of them, who happens to be an Austrian spy, reveals himself and his mission, does she agree. *The Woman Disputed* not only underscores the horrors and sacrifice of war and paints the Russians in a negative light, but it is evidence of Hollywood's concern for certain foreign markets. The setting and the nationalities of the protagonists were changed in order not to alienate the German market. The heroine had originally been French and the villain German, but she became an Austrian along with her love interest and the villain—a Russian.[30]

The Enemy (1927) stands out for its unabashed anti-war message and its middle-class milieu. Based on the Broadway play by Channing Pollock, who had visited postwar Vienna, it does not center on the challenges of a cross-class romance, but on the trials of the Arndt family and other civilians on the home front. The film presents a grim picture of World War I and its consequences, arguing that war arbitrarily creates enemies and tears friends from different nations apart. It turns a pacifist university professor into a pauper and pariah, when he is fired for his anti-war stance. Finally, the film attacks those who profit from war.

Other early movies set in postwar Austria address nostalgic feelings for the "good old days." However, rather than setting the stories in a happier Austria, they take place in the former imperial capital, which has been shattered by war. The stories offer audiences an opportunity to mourn for a lost society. In these movies, Vienna is a place where war profiteers revel in their profits, while the lives of the middle- and upper-classes have been turned upside-down. In both *The Crimson Runner* (1925) and *Night Life* (1927) an impoverished girl is driven to theft by postwar circumstances. *The Greater Glory* (1926), based on Edith O'Shaughnessy's novel *Viennese Medley*, is sympathetic to the losses of the aristocracy and middle-class and views postwar Viennese society critically.

The introduction of sound, the onset of the Great Depression, and the institutionalization of the Motion Picture Production Code brought about the evolution of earlier scenarios. Three films made in 1931 offer new perspectives on earlier criticisms of Habsburg Austria with pre-code type stories of premarital affairs, but with post-code lessons. *Daybreak* (1931), the adaptation of Arthur Schnitzler's novella *Spiel im Morgengrauen* (Night Games, 1926), continued to cast a critical eye on Austrian aristocrats and its military, condemning the officers' gambling and womanizing and their misplaced code of honor that demanded suicide. Yet the film departs from earlier cross-class romances in its more direct dismissal of Old World traditions and the hero's rejection of the limits that society puts on him. With the drastic changes between the literary work and the film, *Daybreak* can be seen as exemplary of the direction that Hollywood's image of Austria was to take in the thirties, perhaps in anticipation of the formalization of Hollywood's censorship. In the novella, when the Austrian lieutenant Wilhelm or Willi Kasda finds himself over his head in debt, he seeks help from his uncle, who has turned his money over to his wife, Leopoldine, a prostitute and astute businesswoman. Unbeknownst to the uncle, Willi had had an affair with her years earlier. Leopoldine, who had truly loved Willi, was insulted when he left money on her bedside and consequently became the person he suggested she was. In the original, unable to pay his debt, the Austrian lieutenant commits suicide. In the film version, some of the more "sordid" details are changed. The female protagonist, Laura, is a poor music teacher, who becomes the consort of a rich gambler in response to the money that Willi left on her night table after their short love affair. However, when Willi is faced with debt, his uncle reluctantly bails him out. Willi retires from the army and true love wins out.

Two stories of female spies, *Dishonored* (April 1931) and *A Woman of Experience* (August 1931) preceded *Mata Hari* (December 1931), the film of the most famous female spy.[31] Both films, set in World War I Austria, highlight the women's strength, while they criticize a government that makes unreasonable demands on them. In both films, the female protagonists are prostitutes enlisted as spies and called on to use their feminine wiles to aid their country. They ultimately sacrifice themselves, not for love of country, but for love of a man.

The Great Depression brought with it a second wave of nostalgia, which led to a more sympathetic portrayal of Austrian aristocracy and

Emperor Franz Josef. It also offered further reflection on gender relations. At the same time, the introduction of sound helped construct Austria as a capital of music. In Ernst Lubitsch's *The Smiling Lieutenant* (1931), a remake of Ludwig Berger's *Waltz Dream* (1925), a singing Austrian lieutenant is forced to marry the princess from the neighboring kingdom of Flausenthurm. Their union appears doomed until his love interest, the leader of a women's orchestra, instructs the princess on love. As she leaves the palace and her former lover behind, the song she sings serves as a warning. Women who stay for breakfast, that is, who stay overnight, do not marry. In *The Night Is Young* (1935) a handsome archduke and a lovely ballet dancer treat the audience to music by Sigmund Romberg with lyrics by Oscar Hammerstein II. At the same time, the film offers lessons in duty and sacrifice for both the male and female protagonists. The emperor convinces the archduke that renouncing his title for love would ultimately belittle him in his lover's eyes. Whereas the women in *The Smiling Lieutenant* and *The Night Is Young* both show their strength through the sacrifice of their love, *The King Steps Out* (1936) offers another take on femininity. In the musical film, based on the wildly successful musical play *Sissy*, the female protagonist, the future Empress of Austria, is portrayed as a determined, fair-minded woman who will not be dictated to by either her mother or the mother of Emperor Franz Josef.

Hollywood's Austria films of the thirties rarely present scenarios in a contemporary Alpine republic. However, there are two that do look on postwar Austrian society with a hint of tempered nostalgia and in which the female protagonists master new challenges. In *Evenings for Sale* (1932) Jenny Kent travels to Vienna in search of a romantic ideal, but chooses duty in Merryville over romance in Vienna. In *Reunion in Vienna* (1933) when the deposed archduke returns to Vienna to celebrate Emperor Franz Josef's one-hundredth birthday, he faces arrest. Throwing caution to the wind, he pursues his former lover, who was once a member of court and is now married. "Cured" of the decadence and allure of imperial life by her psychoanalyst husband, who decries the evils of the monarchy, the former aristocrat chooses her present life, but not without feeling nostalgia for the more glamorous past.[32]

On the surface, films produced in the late thirties and early forties appear a continuation of the imperial scenarios firmly established by the mid-thirties. However, filmmakers drew on stereotypes and clichés in surprising ways to attack the rise of National Socialism in Europe. Emperor Franz Josef, Austrian composers, and Lipizzaner horses appear in films designed to distance Austria from Germany, while still fulfilling the industry's entertainment imperative. *The Great Waltz* (1938) uses Johann Strauss's music as a symbol of the spirit of Austria that has touched an international audience. *Hotel Imperial* (1939), a remake of the 1927 film, depicts Austria as the victim of a foreign power. *Spring Parade* (1940), with a singing Deanna Durbin, depicts a benevolent emperor bringing two quarreling lovers together. *Florian* (1940), with its long sequences of the famous white stallions, suggests that Austria's rich tradition can be saved in the United States. *Bitter Sweet* (1940) revives Noel Coward's 1933 musical set in Vienna, this time in Technicolor. The British heroine Sari runs off to Vienna with her Viennese piano teacher, Carl Linden, on the eve of her engagement to someone from her class whom she does not love. After Linden is killed in a duel defending her honor, Sari successfully has his operetta produced. *New Wine* (1941), a Schubert biopic, suggests that the broader events of the composer's lifetime and of the early 1940s demand a spirit of sacrifice reflected in the composer's music.[33]

Then, just as imperial Austria disappeared from the screen, Hollywood turned to more recent backdrops. *So Ends Our Night* (1941), *They Dare Not Love* (1941), and *Once upon a Honeymoon* (1942) depict the threat of National Socialism to its political opponents, Europe's Jewish citizens, and to democracy. Two additional films from 1943—*Above Suspicion* and *The Strange Death of Adolf Hitler*—offered Americans rare glimpses into an imagined post-Anschluss Austria, in which the brutality of the National Socialists is directed against non-Jewish victims. Based on the thriller of the same name by the Scottish writer Helen MacInnes, *Above Suspicion* has its American heroes travel to former Austria on their honeymoon sometime between March 1938 and September 1939. As a pair of American newlyweds, they will be "above suspicion" or so the British secret service thinks. This film is devoted to showing the importance of American involvement in the fight against National Socialism. With input from refugees and émigrés, *The Strange Death of Adolf Hitler* follows the destruction of the Huber family.[34] Arrested for perfectly imitating Hitler in a derisive fashion, Mr. Huber is forced to be the dictator's double after undergoing plastic surgery. Frau Huber, who has been told her husband was executed and is heartbroken when her two young sons are successfully indoctrinated by the Nazis, decides to assassinate Hitler when he comes to Vienna. Ironically, she kills her husband and is shot herself. With its convoluted plot, the film suggests that action and resistance, rather than a "wait-until-it-passes" attitude, is the only way for Austria to regain entrance into the human family.

When Austria was resurrected in the first films on the postwar screen, no one theme or time dominated. Well aware of the place imperial Austria occupied on the Hollywood screen in the thirties and early forties, Billy Wilder takes the opportunity to make fun of it in *The Emperor Waltz* (produced 1946, released 1948). He inserts the American phonograph salesman, Virgil Smith, into Emperor Franz Josef's Austria to attack racism and intimate the complicity of contemporary Austrians in the Nazi genocide. In 1948, Max Ophuls, known for adaptations of Austrian literature and themes, brought Austrian author Stefan Zweig's *Brief einer*

Unbekannten (1922) to the screen as *Letter from an Unknown Woman*. This study in obsessive love set against the backdrop of a pre–World War I Vienna uses sites such as cafés and the Prater to enhance the atmosphere. MGM's 1949 *The Red Danube*, the first postwar film set in contemporary Austria, focuses on the plight of refugees repatriated to East Bloc countries from occupied Austria. Based on the novel *Vespers in Vienna* by Bruce Marshall, with a screenplay by Austrian émigré Gina Kaus, the film reproduces the clichéd anti-Communist and pro-Catholic plot of the novel. Filmed in part on location, *The Red Danube*, with its condemnation of the Soviets' attempt to repatriate refugees, appears a weak cousin of the highly successful American-British co-production *The Third Man*. When a former Russian prima ballerina and the love interest of a British officer in Vienna commits suicide in the face of deportation, the British occupiers are prompted to take up the cause against the forcible repatriation of refugees.[35]

After a hiatus in the fifties, Austria experienced a slight renaissance on the Hollywood screen in the sixties. A major departure from earlier films, these new films were all shot on location as a response to challenges brought about by the postwar situation domestically and in Europe. Beginning with the 1948 Paramount Decision, which led to the break-up of the film industry's vertically integrated system of production, distribution, and exhibition, the studios were dealt a series of economic blows. The competition from television put a serious dent in box office profits. In addition, European nations instituted measures to keep earnings of American companies in their countries. As Robert R. Shandley explains in *Runaway Romances: Hollywood's Postwar Tour of Europe*, "Foreign film crews could provide much of the labor at lower costs. The higher-paid artists received tax advantages and avoided the gaze of the HUAC by working abroad. More important, the studios would discover that filming in foreign locations, especially in Europe, offered the opportunity to tell the kinds of stories and present the kinds of spectacles that could help them lure American audiences back to the theaters."[36] Moreover, with the increase in the number of Americans traveling abroad, the films could prime travelers for or allow them to relive European adventures.

In addition to dealing with the repercussions of the Paramount Decision, the dominance of television, and the growing wanderlust of middle-class Americans, Hollywood's Austria films of the sixties responded in a variety of ways to domestic interests and issues. Some studios sought to retain an adult audience with serious topics, as evidenced by John Huston's *Freud* (1962), in which Huston compares Freud's exploration of the unconscious to Darwin's discoveries, and Otto Preminger's *The Cardinal* (1963), in which the Austrian-born director delves into topical issues such as abortion, racism, mixed marriage, and the threat of totalitarianism. Paramount assigned Michael Curtiz *A Breath of Scandal*

(1960), the light sex comedy set in turn-of-the-century Austria-Hungary with Sophia Loren as a sex-craved princess, perhaps in part an attempt to profit from the notoriety of Vincente Minnelli's Oscar-winning *Gigi* (1958), set in Paris.

Disney and Twentieth Century-Fox reached out to family-oriented audiences with their Austrian sojourns. Disney's four productions set there draw on the lives of two dead composers and two cultural institutions popular with tourists. The Beethoven biopic *The Magnificent Rebel* was broadcast on Walt Disney's Wonderful World of Color in 1962. Released in theaters in 1962 and then in 1965 on television, *Almost Angels* focuses on the Vienna Boys Choir. *Miracle of the White Stallions* (1963), also first released in theaters and then adapted for television, tells the story of how the famous white stallions were saved first from the Nazis and then from the Russians at the end of World War II. Based on the autobiography of Colonel Alois Podhajsky, the long-term director of the Spanish Riding School in Vienna, it highlights America's role in saving the cultural treasure. Disney's Johann Strauss Jr. biopic, *The Waltz King* (1963), which was made for television but released in theaters abroad, seeks to make the story topical by highlighting the father-son conflict and the son's desire to follow his heart rather than a practical profession. The film that has had the most impact (by far) on Americans' perceptions of Austria is Twentieth Century-Fox's *The Sound of Music* (1965). The singing family who fled to the United States, combined with the stunning scenery in and around Salzburg, have been indelibly imprinted on the American imagination.

Three movies from the seventies filmed on location in Austria were set in an earlier time but colored by contemporary issues and discussions. *The Great Waltz* (1972), Hollywood's third Johann Strauss Jr. biopic and the last film by director Andrew Stone, is yet another fictionalized account of the composer's life. Woven into long dance sequences set in opulent ballrooms, outdoor pavilions, and wine locales, the struggles of Strauss's long-suffering wife Jetty take center stage in an attempt to recognize a woman's contribution to her husband's fame. Herbert Ross's *The Seven-Per-Cent Solution* (1976), with its meeting of Sigmund Freud and the fictional Sherlock Holmes in Vienna, has two great minds solve a mystery through cooperation, ratiocination, and inductive reasoning. At the same time, the film reveals the Austrian aristocratic villain as anti-Semitic. Fred Zinnemann's film *Julia* (1977) deals more directly with Austria's anti-Semitism, when he includes a short segment set in anti-Semitic Vienna before the Anschluss during the country's Austro-Fascist period (1933–38). However, rather than filming it in Vienna, he chose Paris, perhaps, an expression of his antipathy toward his former home.[37]

Postwar and contemporary Austria, nestled between Hungary and what was then Czechoslovakia and Yugoslavia, has shown up in several action-spy movies that emerged at about the time that the covert operations of the CIA and other secret agencies were coming under fire. A neutral country situated between east and west, Austria was known as a haven for spies. Eight years after its success with *The Sound of Music*, Twentieth Century-Fox produced the spy film *The Salzburg Connection* (1972), based on a novel by Helen MacInnes, who also wrote the novel on which *Above Suspicion* was based. *The Salzburg Connection* offers its viewers a more action-packed movie of international intrigue, involving a Nazi treasure as it revisits sites familiar to audiences of *The Sound of Music*. In *Scorpio* (1973) the CIA agent Cross seeks help from a KGB agent in Vienna because the agency has determined he knows too much to live. In *Hopscotch* (1980), which includes some scenes in and around Salzburg, a demoted CIA agent takes revenge by publishing his memoirs. In the James Bond film *The Living Daylights* (1987) "Bratislava" is actually shot in Vienna, and later Vienna makes an appearance as itself. Here a rogue Soviet agent tries to stir up the East-West conflict, but Bond ultimately foils him.

Subsequent action thrillers that traverse Austrian soil, have less to do with the skepticism of agencies such as the CIA or the shadow of Cold War politics, and more to do with international threats. In *The Peacemaker* (1997), a nuclear blast hiding the illegal sale of Russian warheads to Bosnians leads to a short detour to Vienna by the American officials on the trail of the Russian mafia. In *Mission Impossible: Rogue Nation* (2015), Ethan Hunt spends a brief time in the Austrian capital, where he is unsuccessful in thwarting the leader of the mysterious Syndicate, who has the Austrian chancellor assassinated. The James Bond film *Spectre* (2015), with Austrian-German actor Christoph Waltz as the villain, was filmed in part in Austria. In these films the Austrian setting serves merely as an attractive background for a whirlwind tour. These forays into Austria consist of relatively short sequences that hardly engage with that country's citizenry, history, or current state of affairs.[38]

Feature films set primarily in Austria have been few and far between in the last forty years. Three notable films, all set in Austria but filmed in Czechoslovakia (later the Czech Republic), provide unique takes on episodes from pre-1918 Austria. Milos Forman's *Amadeus* (1984) and Bernard Rose's *Immortal Beloved* (1994) both tap into Austria's pre–World War I musical heritage with their unique perspectives on Mozart and Beethoven respectively. In contrast to these historical figures, Neil Burger's *The Illusionist* (2006) fractures Austrian history in ways that imply how distant this historical period is from most viewers. After reading Steven Millhauser's 1990 short story "Eisenheim the Illusionist," Burger became fascinated by the "uncanny sense that nothing is what it seems."[39] He found it "a beautiful cinematic story," but realized that it was "not quite a film."[40] Consequently, he inserted a love story between

Countess von Teschen and the magician Eisenheim and invented the Crown Prince Leopold. "That was the important thing with the character of the crown prince, he wasn't some sniveling weakling of a crown prince, he was fiercely intelligent, but because his father [Franz Josef] is still around he has no power in the empire and it's driving him crazy and he begins to plot his father's overthrow."[41] The emperor makes an appearance when Eisenheim "draws" him on a magic easel during a special performance for the crown prince.

A story originally set in Austria was not the main motivation for Richard Linklater's choice of setting for *Before Sunrise* (1995). The film owes its Viennese backdrop neither to the original story nor to the cultural context, but rather to financial considerations. Although the inspiration for the film came from an all-night walk through Philadelphia, Vienna proved an attractive option when Linklater was looking for a city that could capture the magic of the twenty-four hours the young American male and the French woman spent together. Jean-Christophe Castelli notes that "*Before Sunrise's* integration of the city as a third character is precisely one of the factors that attracted the WFF [Filmfond Wien: Vienna Film Financing Fund] to the project."[42] Surrounding his French and American protagonists at the center of the story, Linklater weaves in many Austrian personalities and unique settings into his Viennese foray and endows the film with a different flavor from films that use Austria merely as an attractive backdrop.[43]

Exploring Hollywood's Austria

As an Austrianist, I have long been drawn to films set in Austria, particularly those where the place is recognizable through fictional or factual personages or when known aspects of Austrian history are identifiable. My original amusement and bemusement at the many fractured projections of Austrian history and Austrians developed into the desire to understand the how and why of these portrayals and the impact of the American contexts. Scholars from a variety of academic fields, from anthropology to literary and film studies, agree that representations and explorations of other cultures and peoples reflect back and comment on the culture of the observer.[44] In his essay "National Types as Hollywood Presents Them," Siegfried Kracauer posits that screen images of foreigners are "more or less identical with the notions American public opinion entertains of the people portrayed."[45] I would argue that, rather than simply duplicating the popular notions, filmmakers play with changing perceptions of Austria, sometimes challenging them, sometimes exaggerating them. From the least commercially successful movies to box office hits, Hollywood's Austria has much to tell us about the relationship between the domestic film industry and historical contexts in the United

States. Set in an imagined Austria, tied to American fantasies, and shaped by an American reality, the films contain embedded messages on changing American mores and gender relationships. The choice of settings, the exaggerated characteristics, and the fractured Austrian history reveal shifting American attitudes toward foreigners as well as the role of the United States on the world stage.

Very little has been written specifically on images of Austria or Austrians in Hollywood films.[46] Books and articles focused primarily on émigré and exile directors in Hollywood deal with their Austria films in the context of their larger oeuvre.[47] The limited number of works on Vienna's place on the screen internationally rarely situates the films in the cultural contexts that shaped them.[48] This book is an attempt to fill the lacunae and consider the industrial and cultural factors that have been instrumental in the evolution of Austria on the Hollywood screen. The scholarship of film historians and historians of Austria and America from World War I to the present has been invaluable in establishing contexts and interpreting the films' subtexts.[49] In addition, archival material, including scripts, memoranda, pressbooks, censorship records, contemporary movie reviews and newspaper articles augmented my efforts to uncover the cultural commentaries in the films.

Two films I do not include in this study, which some might expect, are Erich von Stroheim's *Blind Husbands* (1919) and Carol Reed's *The Third Man* (1949). In the prologue to *Blind Husbands* the location is identified as Cortina D'Ampezzo, somewhere near the Italian-Austrian border, and it is therefore debatable whether it is in Austria or Italy. Consequently, I mark the beginning of Hollywood's Austria with Erich von Stroheim/Rupert Julian's *Merry-Go-Round* (1923), which is unmistakably set in Vienna. On the other hand, I do not include Carol Reed's *The Third Man*, which is set in a post–World War II Vienna, because the American input and context had minimum impact on the film. Despite the efforts of the film's American co-producer David O. Selznick to influence the content and its look, he ultimately had little influence over the decidedly British final product.

Although I do not focus on films, in which Austria as the setting is merely identified by a label, initial stock footage, or through the dialogue, a few words on these films are in order. They reveal that the very name Vienna had a certain currency in the late twenties and earlier thirties. This small body of short-lived films began with Ernst Lubitsch's *The Marriage Circle* (1924) and ended with Edward Buzzell's *Paradise for Three* (June, 1938). Whether comedies or dramas, Vienna must have been seen as an appropriate place for racy scenarios. Most of the plots deal either in a comic or serious way with marital infidelity. In *The Marriage Circle*, a young couple's marital bliss appears threatened through a series of comical situations. In *Her Sister from Paris* (1925) a young wife neglected by her husband is aided by her sister, a star dancer from Paris, who looks exactly like her. The husband falls for the woman he believes is the sister, but before it is too late realizes he loves his wife. In *Serenade* (1927) the wife leads her composer husband to believe that she is having an affair in order to recapture his attention. In the dramas *Her Private Affair* (1929) and *The Firebird* (1934) two women accidently kill a former lover. In *The Kiss in the Mirror* (1933) a lawyer defends a friend who has killed his unfaithful wife and contemplates the same action when he realizes his wife has been unfaithful. In the more lighthearted *The Guardsman* (1931) the suspicious husband of an acting couple masquerades as a Russian noble to test his wife's fidelity. In another pre-code comedy, *Jewel Robbery* (1932), the married female protagonist falls in love with a handsome jewel thief, whom she plans to join in Nice. *Paradise for Three* (1938), based on Erich Kästner's *Drei Männer im Schnee* (Three Men in the Snow), was probably set in Austria to avoid any associations with Nazi Germany. Although these films merit study, they offer little insight into how the funhouse-like distortions of "real" people, a "real" history, and a "real" place are adapted and shaped by cultural contexts.

At the intersection of several disciplines, this study draws on, complements, and ultimately builds upon previous research. It seeks to expand our knowledge of the film industry, and the influence of domestic controversies on images of a foreign country. Finally, it strives to explain the virtual disappearance of Austria from the Hollywood screen. The chapters are arranged roughly chronologically, and each chapter focuses on a theme that delves into the impact of changing historical circumstances on the screen projections and the interplay of the elements that resulted in the "funhouse mirror" distortions of Austria.

Chapter 1, "Erich Stroheim, His Austria(ns) and Their US Contexts," challenges interpretations of the actor/director's Vienna films that focus on his invented pedigree and his published commentary on Austria's capital. It explores how Stroheim played with Americans' notions of the city and criticized post–World War I nostalgia for the ancient régime. At the same time, it argues that Stroheim was sensitive to Americans' vacillating relationship with the European aristocracy in his portrayal of the ruling class on screen as decadent and his off-screen performances as a nostalgic Austrian noble. It also delves into the ways that *Merry-Go-Round* and *The Wedding March* engage in contemporary discussions on marriage, money, sex, and love.

Chapter 2, "Cross-Cultural Encounters of the Intimate Kind: Hollywood's Americans in Love with Austria(ns), 1932–60," looks at Stuart Walker's *Evenings for Sale* (1932), A. Edward Sutherland's *Champagne Waltz* (1937), Billy Wilder's *The Emperor Waltz* (1948), and Michael Curtiz's *A Breath of Scandal* (1960)—four Paramount comedies in which Americans travel to Austria and fall in love with Austria or an

Austrian. When celluloid Americans are confronted with another culture or foreign individuals, personal traits and actions assume metaphorical and metonymic meanings. The symbolic nature of national identities stands out most sharply when an American and Austrian become romantically involved. The romances provide commentaries on the ever-changing historical contexts, including the Great Depression, the rise of fascism in Europe, the ensuing refugee crisis, World War II, genocide, and the Cold War. They also point to the dynamic and changing nature of Austria's currency within Hollywood. This examination of the four comedies traces a shift from a positive evaluation of Austria to a critique of a morally corrupt population and highlights fundamental cultural differences to be adopted, overcome, or rejected. In *Evenings for Sale* and *Champagne Waltz*, the Americans gain from their interactions with Austrians, but World War II and postwar politics change all that. In *The Emperor Waltz* and *A Breath of Scandal* the Austrians have valuable lessons to learn from the American.

Fearful of alienating German audiences and possibly violating the Neutrality Acts as well as facing domestic industry censorship, Hollywood studios were slow to produce openly anti-Nazi films after Hitler came to power in 1933. However, some filmmakers found creative ways to circumvent official and unofficial injunctions. Chapter 3, "The Empire Strikes Back: Imperial Austria Fights Nazis, 1938–41," examines implicit critiques of National Socialism masked in films set in imperial Austria, made between the Anschluss in March 1938 and the entry of the United States into the war in December 1941. Seemingly apolitical films such as *The Great Waltz* (1938), *Florian* (1940), and *New Wine* (1941) draw a clear distinction between Austria and Germany and condemn the machinations of Austria's northern neighbor. The chapter explores the ways in which the fractured historical presentations of the Habsburg monarchy parallel the ever-changing situation in contemporary Europe, and it demonstrates how the trope of Austria as the capital of music is used to distinguish it from its pugilistic neighbor. It uncovers commentary on the place of the United States in preserving venerated Austrian traditions as well as veiled messages for new arrivals.

Although Austria at the time of the Anschluss plays a significant role in only three of the 180 explicitly anti-Nazi films made in Hollywood between 1939 and 1946,[50] these films offer case studies on the mobilization of clichés and popular genres in addressing larger political issues. Chapter 4, "Reflections and Refractions of the Anschluss on the Hollywood Screen, 1941–42," turns to John Cromwell's *So Ends Our Night* (1941), James Whale's *They Dare Not Love* (1941), and Leo McCarey's *Once upon a Honeymoon* (1942), all of which strive to combine propaganda with the industry's entertainment and profit imperative. Those in Hollywood who wished to reach a wide audience with political messages were very aware of the existence of widespread isolationist sentiments, of anti-Semitism, of restrictive immigration regulations in the United States, and (of course) of the public's desire for entertainment. In an attempt to balance entertainment and market concerns with a message, the filmmakers employed popular genres, made strategic choices in casting, and created dramatic publicity in their fractured version of events in Austria. Each film presents a love story against the backdrop of a distorted version of history to address the threat that National Socialism posed for humanity and democracy.

When Otto Preminger and Robert Wise return to Austria at the time of the Anschluss in *The Cardinal* and *The Sound of Music*, theirs is not a call to arms. Chapter 5, "Confronting and Escaping History: *The Cardinal* (1963) and *The Sound of Music* (1965)," examines how the portrayal of this period of Austrian history in the two high-budget films responds to both industry crises and the political and social upheaval of the sixties. Made on location as part of a larger Hollywood trend of filming abroad, both films take viewers on a virtual tour of some of Austria's tourist attractions and its stunning scenery. At the same time, the directors have very different takes on and uses for this period of Austrian history. Preminger sets out to confront and consider the necessity of remembering this past; at the same time, he ties this return to Vienna with contemporary issues, such as racism and the threat of totalitarianism. By contrast, Wise offers viewers an escape from contemporary controversies with the story of the von Trapp family.

"Hollywood's Austria—Its Past, Present, Future," the concluding section, highlights factors that contributed to the protean character of Austria and Austria-Hungary on the Hollywood screen and its fluctuating popularity. It considers reasons for Austria's rare appearances on the contemporary Hollywood screen and Austria's marginal and ultimately diminishing position in the American imagination.

1: Erich Stroheim, His Austria(ns), and Their US Contexts

ERICH VON STROHEIM, the Viennese-born director/actor with a fictitious pedigree, introduced the Habsburg capital to the American screen in 1923 with *Merry-Go-Round* and revived prewar Vienna again in 1928 with *The Wedding March*. When he disembarked at Ellis Island in 1909, Erich Oswald Stroheim, born in 1885 to Jewish parents, reinvented himself as an Austrian aristocrat. Throughout his life, he varied the stories of his past in Austria, but in all of his personal fictions, he was an aristocrat who had been a high ranking officer serving Emperor Franz Josef in the army. Stroheim's confabulated past, which served him well in Hollywood, invited psychological interpretations of his two Vienna films. Richard Koszarski views *Merry-Go-Round* as a cathartic gesture that expressed the director's desire to deal with a society that excluded him. "In rebuilding Vienna, von Stroheim was not just outdoing De Mille or Griffith in details of realistic splendor. He was exorcising some of his deepest feelings, dredging up conflicts so intense that he no longer could keep them fully bottled up.... Whatever the truth of his days in Vienna, the ambiguities of *Merry-Go-Round* reveal a continuing internal struggle. He faced the fall of this dynasty with all the emotion of a true convert."[1] Along the same lines, Koszarski considers *The Wedding March* "a great, nostalgic homage to prewar Vienna."[2] In a similar vein, Arthur Lenning maintains that *The Wedding March* "allowed Stroheim to act the role of his dreams: an aristocratic rake in the doomed prewar Vienna of his youth. It was his greatest wish-fulfillment."[3] Frieda Grafe also explains how Stroheim's adopted persona and his directorial ambitions coincided. "By slipping on the uniform he turns himself into the leading man. With this act, the rejected, illegitimate son uses his own trade to appropriate that which had been denied him."[4] Stroheim's published remarks on his relationship to Vienna encouraged such interpretations that ignore the impact of domestic contexts on his films.[5] In the rare examples when *Merry-Go-Round* and *The Wedding March* have been examined within the context of the Hollywood system, film scholars have focused on the director's personal battles with the studio bosses, which they viewed as emblematic of an industry in which commercialism so often wins out over artistic ambitions.[6]

Such interpretations fail to consider how Stroheim's vision of Vienna, his presentation of pre–World War I Viennese aristocratic society, and his off-screen performance as a nostalgic in the late twenties and early thirties drew from and commented on perceptions of Austria, its past, and its citizenry, then circulating in the United States. At the same time, they overlook how the films weigh in on contemporary discussions on marriage, money, sex, and love. In his essay "National Types as Hollywood Presents Them," Siegfried Kracauer argues that as capitalistic enterprises studios give audiences what they think they want. But he also maintains that "in the long run audience desires, acute or dormant, determine the character of Hollywood films."[7] Taking this a step further, he stresses that "the audiences also determine the way these films picture foreigners" and consequently "any such image is more or less identical with the notions American public opinion entertains of the people portrayed."[8] Kracauer's assessment can also be applied to the image of foreign places. However, although images of foreign peoples and places are drawn from public opinion, they are not necessarily identical with it. Stroheim offers such an example. He sometimes reinforces and sometimes challenges the public's notions of the city and its inhabitants circulating in the postwar period.

World War I and Nostalgic Thoughts on Vienna

World War I was a watershed event. Because of the seismic shifts in postwar society, many in the United States were left disillusioned or alienated. The influx of immigrants, particularly from southern and eastern Europe, was viewed by many, particularly white Protestants, as a threat to their dominant societal position.[9] The disillusionment and alienation resulted in the emergence of nostalgia for a simpler past and a celebration of traditional values. Concomitantly, it led to a disdain for and abandonment of conventions as well. According to Christopher Lasch, the word nostalgia, referring to "a sentimental view of the past . . . was firmly established by the 1920s." He points to the "historical events that made the prewar world appear innocent and remote."[10] Certainly, the twenties were rife with waves of nostalgia, which Svetlana Boym defines as "a defense mechanism in a time of accelerated rhythms of life and historical upheavals."[11] Pre–World War I Vienna appeared to strike nostalgic nerves in the United States for those who saw it as a symbol of a lost world of grace. For example, Charles J. Rosebault lamented the demise of pre–World War I Vienna in nostalgic terms in a 1919 article in the *New York Times Magazine*, predicting, "It will be a world less fragrant, a world that has lost much in color, in quaintness, in picturesque simplicity and alluring coziness, when Vienna, as seems likely to be its fate, has sunk from its once unique place among the capitals of the world to helpless insignificance."[12] The 1928 *Times* article "Vienna Lives Again" on E. A. Dupont's film *Love Me and the World Is Mine* appeals to the public's nostalgia for prewar Vienna. "Vienna, long hailed by poets and novelists as the most colorful and fascinating city in the world, and an international capital of culture, music and art, has been reproduced once more on the screen." A moribund Vienna is resurrected, "not the city of today, struggling with poverty, political turmoil and readjustment following the war but the gay and brilliant city of 1914." With a past and present far enough away, pre–World War I Vienna could serve as a repository for nostalgic feelings and an ideal city for sentimental excursions into the past. On the other hand, for some Americans postwar Vienna might have been another example of the failure of World War I to fulfill its promise of American style democracy. As reported in the print media, it was no longer the capital of a multiethnic empire, but a city run by socialists in a country facing economic ruin in the midst of political strife.

Rethinking Nostalgia in Stroheim's Vienna

In *Merry-Go-Round* and *The Wedding March*, Stroheim famously recreates pre–World War I Vienna, a city that he emigrated from in 1909 and did not see again until 1930. From stock footage of shots in and around the city's center that introduce the films, to elaborate reproductions of famous sites and ceremonies, to familiar tourist draws, great care was given to transport viewers to a far-away place and time. However, while the director seeks to fulfill audiences' desire for vicarious adventure and spectacle, he undermines nostalgia for a pre–World War I past and addresses topical issues. He exposes Viennese society as corrupt and hollowed-out. In eye-pleasing scenes, he inserts topical commentary on marriage, money, sex, and love. By contrast, Stroheim's invented biography, his presentation of self and comments on contemporary Vienna, and his celluloid male aristocrats conform to and reflect ambivalent feelings circulating in the United States vis-à-vis Austria's aristocrats. His off-screen performance as the one-time titled Austrian taps into the nostalgia for a lost era in the face of contemporary reports on socialist Vienna.

When Stroheim transports viewers to his Vienna, he both speaks to and plays with the nostalgia that many felt for Vienna. The filmmaker frames the city as one of stark contrasts and presents viewers with a version of Vienna that is both gay and grim—and above all decadent. In *Merry-Go-Round* the filmmaker begins his tour of Vienna with an iris shot of St. Stephan's Cathedral, followed by a short action shot of pedestrian and horse-drawn commercial traffic in the square in front of the cathedral. Moving on, as part of his impressively realistic sets, Stroheim includes a long action shot of the Prater Amusement Park with its famous Ferris wheel, and one of the imperial palaces as the "emperor" exits. In *The Wedding March*, after place and time are announced with the intertitle "Vienna—Anno

Domini—1914," the camera proceeds to give an abridged tour of the First and Second Districts, highly trafficked areas of the city. The audience first sees the State Theater (Burgtheater), then a side view of the State Opera (Staatsoper) with a view of the Kärntnerstrasse, a major street with shops that leads to the cathedral. The camera jumps to a shot of an inner-city square: the Graben. This transitions to the Danube Canal, quickly followed by a shot of the Prater, Vienna's famed amusement park. Here the camera moves, as if from the perspective of someone on the Ferris wheel. The visuals of the major landmarks confirm the "personality" that Vienna had acquired in the United States, and this selective realism includes landmarks that tie the capital of Austria-Hungary to its Catholic and imperial heritage and its more frivolous side.[13]

Text panels complement the introductory images. In *The Wedding March* Stroheim draws on Austria's aristocratic and musical heritage to help situate his story. Vienna is labeled "Glorious and Proud" and the seat of the Habsburgs. He taps into a legacy that goes back centuries. Although he takes viewers to sites along the Ringstrasse, he skips the Parliament, which is situated between the State Theater and the Opera, and removes any suggestion of a different center of political power. In declaring Vienna "The town—that gave the world Beethoven—Mozart—Schubert—Haydn," Stroheim anchors the city's musical identity in the eighteenth and nineteenth centuries. This Vienna appears to have no knowledge of composers active in the early twentieth century, including Gustav Mahler, Arnold Schönberg, Alban Berg, and Anton Webern. Vienna is also presented as "the town of waltzes, laughter, and of pure, sweet love." As a city "with a code of morals all its own," Stroheim's Vienna promises the luscious decadence often denied American protagonists.

Stroheim also tempers clichés of Vienna as the one-time capital of gaiety and reveals the darker side of "gay" Vienna. In *Merry-Go-Round*, Vienna is identified as "the town of joy—of gladness—and of mirth," which is followed by a shot of the Prater. This is juxtaposed to the pronouncement that Vienna is also a place "of sordid sorrow—and of grief," followed by the short dramatization of a suicide. In *The Wedding March* the filmmaker sandwiches images and text on two contrasting and competing landmarks between the virtual tour of the city and the reference to the city's imperial and musical heritage. St. Stephan's, the city's "oldest guardian" offers solace as it is "guiding—comforting—consoling." By contrast, "Iron Man," supposedly "a remnant of the Middle Ages," is "heartless—soulless—threatening." This knight in not-so-shining armor appears to Mitzi (Fay Wray) when she expresses her fears to her aristocratic admirer, Nicholas Erhart Hans Karl Maria, Prince von Wildeliebe-Rauffenburg (or Nicki for short, played by Stroheim), during her first evening rendezvous with him. The Iron Man reappears after Nicki seduces her, and again when Nicki weds someone else for money.[14]

In addition to these dramatic contrasts, Stroheim further questions nostalgic feelings for this place when he interjects subtle jabs at the glory of the imperial capital city and its titled inhabitants. In *Merry-Go-Round* the first adjectives he attributes to the city—"old—gray—historical"— hardly seem fitting for Vienna. They suggest a musty, staid place and not the grandeur or decadence expected of the capital of an empire of over fifty million and a city of two million in the prewar years. In both films, descriptions of Vienna are introduced with "The Town," diminishing the glory of the imperial city, not letting it be taken too seriously. Similarly, by beginning *The Wedding March* with images of the State Theater and the Opera, the filmmaker implies the staged nature of his own creation and the fiction of the film.

Constructing the city as one of contrasts, Stroheim takes elements of a real place that have assumed a special place in the American imagination and includes texts that both engage with and counter circulating clichés. While he confirms romantic associations with the city, he shows a flip side to Vienna, suggesting a more complex "personality" than the clichés impart.[15] Stroheim creates a fiction, but a fiction combined with aspects of Vienna's Habsburg past, the actor/director's own personal fiction as an aristocrat, and American projections of Vienna and its inhabitants.

In both films, Stroheim conveys the decadence of the society in elaborate, visually captivating, censor-challenging orgy scenes, which serve to undermine nostalgia for the imperial past. Both reveal the debauchery of the upper class, as society's male elite cavort with prostitutes and swill down alcohol. In *Merry-Go-Round*, uniformed officers are seated at a table surrounded by attractive, scantily dressed women. The champagne is flowing, and the men are all obviously inebriated. When Madame Elvira asks Count Franz von Hohenegg (Norman Kerry), the film's main male protagonist, to stir the "love pot," he pours multiple bottles of champagne into a large vessel that had been brought to the table. Two arms emerge followed by the torso of an attractive woman who appears nude. In *The Wedding March* Stroheim stages an opulent orgy that explores the connection between sex, money, and marriage. When the "little crooked house— in that little crooked street" is introduced about an hour into the film, a Mother Goose story does not await, but a brothel and an eye-pleasing sequence. Nicki is surrounded by fawning women in exotic costumes, whom he has to pull himself away from before he leaves for a midnight rendezvous with Mitzi, the sweet maiden from a lower class; Nicki's father shows up at the brothel, nods to his son and then joins in the merriment, crawling on the floor with women riding him like a horse; the rich Schweisser appears at the party that he is apparently financing; soon drunk and on the floor, he negotiates his daughter's marriage with Nicki's inebriated father. When the drunken fathers arrange the union of their children during an orgy, the director casts this marriage of decadence and commerce in a critical light. Nicki will be well taken care of and Nicki's father will "earn" a million *Kronen* from the deal. Later when Nicki is presented with the deal, he objects, at first. However, when his mother reveals the amount involved, he stifles his protests and marries.[16]

At the same time, the filmmaker connects the titled class to vices of excess that visually echo the hedonism of the roaring twenties. Spliced into the brothel sequence are montages and double exposures with armies of champagne glasses being filled by African slaves chained to each other, disembodied hands wildly playing various instruments, and face shots of a lively black piano player, all of which convey the wantonness and decadent abandon of the evening. Neither the illegal consumption of alcohol nor prostitution were rarities in the United States.[17] Indeed, Stroheim supposedly hired sex workers and had alcohol served when filming both scenes. In a letter from September 3, 1926, Pat Powers, the producer of *The Wedding March* complained after an inquiry from federal agents. "I have had a visit from the Dry agents, who have evidently been informed by someone as to the libations occurring during the taking of the production."[18] Although Hollywood mores may be an exaggeration of practices in the United States, Stroheim conjures up images of behavior not necessarily foreign.

In a visually stunning sequence reminiscent of a film within a film that comes earlier in *The Wedding March*, Stroheim recreates the drama and the pageantry of the celebration of Corpus Christi. Announced in the film as "the greatest religious and military celebration of the year," in reality the ceremony held great symbolic meaning for the Habsburgs during their reign. "Veneration of the Eucharist was a leitmotif of Habsburg piety. The Corpus Christi procession was always celebrated with great opulence; it was not only a resplendent spectacle for the general public, but the event for demonstrating the way the Habsburgs saw themselves as Catholics."[19] Its inclusion in the film would appear to argue for the religiosity of the society; however, Stroheim has something else in mind.

In the impressive reenactment, Stroheim uses the Corpus Christi sequence to expose the hypocrisy of the aristocracy and the emptiness of the ceremony for them. First, ringing bells announce the ceremony; military and religious groups file into the church; the arrival of the emperor is announced and greeted with great pomp; the emperor exhibits his piety by bowing before the bishop and kneeling at the altar; large choirs rise to honor the occasion; outside a mounted honor guard keeps the crowds at bay. At some point, more bells ring to announce the end of the church proceedings and the next shots are in opulent Technicolor. Religious and military dignitaries exit the church as the onlookers watch; the emperor follows the bishop carrying the monstrance, and the crowd bows as their ruler walks by. The shift from color back to black and white marks the resumption of the story, as it highlights the superficiality and theater of the ceremony.

Figure 1.1. Drunken fathers arranging their children's marriage at a brothel in *The Wedding March*. © Paramount Pictures. All rights reserved. Courtesy of the Margaret Herrick Library, Academy of Motion Picture Arts & Sciences.

The ceremony is without spiritual meaning for the major protagonists and would have little emotional or spiritual meaning for non-Catholic American viewers. With perhaps the exception of the lame Cecilia, shown in church poring piteously over a prayer book, none are particularly devout or interested in the religious content of the day. Essential for plot development, the ceremony is a place to see and be seen. Mitzi, one of the onlookers, flirts with the dashing officer Nicki, who, on his mount, is one of the many separating the spectators from the participants. When a salvo scares Nicki's horse, Mitzi is injured and shuttled off to the hospital, where Nicki visits her and the seeds of the romance sown at the ceremony begin to sprout.

The hypocrisy of the aristocrats and the emptiness of the religious ceremony is further emphasized when Nicki's parents discuss his future prospects during the ceremony. While still in the church, Nicki's parents spy the wealthy Schweisser, who has made his fortune from people's feet with his famous corn plasters. Nicki's parents exchange thoughts that the daughter, although lame, might be a suitable match for their son because of her father's millions.

In *The Wedding March*, the excursions into the worlds of debauchery and religious spectacle seek to counter a longing for this past and weigh in on shifts in attitudes toward marriage. The epigraph, "O Love, without thee, Marriage is a sacrilege and mockery," quoted at the beginning of the movie and before Cecilia and Nicki's wedding at the end, speaks to the "sacrilege and mockery" of the unions in the film. Stroheim uses his aristocrats for a critique of marriages not founded on love, tying them to the practice of arranged marriages. When Prince Ottokar and Princess Maria Immaculata von Wildeliebe-Rauffenburg are introduced, they are presented as warring parties. Their marriage, sarcastically referred to as "this ideal, blissful union," has nothing to do with love. When Nicki first comes to them, hoping to pump them for money, they both encourage him to "marry money." Later when he protests the marriage his father has arranged and exclaims "Did it ever occur to you that I might be in love with somebody else?" his mother declares, "but marriage is *one thing* and love *another*!" Turning to her husband, she seeks and receives affirmation.

By using a tradition associated with the Old World, Stroheim rails against loveless marriages and casts the New World in a positive light.[20] Whereas there appears to be little choice in the undemocratic monarchy, the United States potentially offers more freedom. As the historian Nancy Cott notes, even "European immigrants themselves, when they came to write memoirs and fiction, often used the contrast between arranged marriage and the love match to stand for the difference between the Old World and the New, between outdated tradition and modernity, between falsity and truth, tyranny and freedom."[21] However, Stroheim is not simply aligning arranged marriages with Old World practices. In a world where the wealthy can buy titles and the titled can profit from the accident of birth, these transactions hold a contemporary message. If the film's epigraph does not convey that, a declaration in the pressbook does. "No marriage is lasting which is not founded upon love and any union for social or financial purposes is doomed to failure."[22] The film's message is leveled against those who press their children into unhappy unions or who themselves enter a marriage based on social status and financial gain.

Just as Stroheim finds marriage without love "a sacrilege and mockery," satisfying sex must also be a component of a happy marriage. In both *Merry-Go-Round* and *The Wedding March* the two dashing bachelors, Count Hohenegg and Prince Nicholas von Wildeliebe-Rauffenburg, are depicted as carrying on amorous affairs and frequenting brothels, and their original attraction to the sweet young women is also decidedly sexual. However, when both men do fall in love with the women, the sexual attraction becomes more than a base drive. By the same token, the attraction that the young women feel for the men also triggers erotic stirrings. In the twenties, "a new type of marriage was evolving that highlighted love and companionship as the principal conjugal bond. Furthermore, love was thought to be anchored in mutual sexual attraction and gratification. Sex was not merely a sign of love but its origin, underpinning and essential ingredient."²³ After they fall in love, the male protagonists see a connection between love and sex and the young women fall in love with the men in part because of the sexual chemistry. Their love has the potential for a new type of union, which, however, cannot be realized in a corrupt, hierarchical society that disallows personal choice.

Stroheim's depictions of Vienna and its citizenry may contain echoes of public perceptions, but the director adapts them for his intended message. He invites audiences to rethink nostalgic feelings toward Vienna and perhaps toward the realization that earlier was not necessarily simpler. The audience could also view the removal of such a system as a positive result of World War I. At the same time, he offers viewers visual pleasure and contemporary messages on the necessity of coupling love, marriage, and sex.

Stroheim's Aristocrats Respond to American Tastes

Erich von Stroheim played equally with audience expectations in his onscreen and in real-life performances as an Austrian aristocrat, which spoke both to Americans' fascination with and their disdain for Austria's nobles. At the turn of the century and into the first decades of the twentieth century, Europe's aristocrats had attained a certain level of admiration in the United States. Tales in popular literature and early films presented fictitious kingdoms and chivalrous protagonists.²⁴ Emperor Franz Josef, who had been viewed harshly by American journalists in his early years on the throne, was looked upon much more benevolently in the late nineteenth and early twentieth centuries.²⁵ Romances between America's wealthy and Europe's titled garnered interest.²⁶ In the late 1800s and early 1900s interest in titles among wealthy Americans prompted the publication of *Titled Americans* in 1890 and a revised version in 1915.²⁷ When Erich Stroheim arrived in the United States in 1909 at the age of twenty-four, he must have understood that Americans would be impressed by titles and less sympathetic to a penniless Jew. Concerning Stroheim's fictitious knighthood upon arrival in the United States, Richard Koszarski speculates on Stroheim's thinking: "It might not help immediately, but Americans were notoriously title crazy, and who could tell what opportunities might present themselves."²⁸ By inventing his biography, Stroheim tapped into Americans' fascination with European nobility.

After the dissolution of the monarchy and the US declaration of war on Austria-Hungary, the elevated position of Old War aristocrats was reevaluated. Previous romantic attributes ascribed to nobles were replaced with harsh assessments in the wake of World War I. In the *New York Times* article entitled "Fading Hopes of a Once Proud Aristocracy" from February 15, 1920, Charles J. Rosebault condemned the decadence of the Austrian aristocracy while bemoaning the demise of "gay" Vienna. In his unflattering portrait, the author singles out the nobles' inability to adjust to their new situation and their dependence on "privilege and tradition," which are anathema to the American work ethic. According to him, Austrian royals were loath to enter a trade or assume a profession, and the military and civil service were the only two professional avenues the elite deemed suitable. Rosebault points to gambling and other aristocratic pastimes, which, he implies, upstanding Americans abjure. He also lampoons aristocratic notions of honor by which suicide is preferable to financial ruin.

In Hollywood Stroheim capitalized on his title and his fabricated time in the military. As a supposed officer in the Royal and Imperial Army, he offered his expertise as a military advisor and with his convincing officious, aristocratic pose, he garnered some juicy roles as a reprehensible German officer in World War I films.[29] In his directorial debut, *Blind Husbands* (1919), he not only directed, but also played an aristocratic Austrian lecher who preys on the neglected wife of an American surgeon.

In both *Merry-Go-Round* and *The Wedding March*, Stroheim's dramatic presentation of the decadent aristocracy echoes some of Rosebault's pronouncements.[30] The male protagonists, Count Franz Hohenegg (*Merry-Go-Round*) and Nicholas Erhart Hans Karl Maria, Prince von Wildeliebe-Rauffenburg (*The Wedding March*), both profligate aristocratic officers, are occupied at court in duties that are without content and certainly out of sync with the American work ethic. In *Merry-Go-Round*, when the young protagonist, Count Hohenegg, stands beside the seated Emperor Franz Josef, the audience is told "To Count Hohenegg, 'work' meant an elaborate and pompous idleness, while the court went through its daily round of empty ritual." Indeed, the audience is provided with no evidence to the contrary. In *The Wedding March* Nicki, who is identified as "His Majesty's Chamberlain and First Lieutenant of the Imperial and Royal Life Guard-Mounted," executes one official duty during the film and that is sitting on a horse as part of the honor guard at the Corpus Christi procession. Even this duty he fulfills shoddily. He appears to have trouble controlling his horse and he spends a great deal of the ceremony flirting with Mitzi. In their spare time, Hohenegg and Wildeliebe-Rauffenburg both frequent brothels along with their uniformed brethren. Nicki spends his money too freely on cards and women. In debt, he is advised by his father to either shoot his brains out or marry money. In both films, the profligate aristocratic officers fall for a sweet young thing (süßes Mädel), reminiscent of female protagonists in the works of the Austrian writer Arthur Schnitzler. While such dalliances may be tolerated, the men are expected to marry within their class, which both do.

Stroheim uses both subtle and blatant methods to criticize Austria's upper-crust. In *Merry-Go-Round* and *The Wedding March*, Stroheim invents family names that associate decadent qualities with the royals, while he pokes fun at Americans' fascination with the titled class. Although only spelled out in the credits, in *Merry-Go-Round* his secondary aristocrats are given telling surnames—Baron von Lechtzinn (a bastardized rendition of Leichtsinn = foolishness), Baron von Uebermut (Übermut = arrogance or cockiness), Prince Eitel Hochgemut (eitel = vain and Hochmut = arrogance or haughtiness). If foolishness, arrogance, and vanity are singled out in *Merry-Go-Round* as features of Austria's aristocrats, in *The Wedding March* the family name "von Wildeliebe-Rauffenburg" wittily characterizes them. Wildeliebe or free love describes the behavior of the young prince played by middle-aged Stroheim.[31] The second part of the name Rauffenburg, a combination of raufen = to brawl and Burg = fortress, applies more to the parents and their acrimonious relationship.

If Stroheim's rendition of Nicki von Wildeliebe-Rauffenburg in *The Wedding March* fits the postwar profile of the decadent aristocrat, the actor/director assumed the pose of a nostalgic off-screen, tapping into a second shift in attitudes. As Christopher Lasch contends, "disparagement of the present" is "the hallmark of the nostalgic attitude," and Stroheim is a nostalgic par excellence.[32] His stance speaks to the continued power of the myth of "gay Vienna" and the rebirth or reemergence of a more sympathetic view toward Europe's titled. Nostalgia was first ascribed to Stroheim in a *New York Times* article from January 2, 1927, entitled "Old Pre-War Vienna Reproduced in Film," which describes the set of *The Wedding March*. After enumerating the places "visited" in the film and describing the luscious interiors and exteriors, the article turns to Stroheim's alleged spontaneous reaction to the set. "'It is Vienna,' exclaimed von Stroheim as he walked about through the various sets and scenes, and those with him observed a sad note in his voice—'Vienna, before the great war of 1914—Vienna the melodious, the romantic, the dramatic—my Vienna!'" Stroheim's performance endows the set with authenticity and, at the same time, its supposed authenticity elicits a nostalgic tone in this solipsistic gesture. With his nostalgic pose, he substantiates his claim that "his" Vienna existed. The reconstructed Vienna allegedly had the ability to transport him back in time, but also to remind him that his Vienna no longer (or never) existed.

The native Viennese and would-be aristocrat embraced nostalgia. In a piece published in *The Hollywood Filmograph* from April 7, 1928, Stroheim claims, "*The Wedding March* is an expression of my own homesickness, the nostalgia of one who revives dear memories with a catch in his throat and a pain in his heart." He continues, "It is as if I were living my youth again, as if by some miracle I am once more the young officer I portray in the picture, just as I was years ago when as a Dragoon, I was attached to the Emperor Franz Josef's personal staff as a Life Guard Mounted."[33] Just as he claims the film transports him to an earlier time and pulls at his heartstrings, he recreates a city that has been viewed by many in nostalgic terms and promises (falsely) a nostalgic excursion into the past.

In an article published in April 1930 in *Motion Picture Classic*, Erich von Stroheim again conjured up a lost Vienna that resembles and reiterates the contrasts found in his films. The very title—"T*he* Vienna *of* Von Stroheim. It Was—It Is Not Now—A City of Romance And Pageantry And Waltzing"—evokes a clichéd Vienna tied to the director and his film.[34] The note following the title—"As told by Eric Von Stroheim to Dorothy Calhoun"—assures readers of its authenticity. In offering an "authentic" insider's view of the city he left in 1909, Stroheim perpetuates stereotypes and American misconceptions and prejudices. If, as Kracauer claims, notions of the viewing public determine the depiction of foreigners in Hollywood's films, it appears that they have also affected Stroheim's off-screen Viennese persona.[35] In his responses in the interview, he recycles common perceptions of the city.

Beginning with his usual dramatic flair, Stroheim announces that the Vienna he speaks of can only be spoken of "in the past tense, as a man speaks of a woman he has loved and who is dead." He continues, "For my Vienna is as different from what they call Vienna now as the quick is different from the dead. The streets are there and the buildings and the parks, but it is not these things that make a city." Stroheim mournfully enumerates the sounds, sights, and people no longer there that made Vienna so special for him.

> Unless there were the military sound of the feet of officers' horses on the cobblestones, and the wheels of fiacres carrying beautiful women to some rendezvous . . . and the clatter of jeweled scabbards and spurs on the pavement, it would not be Vienna. Unless the grey stone palaces on the Ringstrasse were occupied by splendid names, names that go back to the Crusaders, names that belong to Austria's history, it would not be Vienna. Unless the Stadtpark were bright with uniforms and soldiers strutting and pulling their mustaches for the admiration of red-cheeked nursemaids and the air was filled with laughter and songs and music, it would not be Vienna.[36]

Here, Stroheim presents himself as the model nostalgic. According to Lasch, "Nostalgia appeals to the feeling that the past offered delights no longer obtainable." The absence of the Habsburg military grieves Stroheim. The director sketches out multiple reasons why his past is "a time irretrievably lost and for that reason timeless and unchanging."[37] True to form, Stroheim pronounces "I shall never go back to the city where I was born" for it "would be like going to the morgue to identify the body of a sweetheart one remembers as a lovely living woman with whimsical ways and a thousand dear beauties."[38] The buildings may still be there, but for the nostalgic Stroheim there is just no comparison.

However, Stroheim did return to Vienna in summer 1930, not long after the published article appeared. In the *New York Times* article

"Vienna Makes Director Sad," appearing on October 12, 1930, Stroheim does little to revise his earlier remarks. He remains the nostalgic, this time echoing US news reports. Although it is much shorter than the interview with Calhoun, the pathos is the same. "'They say Vienna is dying,' he said, 'But it is a half-truth. Vienna is dead. Her people are sodden and weary; they have the stamp of defeat on their faces, the faces of the once bright Vienna of the old days. They are licked. They have no hope. And they don't care.'" He notes that the buildings are the same and conjectures that the lilacs bloom as usual. Although on the surface the city may appear the same, according to Stroheim its one-time essence is gone. "'But the gayety of Vienna is gone and the people never hope to rise.'"

When Stroheim discussed prewar Vienna with Calhoun in the *Motion Picture Classic* article, his "Vienna" resembled the fictionalized city that he brought to life in his films, and it coincided with the place of Vienna in the collective imagination. "Some few cities have sex, and the love they arouse is warm, ardent, passionate. Everywhere I go, people seem to have that emotion for Vienna." Stroheim's Vienna is not a real city, but a cipher or idea and ideal for the Hollywood screen. "It stands to the whole world for romance." The pre–World War I Vienna that Stroheim describes has more to do with the city he created in his two films than with the real capital. His ambivalent language erases the difference between fact and fiction when he pronounces, "For the drama and romance of *my* [my emphasis] Vienna were based upon its contrasts." He paints a city "of the very rich and the very poor" and concludes, "whether you approve of such a social structure or not, you will admit it makes for color in life, for picturesqueness and romance."[39] What began as a nostalgic performance morphs into a descriptive explanation for the drama in "his" Vienna. He implies that romantic associations and an unfair, undemocratic class system make for great cinematic drama.

In his closing remarks in the Calhoun piece, Stroheim returns to elements from his films and clichés to describe prewar Vienna and "correct" any uncritical assessments of the feudal society. "My Vienna was a city of crassest contrasts." He then turns to contrasting images that appear taken from *The Wedding March*. "It was sentimental, easily moved to tears and laughter. We believed in the Danube Maids who danced on spring nights by the river, and all such innocent childlike things." His romantic view of Vienna did not prevent him from reminding readers of its darker side, also present in his films. "Yet my Vienna had another side. High against the sky above the Rathaus, the beautiful medieval City Hall, stands The Iron Man, a sullen figure in heavy battle armor, symbol of intolerance and prejudice and cruelty and hate."[40] Tales of the Danube Maids and The Iron Man atop the town hall did indeed exist.[41] However, the town hall is not medieval, but an example of neogothic historicism from the latter part of the nineteenth century, and The Iron Man was placed there by the architect to watch over the city. Indeed, American readers would not necessarily know this, but some might remember the threatening Iron Man from *The Wedding March*.

As a displaced Austrian "aristocrat," Stroheim would naturally be inclined to disapprove of Vienna in the interwar period. In this persona, he sees Vienna as impoverished and lacking the earlier drama. "Those who were at the heads of the government perhaps wait on the tables [in cafés] now and bring their wine to pompous bourgeois and tourists from America."[42] Just as the Habsburgs and dashing officers have been displaced, the mercantile classes have supposedly profited from the war and have ended up on top. The "beer barons and shopkeepers enriched by the war and ennobled by their money live in the crumbling palaces of the Rings and the streets that radiate from them like the spokes of a giant wheel."[43] While his pronouncements conformed to his aristocratic persona, they were not particularly original. The reversals of fortune of the professional and titled classes in postwar Vienna had been reported in the news, written about in fiction, and brought to life in other Hollywood movies. For example, Anne O'Hare McCormick stated in a *New York Times* article from August 12, 1923, "Every one between the bankers and war profiteers and the laboring classes is starkly poor." Edith O'Shaughnessy, who had lived in Vienna as the wife of a diplomat, "bewails both the loss of empire and the plight of the Viennese bourgeoisie" in her novel *Viennese Medley* (1924).[44] Curt Rehfeld's *The Greater Glory* (1926), based on O'Shaughnessy's novel, deals with reversals of fortune for a well-to-do family impoverished by the collapse of the monarchy and their working-class counterparts who have come out on top. The films *The Crimson Runner* (1925) and *Night Life* (1927), also set in an impoverished postwar Vienna, play on feelings of loss.

Not having visited Vienna since 1909, Stroheim parroted and exaggerated what others had said and written about Vienna when he spoke to Calhoun. The most blatant fictions are those involving the Socialists. In his version of postwar Vienna, the palace has "become a storehouse" and the Socialists "can spit on the marble floors and wear their hats in Old Franz Josef's bedchamber itself."[45] Just as he repeats clichés accepted by Americans in his films, he duplicates a false picture of the horrors of a socialist Vienna. Ignoring the major contributions the Social Democrats had made since 1919, Stroheim apes the prejudices and fears of many Americans. In 1921 an author of historical novels, Kenneth L. Roberts, reported in his documentary *Europe's Morning After*, "The governing class in Austria, being Social Democrats—and Social Democracy is so close to a dictatorship of the working classes that a knife blade can scarcely be pried between them—is fearful of tying up with Hungary, because if it had a monarchy wished on it the working classes would not continue to be the ruling classes to any noticeable extent."[46] In an article from

February 2, 1925, Edwin L. James, the *New York Times* editor, depicted a once splendid city, made pathetic by the ruling Socialists. He lamented, "About all the joy that was left in Vienna has been taxed to death." James concluded that the "proletariat had certainly put the city's high life next to ruin. Somehow, it seemed a shame to do that to Vienna."[47] The statements reveal a very slanted, simplistic view of Social Democracy and little or no understanding of Austrian Social Democracy. Stroheim capitalized on this and his negative images combined tendentious reports with a hefty bit of imagination.

In reality, devastated by four years of war, the country faced continued food shortages; starvation along with tuberculosis were major killers in the postwar years. The population also suffered from inflation and widespread unemployment. The Social Democrats, who dominated politics in the capital until 1934, set about to improve the conditions of the population, particularly of the working class. Consequently, great progress was made in the areas of public housing, health, and education, for which the city earned the moniker "Red Vienna."[48] However, the political leanings of "Red Vienna" made it unattractive for the Hollywood screen and trickier as a place for commenting on the issues then dominant in the United States.

Conclusion: Perpetuating and Questioning Nostalgia

In his films, Stroheim reconstructed a world of yesteryear, speaking to the nostalgia associated with Austria's capital city. At the same time, with his city of contrasts, the story of doomed lovers in an intractable society, and his decadent aristocrats, he questioned nostalgia for an earlier time and distant place. By contrast, Stroheim's off-screen performances as an aristocrat suggested he was catering to the ambivalent views of the Austrian aristocracy circulating in the United States. In assuming a new identity when he came to the United States in 1909, Stroheim realized an aristocrat would have more social currency than a poor Jewish immigrant. In the early postwar years, when feelings against the titled ran high, Stroheim could offer an "authentic" picture of the time. In the 1920 article "Fading Hopes of a Once Proud Aristocracy," in which Rosebault describes a decadent group unable or unwilling to adjust to the new times, he predicts that the general antipathy toward these aristocrats will probably evolve into nostalgia. In fact, he maintains that Americans "may grow indulgent toward the poor remnants of an aristocracy that once filled the eye and appealed to the imagination."[49] By the second half of the twenties, the pendulum had indeed begun to swing back to a more positive assessment.

Stroheim's biography, both real and invented, has distracted many from the ways in which his Vienna and aristocrats are tied to contexts in post–World War I United States. The actor-director's off-screen nostalgic performance registered a general shift in attitude toward the aristocracy and anticipated the softer, kinder portrayals of Austrian aristocrats that emerged on screen in the thirties. Instead of decadent hypocrites trapped in a hierarchical system, the aristocrats come to represent qualities lost or needed in light of the challenges in the twenties and thirties. A former aristocrat in post–World War I Austria learns how to deal with displacement (*Evenings for Sale*, 1932); a nephew of Emperor Franz Josef chooses duty over love (*The Night Is Young*, 1935); the future emperor finds love and self-determination despite a domineering mother's orders (*The King Steps Out*, 1936). In the late thirties and forties Austrian aristocrats and monarchists stand in for the better Germans (*Florian*, 1940; *They Dare Not Love*, 1941). This was to change again after the United States entered the war. The subsequent chapters explore how the symbolic function of the country and its inhabitants, aristocratic and not, responded to the historical and industrial contexts.

2: Cross-Cultural Encounters of the Intimate Kind: Hollywood's Americans in Love with Austria(ns), 1932–60

WHEN CELLULOID AMERICANS travel to Austria, personal traits and actions assume symbolic meanings that stand out most sharply in cross-cultural romantic encounters.[1] In four Paramount comedies—Stuart Walker's *Evenings for Sale* (1932), A. Edward Sutherland's *Champagne Waltz* (1937), Billy Wilder's *The Emperor Waltz* (1948), and Michael Curtiz's *A Breath of Scandal* (1960)—the Americans' foreign adventures and cross-cultural romances result in humorous situations that offer more direct commentaries on topical issues circulating in the United States than Hollywood's other Austria films.[2] The filmmakers mobilize clichés and stereotypes that highlight supposedly different national traits to weigh in on the ever-changing historical contexts, including the Great Depression, the rise of fascism in Europe, the ensuing refugee crisis, World War II, genocide, and the Cold War. Sometimes implicitly, sometimes explicitly, the Austrian-American encounters reflect on contemporary attitudes toward Europe, specifically Austria.

Although Paramount had already produced a number of films set in Vienna before *Evenings for Sale* and *Champagne Waltz*, the two are quite a departure from the studio's earlier Vienna films, dramas set in Franz Josef's empire.[3] By contrast, in *Evenings for Sale* and *Champagne Waltz* American protagonists travel to postwar Austria, which may seem an unlikely setting for a Hollywood romantic comedy.[4] Having never fully recovered from World War I, the fledgling republic was faced with an extreme economic crisis and torn by political strife.[5] Both films conjure up a mythic postwar Vienna with slight nods to the city's reality while suggesting deeper messages. *Evenings for Sale*'s portrayal of postwar Vienna offers commentary on the Depression with its impoverished, deposed aristocracy. Using the "invasion" of an American jazz band into a staid Vienna in the twenties, *Champagne Waltz* responds in a unique way to US immigration policies and Nazi Germany's inhumane emigration policies, which made it difficult for refugees to come to the United States.

The events of World War II and the ensuing Cold War resulted in multiple reversals in Paramount's subsequent Austrian-American romances.

Whereas the Americans gain from their interaction with Austrians in *Evenings for Sale* and *Champagne Waltz*, the Americans have lessons to teach the Austrians in *The Emperor Waltz* (1948) and *A Breath of Scandal* (1960). Although these two Austrian-American romances are both set in Emperor Franz Josef's Austria-Hungary, they contrast with Hollywood's positive depictions of the empire of the late thirties and early forties, which used the Old World to attack Nazi Germany's policies. Here, the Old World-New World conflict is used to condemn the behavior of the Europeans, while commenting on discussions of sexuality in the United States. *The Emperor Waltz* takes potshots at anti-Americanism, European snobbism, and National Socialist racist policies. In *A Breath of Scandal* the morals of the haughty Austrians are tied to Cold War discussions that connected female sexuality with the health of a nation.

Reflections on the Depression in *Evenings for Sale*

When Jenny Kent (Mary Boland), a rich middle-aged American widow, seeks her romantic ideal in Vienna and her path intersects with that of the younger, impoverished Count Franz von Degenthal (Herbert Marshall), *Evenings for Sale* engages in debates on gender roles and attitudes toward work, charity, and relief during the Depression. It also comments on the role of the United States on the world stage. The film calls on women to put duty before pleasure and admonishes them to be more understanding of the plight of the displaced men in their lives. Indeed, the film functions like the woman's film, which according to Jeanine Basinger, "drew women in with images of what was lacking in their own lives and sent them home reassured that their own lives were the right thing after all."[6] Widowed for ten years, relieved of her duties as a mother now that her daughter is married, and extremely wealthy thanks to her husband's wise investments, Jenny Kent views her trip to Vienna as the opportunity to assume a new identity. According to William W. Stowe, "Travelers are performers, actors of well-known scenes, players of well-known roles, and adopters of approved attitudes, all of which are laid out for them in the guidebooks' liturgy."[7] For Jenny, her script does not come from a guidebook, but from her memories of *The Merry Widow*, which she erroneously believes was set in Vienna. As she heads off to Vienna, Jenny has almost all the makings of a merry widow herself, a role she wishes to assume, perhaps permanently. Only when confronted with the roles of grandmother and merry-widow-bride, which she views as incompatible, does she rethink and reject her fantasies and head for home.

Blinded by her naiveté and the power of a romantic ideal promulgated in popular culture, Jenny remains blissfully unaware that the Vienna of her dreams is a commodity that tourists and the wealthy can buy. Though this is repeatedly disclosed visually and in actions, when the American meets Count Franz von Degenthal, she believes she has found her dream. Once in Vienna, the hotel receptionist informs her that Maxim's is not in Vienna, but in Paris. Recognizing her disappointment and loneliness, he picks up a brochure for the Café Zassania. He then reads about their "Widow's Evenings," which afford unaccompanied women the opportunity to meet "officers of the former Imperial Guard" or "perhaps a baron or a duke" in a respectable setting.[8]

The first shot of the Café Zassania, a revolving door, doubles as the entrance to the establishment and signals that it is a type of stage where the interactions are more or less scripted. Here, Jenny can play the merry widow. However, unaware of the "rules" and blinded by her romantic projections, she fails to realize that the café is a place where impoverished aristocrats make money as gigolos, where they are to be paid for each dance and for conversing and drinking with the customers. In this arena Jenny's clichéd notions of Vienna frame her interactions with the Viennese, and her reactions to "Viennese" customs are very much defined by her position as an older American female with little experience of the world. By the same token, her American naiveté suggests how ill-suited she is for the role.

Jenny's romantic ideal of Vienna appears confirmed throughout the evening even as the audience is repeatedly made aware of the artifice behind it. The café is just as she had imagined gay Vienna. Upon being seated, she exclaims, "Whenever they played 'The Blue Danube' at home I always imagined a place like this." There she receives the royal treatment. When Bimpfel (Charles Ruggles), the head waiter and Degenthal's devoted former orderly, instructs the orchestra to play "The Blue Danube Waltz" and when the former count asks her to dance and spends the evening with her, she has the illusion of having stepped into a Viennese operetta.

Enamored by her surroundings, ignorant of the Austrian postwar reality and consequently unaware that Franz von Degenthal, her "Danilo," must charge her for his attention and should be treated to the drinks consumed, she is mystified when handed a bill at the end of the evening. This does not fit into her romantic vision of Vienna or her experience of the world. Nor does she comprehend Degenthal's response after she remarks at the end of the evening, "It's all been so charming, you and everything. I wish I could carry it all back with me to Merryville." He cynically replies, "You can, if you have the money. Everything here is for sale." Ready to live her romantic ideal, Jenny is ignorant of the artifice of this world, even though the audience is not. In this Vienna, members of the former aristocracy have lost their wealth and social standing, but not their cachet and manners, allowing wealthy patrons—tourists, the Viennese moneyed middle-class and nouveau riche—to hobnob with the once royal.

If Jenny's expectations of Vienna blind her to the Austrian reality, her American values and socialization as a middle-aged American make it difficult for her to adjust to the continental customs and embrace the desired role fully. Although seeking the royal, her democratic nature interferes with her becoming the merry widow of her fantasy. After Bimpfel shows her to the "royal box," where he asks her for her coat, she initially does not know what he wants. When he tells her, she replies delightedly, "Anyone would think I'm a queen or something." She then thanks him and asks him for his name, something which obviously surprises the Austrian, used to ceremony and strict social hierarchy. Later, Jenny's maternal side places her at odds with foreign notions of motherhood and her desire to play the romantically desirable merry widow. When she visits the Degenthal castle the day it and its contents are being auctioned off, Franz shows her the nursery. Here, she admires all the toys and finally a picture of the young Degenthal with his mother:

JENNY: My, what a handsome boy you were. Of course, you still are.
FRANZ: That's when I was five.
JENNY: Did she used to put you to bed every night?
FRANZ: Oh no. I had a nurse for that.

At this point she looks away embarrassed and then asks, "Well, didn't she tuck you in, kiss you goodnight?" When Degenthal responds, "Sometimes before going to bed the nurse would take me to her room and let me kiss her hand." Jenny looks aghast and responds "Kiss her hand?! Oh, oh, I'd have squeezed the daylights out of you." And then somewhat embarrassed at the possible misunderstanding of sexual connotations, she quickly adds, "I mean, that is, if I'd have been your mother." She cannot comprehend Degenthal's distant relationship to his mother. Although such behavior was not unknown in the United States, the film narrative rejects this custom as a remnant of a decadent Austrian aristocracy, strangely foreign to the warm-hearted American.

Vienna's romantic hold on Jenny is strong despite repeated signs of its staged nature. Only when she finds herself unexpectedly faced with a major life choice does she realize she does not belong in this world. Still entranced by the romance that Vienna offered even when she finds out that Franz's original attentions had mercenary motives, it takes a call from the United States to make her look in the mirror. Immediately after she mistakenly believes that Degenthal has proposed to her, a telephone call interrupts them, and she finds out she is a grandmother. Excited, she shares the happy news with the count, who seizes the moment and asks if she has told her family about them. If her face showed great disappointment when she found out Maxim's was not in Vienna, here it expresses

Figure 2.1. Jenny Kent and Count Franz von Degenthal in the nursery of the Degenthal family castle on the day of its auction in *Evenings for Sale*. © 1932 Paramount Publix Corporation. Credit: Universal Studios Licensing LLC. Courtesy of the Margaret Herrick Library, Academy of Motion Picture Arts & Sciences.

extreme embarrassment. In her world the roles of bride and grandmother are incompatible, and Jenny's original quest for an operetta-like adventure becomes a more profound journey. The American adjusts her self-image from the marriageable merry widow to a more conventional role. Searching for the right words, she states, "No use fooling myself. At heart I'm just a grandmother and nothing else and I belong in Merryville. I'm afraid it's too late for this." Her encounter with Austria allowed her to experience her romantic ideal, if only briefly. Somewhat wistfully, she remarks, "Everything that's lovely over here would seem just, just funny over there." Jenny does not reject the pleasure that Vienna has offered her, but she realizes that remaining would mean behaving inappropriately for her age, gender, and home culture. Her realization allows her to accept the mundane over the romantic, duty over pleasure, reality over the realm of imagination. Moreover, Jenny does not totally abandon the role of merry widow, only redefines it, as we will see in the following discussion of Degenthal.

Although set on foreign soil, Franz von Degenthal's story engages the topical discourses concerning men and work that resonate with the situation of many men in the early thirties in the United States. "By early 1932 well over ten million persons were out of work, nearly 20 percent of the labor force."[9] The gravity of the financial downturn was devastating. "The country had never before known unemployment of these magnitudes or of this duration. It had in place no mechanism with which to combat mass destitution on this scale."[10] Like many of US men, Degenthal has been stripped of his old identity and had a new one foisted upon him by circumstances. He had lost his title, his fortune, his position, and his self-respect. His initial loss of identity and sense of purpose in life was not atypical for men who lost their jobs in the first years of the Depression. The historian Philip Hanson writes, "Wrapped up as identities are in profession and finance, having one's identity revised against one's will was a frequent and bitter occurrence in the thirties. In cases where a revision was not absolute, the threat, in the form of reduced job hours, potential layoffs, or plant closings, created persistent tension."[11] When Franz first appears on screen he is obviously contemplating suicide, but being stereotypically Viennese, he allows himself one more night of enjoyment at a masked ball before executing his plan. There he unexpectedly falls in love with the beautiful Lela Fischer (Sari Maritza) and regains his desire to live. Bimpfel, his former orderly and now the head waiter at the Café Zassania, proposes that Degenthal consider working there as a paid dancer. After Degenthal accepts the job of gigolo, he somewhat sarcastically responds to Bimpfel and his new boss, "Gentlemen, I thank you, it is a great moment in a man's life when he discovers his real work in this world." Stripped of his title and fortune, his bitterness suggests a false truth he has internalized, that is, a man's worth in the eyes of others and perhaps in one's own eyes is reduced to what he does and not who he is. However, in the course of the film, Degenthal proves again and again that a man's value depends on his character and not his position. For example, when he realizes that Jenny has no idea that his attentions carry a fee, the impoverished former count pays the bill in order to hold on to his dignity.

Ultimately, the film argues for a more tolerant attitude toward men who have to accept work that might be considered distasteful or beneath their dignity. At the same time, it pits concepts of honest work against relief, when Degenthal refuses to accept employment that is exclusively for show. Thus, despite his distaste for the job of gigolo and the fact that he has to work for his former butler, he turns down a job offer from Lela's father. Later, Lela confronts Franz at the café:

LELA:	How can you bring yourself to do this kind of work?
FRANZ:	One must live.
LELA:	Would you rather do this than accept father's offer?
FRANZ:	I can't be of any use to your father. After all I can dance. Here at least I'm not taking money under false pretenses. Are you so terribly disappointed in me?
LELA:	Yes, I thought you had pride. (Looks back) And I find you selling your charming manners, your smile, yourself in a nightclub.

What Lela does not realize is that he refused her father's job offer because of his pride and strength of character. Although she finds his work as a paid dancer beneath him, her position is criticized. Her sympathetic father, who initially appears surprised and disappointed, later comments that it is none of their business how a man makes his money. So, though it is not an ideal job, it is at least honest work.

The film, based on "Widow's Evening" by I. A. R. Wylie, differs from the short story in significant ways that underscore the film's intention to call on women to support those men who have been demoted and displaced because of societal upheavals. Although both male protagonists work as professional dancers and escorts, they have taken the job for different reasons. Finding himself impoverished after the war, Egon von Arnstalt, the story's aristocrat, views selling his charm and sad story as an easy way to make money. By contrast, Franz von Degenthal chooses to work as a gigolo after he falls in love with Lela and has a reason to live. In both story and film, the deposed royal refuses a job offer from Mr. Fischer, the father of his love interest. In the story, the young man feels it would be beneath him and too middle-class. In the film, the male protagonist refuses the offer because it is charity and the money earned would be "under false pretenses." Consequently, the film's protagonist does not possess the same flawed character as his counterpart in the story. Unlike the titled class in Stroheim's films, here the aristocrat is not painted as decadent. Rather the film uses the plight of the count to garner sympathy for the men economically displaced by the ravages of the Depression.

Although making money "under false pretenses" is likened to receiving relief and something Degenthal considers dishonest, working for his former unsympathetic butler, who delights in humiliating him, is problematic within the film's narrative and in conflict with conservative American values. Whereas the wealth of Lela's father, someone who has always been middle-class and has not taken advantage of others' misfortunes, is positively coded, the advancement of the former butler is viewed negatively. While not a realistic picture of postwar Austria, the negative portrayal of the former butler, who gloats that workers are now on top and Degenthal's class is on the bottom, conforms to Hollywood's dislike of social upheavals that would threaten the status quo. When the former butler capitalizes on the commodification of the manners of others and markets a romantic notion of the city and its past glory, he is taking advantage of an unfortunate shake-up of society.[12] At the same time, working as a gigolo alienates Degenthal from Lela, the woman he loves. The solution for his financial and romantic woes comes in the form of foreign aid and suggests the importance of American involvement abroad.

Ready to embrace the less romantic role of grandmother, Jenny does not totally abandon the role of merry widow. She merely redefines it and implicitly supports a position that the United States had taken on the world stage in the wake of World War I. As Jenny is leaving the Degenthal castle, which she had recently acquired at auction, Bimpfel asks what she plans to do with her acquisition. Giving it to the count outright would not do, because he could neither afford its upkeep nor would he accept charity. Turning it into a smart investment holds the answer. She names Franz manager and Bimpfel his assistant. True to form, the American suggests they modernize the castle and transform it into an apartment hotel, installing central heating and bathrooms. If we see Jenny metonymically as the United States, then her largess can be read as a positive spin on the country's engagement on the world's stage. Jenny makes a wise investment, which appears to call for minimal American involvement with a potentially high return. It also promises to stabilize an unstable society, and it indirectly challenges the upstart butler. From a mainstream American perspective, this is certainly preferable to having Franz work for his former butler. Although the former count will still earn his keep from his manners and his family's history for another employer, the circumstances have changed. No longer is it the worker turned boss who will profit from the count's performance, but Franz von Degenthal himself—and his American investor.

Evenings for Sale transports viewers to a Vienna in transition, where former roles are in flux as in the United States and where the clichés have been turned into commodities. Like Lela, women are asked to be more tolerant toward the men in their lives, and like Jenny, women are called upon to accept narrowly prescribed roles that rank duty higher than pleasure or personal fulfillment. Jenny is also a stand-in for those desiring escape, and her journey is reminiscent of the role cinema played for American women in the thirties. Like Jenny, the American public could escape to an imagined world that seemed real because of its tenuous basis in reality. Vienna—and movies—are presented as commodities to be consumed and enjoyed—in moderation and with ironic distance.

Clashing and Melding Cultures in *Champagne Waltz*

In a *New York Times* article from February 3, 1935, an Austrian guest mused that the only place a happy Vienna existed anymore was in foreign-made films or in memories.[13] A. Edward Sutherland's *Champagne Waltz* (1937) appears to substantiate the Austrian's claim. Set in a world unscathed by economic hardship and untouched by political instability, it bears little resemblance to contemporary Austria. The initially packed waltz palace, the bustling wine garden, and the lively street scenes all suggest a healthy economy and political calm. In this story, Vienna's equilibrium is not shaken by domestic upheaval or threats from its northern neighbor, but by an American jazz band.

When *Champagne Waltz* reenacts the jazz invasion, it attaches gender to the nations involved. The United States is the home of the more aggressive low culture genre, exemplified by the male jazz band, while Austria is viewed as the home of "high" culture, associated in the minds of many Americans as feminine and embodied here by a female opera singer.[14] When the American jazz band takes Austria by storm, it threatens what is presented as a venerable Austrian music tradition. After the band leader Buzzy Bellew (Fred MacMurray) is transformed by his romance with the warbling Elsa Strauss (Gladys Swarthout), he convinces the American and Austrian impresarios to bring the Austrians to New York. There in the closing scene the two musical idioms are united and the two lovers reunited.

Champagne Waltz revives the cultural clash at a time of social upheaval in the United States and Europe. Unemployment remained high in the United States, which led to a stricter enforcement of an earlier immigration law that demanded that visas be issued only to those who would not become a public charge. At the same time, the Nazi takeover resulted in an ever-growing number of refugees desiring to come to the United States. The Austrian-American romance prompts reflections on American chauvinism and argues for the contributions that Austrians and others fleeing Europe could make in the United States. The film views the melding of two seemingly opposing musical idioms and the cross-cultural romance as rooted in the fabric and diversity of the United States. Moreover, it depicts the integration of the newcomers as economically profitable.

The incursion of American jazz into Vienna is performed spatially and aurally as a type of takeover unwittingly carried-out by benevolent male aggressors. The film begins in a world where the waltz, undisturbed by outside forces, rules supreme. It opens with a still, a distant shot of the back gardens of Schönbrunn, the baroque summer palace of the Habsburgs. The word "Vienna" is immediately superimposed over the palace. The shot fades to the sign "Viennese Waltz Palace, founded in 1867 by Johann Strauss and now under the direction of Franz Strauss." In these shots two traditions are tied together—Austria's imperial past and its musical heritage, which would have been familiar to American moviegoers of the time. The establishment of place allows the audience to appreciate the impact of the ensuing jazz invasion and the solution to the clash of cultures.

Although Vienna is clearly identified as the setting, the film leaves the exact time purposefully open. While the first shots might suggest a pre–World War I Austria, viewers can assign the action to some unspecified time during the Austrian First Republic after the first spoken temporal reference. Showman that he is, the American impresario Happy Gallagher (Jack Oakie) wants Buzzy Bellew's entrance into the city to match his celebrity status. "By the way, I want every big shot in this town down at the railroad station tomorrow. . . . I want the mayor, the governor, I want the king." To this, his Austrian counterpart Max Snellinek (Herman Bing) replies in a thick accent: "There is no king. This is a republic." Only later is it possible to pin down the exact year. When Buzzy informs the two businessmen that the Waltz Palace has been in the Strauss family for fifty-five years, viewers with good memories and quick math skills can pinpoint the year as 1922.[15] However, it is unlikely that many viewers would care or be able to figure it out. Audiences in 1937 could assign the situation to the recent past or the present, ignoring the fact that after the dissolution of the parliament in 1933 Austria was a fascist state.

The opening scene captures the extent to which the tradition of Johann Strauss Jr. is supposedly venerated in Vienna, providing a stark contrast with the coming violation of Austria's musical heritage. From the sign of the "Viennese Waltz Palace," the camera cuts to a statue of Strauss holding a conductor's baton. Just then a rose is placed at its base by a disembodied hand, later identified as belonging to Fräulein Elsa Strauss, when the doorman greets her. When Franz Strauss, Elsa's grandfather and director of the Waltz Palace, arrives shortly afterward, a group of children beg him to make "him," the statue, play. Gladly acquiescing to their pleas, he sets the mechanism in motion that animates the statue of his famous ancestor. The impressive baroque-looking doors of the Waltz Palace open as Franz Strauss enters the lavish hall and underscore the late composer's status. Once inside, the interest shifts to Elsa Strauss. As the camera follows Franz Strauss, he passes admirers eager to know when his granddaughter is going to sing, building up the anticipation. As her grandfather raises his baton, the strains of Elsa Strauss singing a waltz in praise of Vienna are heard. However, the camera does not yet show her. The camera slowly pans over a rapt, rather strait-laced audience, until it finally reaches the beautiful descendant of the Waltz King, warbling "Paradise in Waltz Time" after the long build-up.

Immediately after this scene in the Waltz Palace, the impending cultural conflict with the American competition is foreshadowed and revealed as a business transaction. The camera cuts from a final close up of Elsa to two men as they emerge from the Waltz Palace. They walk next door and stop in front of a sign announcing the arrival of Buzzy Bellew and the opening of a jazz club. The Austrian impresario Snellinek expresses fear about his recent business venture, having invested heavily in the adjacent jazz club. Bellew's manager, the 100-percent oafish American Happy Gallagher effusively assures him that Buzzy is the greatest. When Snellinek asks him to compare Buzzy to Beethoven, Mozart, Schubert, Gallagher shows his ignorance of classical music and enthusiastically replies, "Schubert, he's better than both the Schuberts." Although Snellinek may be a little less parochial than his partner, both are equally concerned with profit associated with their investments in the entertainment industry.

The apparent spatial security and acoustic dominance of the "classical" idiom in the previous scenes are decidedly upset by Buzzy Bellew's invasion-like entrance. Snellinek has assembled the *Männergesangverein* (Men's Singing Club) and Austrian and American dignitaries alike at the train station to welcome the American jazz band. As Buzzy's train pulls in, the chorus intones the melodious and staid greeting, "We welcome you, we welcome you, we welcome you into our hearts." The crowd does not know what awaits them. When Gallagher finally rousts the American combo from the train, Buzzy sets off an acoustic explosion. He jumps off the train, clarinet in hand, and literally blows the Viennese away. The following shots show how foreign and initially alarming the music is. A woman emerging from a train car retreats back on board when she hears the music's strains. A dachshund runs from its cacophony. The city fathers lined up to greet the band stiffen. However, their reserve is soon worn down by the music and the antics of the band. By the end of the sequence, the Austrians welcoming the Americans become indistinguishable from their foreign guests as all move in time with the music.

If the band's arrival is performed as an invasion, their success is presented as an occupation, welcomed by many, but deplored by the neighbors. Four months after their arrival, the jazz locale is hopping, but the Waltz Palace is woefully empty. Not only has the public flocked to the hall next door, but the foreign music invades their space. Franz Strauss takes stock of the situation and grimly realizes it is not the weather or the day of the week that keeps people away. "No, no, ever since that American band came here I've been telling myself it's the weather, it's Monday, it's Friday, making one excuse after the other. Listen. They play so loud it comes through the wall. I've asked them to play more quietly. I've written letters, I've protested. That's not music, that's noise." The gentle waltzes cannot hold their own against the more aggressive popular music, and the demise of the Waltz Palace appears imminent.

However, just at the moment when the Waltz Palace is threatened with closure, Buzzy is awakened to the beauty of Austria's rich past in an almost spiritual revelation. Just after Buzzy Bellew, who had originally pretended to be the American consul, "confesses" that he is a refrigerator salesman, Elsa asks him if he can be serious for a moment. She wants to show him something very important. They then enter the Waltz Palace and the camera cuts to a vast and impressive empty space, whereupon Buzzy utters a monosyllabic, "Gee." Elsa explains, "This is what the Strauss name stands for. And this is what those people next door are destroying. Things have happened in this room. Great things, things to be proud of." Buzzy, duly impressed by the empty space, replies, "I can see that now, Elsa." However, she insists, "No, all you see is with your eyes. I want you to see it with your heart. I want you to see it as Johann Strauss saw it. . . ." As the camera cuts from a medium shot of them to a long shot from behind them into the vast and empty room, she completes the sentence, ". . . that night so many years ago when he first played his Blue Danube for the emperor." Elsa's desire that Buzzy see it with his heart along with the revered space works magic. A film within a film presents a memory handed down over generations, a memory so powerful that Buzzy and the audience see what Elsa Strauss wants him to see. As the screen fills with festively-dressed people, Elsa and Buzzy fade from view. The emperor enters, Strauss plays a waltz, and the crowd dances.[16] In this two-minute-and-forty-second-long sequence, the glory of the past is multiplied through shots of the dancers taken from various heights and angles as well as a long shot of the ballroom crowded with dancers reflected in a mirror. As the last strains of the waltz are played and the image of the dancers fades, the camera cuts back to Buzzy and Elsa in the empty hall. The otherwise loquacious Buzzy can only utter a hushed and reverent "gosh." He kisses Elsa not on the mouth as in an earlier scene, but on the forehead, a sign of respect for this past.

Figure 2.2. Ballroom flashback in *Champagne Waltz*. © 1936 Paramount Pictures. Credit: Universal Studios Licensing LLC. Courtesy of the Margaret Herrick Library, Academy of Motion Picture Arts & Sciences.

The scene serves multiple purposes. It comments on the power of love, space, and the imagination as well as the magic of cinema and the importance of the endangered music. Love and the "sacred" space open Buzzy's eyes to another world. Although in earlier versions of the script, Elsa narrated what viewers saw, here Buzzy is moved by a past transmitted to him mysteriously through the power of suggestion and the very space itself. The audience, too, is privy to the magical and mystical scene shared between Elsa and Buzzy. At this point, Buzzy's romance with Elsa takes on new meaning for him, giving him and ideally the audience a new appreciation of the threatened Austrian culture. Performing becomes empty for Buzzy, if it means the ruin of the Waltz Palace. Unable to convince Snellinek or Gallagher of the importance of their musical neighbors, Buzzy breaks his contract and returns to the United States where he ends up playing in dives. Yet, Buzzy's new principles and resulting sacrifice cannot revive the waltz or reverse the misfortunes of Elsa and her grandfather, who are reduced to giving music lessons to untalented children.

The film does not simply argue for the cultural importance of the music, but its financial potential and adaptability. The only hope for the endangered music lies in finding a new audience with money, that is, transplanting it to the United States. When Buzzy tips Gallagher off to a great business prospect in New York, Gallagher and Snellinek bring the Waltz Palace to New York. In contrast to the jazz invasion of Austria, this is not staged as a take-over, but as a combined cultural and financial opportunity that will thrive alongside other forms of popular entertainment. Unlike the "jazz invasion" that threatened hallowed traditions in Vienna, the Austrians are easily integrated into the cultural scene in New York. They even adopt slicker performance styles. From the flashing lights high atop the Blue Danube Roof advertising Elsa and Franz Strauss's first appearance in the United States, the picture fades to a medium close-up of the club's doors that replicate those of the Viennese Waltz Palace. A long dance sequence between the American dancer and his Austrian partner introduces the new floor show, which begins and ends with gestures more sensual than any shared between Buzzy and Elsa. Next comes a musical offering—Elsa's reprise of "Paradise in Waltz Time" from the opening scene, but with different staging. In a setting reminiscent of Busby Berkeley films, Elsa looks like a decoration on a wedding cake, singing atop a structure surrounded by five "layers" of violin players.

However, for a truly happy ending the lovers and the idioms must be united. When Buzzy and Elsa are reunited in the final scene, both the earlier spatial antipathies and aural cacophony are resolved in the blending of the two musical idioms. From the new neon sign that combines jazz and waltz through the shared "a," the camera fades to a long shot of Franz Strauss on a podium conducting a waltz and playing his violin with a huge string orchestra. The orchestra members sway as they play the classical waltz. This is followed by an extreme long shot of the Austrian conductor and the orchestra as well as a long shot of the orchestra from the side. Then the camera pans quickly to Buzzy, who in tails is conducting "The Tiger Rag" and playing a saxophone in front of a sizable brass and percussion orchestra. The camera mirrors the earlier takes of Strauss's orchestra with shots of the jazz orchestra, before it cuts to an extreme long shot of the ensembles side-by-side. As the camera alternates from the huge waltz orchestra to Buzzy's equally large ensemble, the music style, too, alternates, shifting between the classical waltz and big band style. When the two orchestras merge together as they play, the styles also merge, and they play the waltz in a decidedly big-band rhythm. When they have been totally united, the members of the newly formed orchestra stand up, and Elsa emerges from the floor. The camera zooms in on her and backs out as the two conductors' podiums move toward her. Franz Strauss and Buzzy Bellew, the former warring representatives of the two cultures, are brought together by Elsa. She switches their instruments, giving Strauss a saxophone and Buzzy a violin. Each man plays a phrase, with a nod to the other's musical genre.

The last words spoken in the film signal that the union of the two idioms and reunion of the lovers carries meaning that extends beyond any personal relationship. During a final close-up, Elsa quotes the motto of the United States: "E pluribus unum." Earlier Buzzy had used it as a type of battle cry when pretending to be the American consul on the war path against that dastardly Buzzy Bellew. However, when he used it, it was without meaning. By contrast, the final scene embodies the phrase. "Out of the many is one" or in this case, out of the many is something new. Not only is Austria's rich tradition viewed as something worth importing to the United States, but both it and jazz become something new. At a time when many were seeking refuge in the United States from Hitler's tyranny, the film offers a serious message. *Champagne Waltz* is a call for acceptance of different cultures and a reminder of the belief that America was built on the idea of strength in diversity.

The on-screen cross-cultural encounters and melding of cultures were indebted to off-screen cross-cultural encounters that extend back to Paul Whiteman's trip to Vienna in June 1926. A then young Billy Wilder, who co-wrote the story "Moon Over Vienna," on which the film was based, was among the crowd who met the band leader at the train station.[17] A huge fan of Whiteman's, Wilder shepherded the band leader around Vienna and followed him to Berlin to report on his performances there for the tabloid *Die Stunde*. In the article he wrote about the visit he poses questions that had been circulating in Europe since the introduction of jazz. "For jazz? Against jazz? The most modern music? Kitsch? Art?" His answer swiftly follows: "A Must! A necessary renewal of the blood of calcified Europe."[18] In the cultural debates in the twenties, Wilder came down on the side of the American genre as necessary to rejuvenate old Europe. However, a decade later he highlighted the cultural and entertainment value of the older European idiom. Having arrived in the United States in 1934 as a refugee from Hitler, Wilder advocated the contribution that Europeans could make to the entertainment industry.[19]

In his *New York Times* review from February 4, 1937, Frank Nugent found little new in Paramount's attempt at semi-high-brow entertainment. When he argues that *Champagne Waltz* rehashes "the old feud between classical music and jazz," he overlooks the symbolic and timely quality of the Austrian-American fusion. *Champagne Waltz* returns to these debates to comment on the United States, but with a definite timely American take on the topic. A comparison with Emmerich Kálmán's Viennese operetta *Die Herzogin von Chicago* (The Duchess of Chicago) from 1928, in which the composer integrates jazz à la Paul Whitman, illustrates how each is addressing a particular cultural context.[20] The operetta, with a libretto by Julius Brammer and Alfred Grünwald, has parallels with Paramount's cross-cultural romance. In the Hungarian's take on the jazz craze, an impoverished prince from an imaginary European kingdom falls in love with an American heiress, but not before there is a musical culture clash. The royal, a lover of the czardas, is incensed when the rich American demands to hear jazz and dance the Charleston in his favorite café. But in the end both learn from the other and are reconciled in love. As the musicologist Stefan Frey argues, Kálmán turns to the American idiom to revitalize operetta.[21] The cultural conflict and resolution in the Hollywood film fulfills other goals. In *Champagne Waltz*, the "real" backdrop and reversal of sexes are more than cosmetic differences. The setting in a republican Vienna with a male American protagonist and a European female has symbolic consequences. In this scenario where the "male" culture initially threatened the "female" culture, the American learns its value and rescues it in the end. In the "E pluribus unum" musical finale, a new idiom emerges from the two.

The tale that begins in Hollywood's Austria and ends in a cinematic New York offers a contemporary parable in fancy dress. At a time when Europe was becoming increasingly dangerous for many of its citizens, the romantic liaison in *Champagne Waltz* humorously criticizes cultural ignorance and insensitivity toward other cultures and argues for the recognition of the contributions of the new immigrants in the United States. Just as the American Buzzy Bellew has gained from his contact with Austrian culture, so too can society at large be enriched through the contribution of this foreign contingent. For those who are not moved by altruism, the final scene lavishly suggests that integrating and adapting the Austrian idiom can also bring financial gain.

Red-Blooded Americans in *The Emperor Waltz* and *A Breath of Scandal*

Circumstances in the intervening years led to realignments in the cross-cultural romances. In Billy Wilder's *The Emperor Waltz* and Michael Curtiz's *A Breath of Scandal*, released in 1948 and 1960 respectively, the Austrians learn important lessons from the Americans in an imperial setting. There is neither a positive view of the European empire nor a possible melding of cultures. In contrast to *Evenings for Sale* and *Champagne Waltz*, the two movies tie actions of individuals more directly to the country's elite. Moreover, they stand in stark opposition to the empire-affirming pictures of the late thirties and early forties, which use imperial Austria to distance the country from its pugilistic neighbor Germany.

Both *The Emperor Waltz* and *A Breath of Scandal* trace their roots back to Ferenc Molnár's 1928 play *Olympia*, which attacks snobbery and hypocrisy through the doomed romance of a princess and a "lowly" Hungarian captain. The filmmakers reworked the original scenario to hail "American" virtues and attack attitudes and behaviors they associated with Europe, each reflecting the historical juncture of their production. However, each has a different take on the cross-cultural affair. In 1943 Wilder and Brackett had Paramount buy the rights to *Olympia* from MGM, which had filmed it as *His Glorious Night* in 1929.[22] Wanting to make a musical comedy out of it, they decided that Kovacs, the Hungarian officer, had to be changed to an American. Brackett noted in his diary on May 15, 1944, "In the afternoon, having crystallized our difficulty (or we hope) into the fact that the difference between a Princess heroine and a Captain (untitled) hero is too pastel for the grasp of an American audience, we set about finding a job for Kovacs. Considered a Ford car salesman, but gave it up for a Victor phonograph salesman with Master's Voice fox terrier."[23] The two appear to have drafted a basic outline by October 3, 1945, when Brackett notes, "Told an old story of ours—one suggested by *Olympia*, in which a traveling salesman for phonographs in 1905 tries to get the endorsement of the Emperor Franz Joseph and wins the heart of an Arch Duchess."[24] It was at this session that Wilder also envisioned Bing Crosby as the salesman.

Although not set in contemporary Austria, this tale nonetheless addressed topical issues circulating between the time the project was conceived in 1943 and shooting was completed in June 1946. In the turn-of-the-century setting, the film makes fun of European anti-Americanism, attacks Nazi racist ideology, debunks the myth of Austria's innocence, and hails American economic strength, simplicity, and moral character. In this light-hearted "film with music" the American phonograph salesperson, Virgil Smith (Bing Crosby), travels to Austria-Hungary with his mongrel dog Buttons. The enterprising Smith thinks that if the emperor (Richard Haydn) buys the new invention, all Austria will. However, things do not quite work out as expected. When he meets Countess Johanna Franziska Augusta von Stolzenberg-Stolzenberg (Joan Fontaine), every bit as proud as her name suggests (stolz = proud; Berg = mountain), the blue-blood, along with her poodle Scheherazade, insult the red-blooded American and his dog. Later they toss differences aside and fall for each other, but not without some lessons for the celluloid Austrians and commentary on their behavior. As representatives of their countries, Virgil and Johanna and their four-legged counterparts are tied to particular discourses on national identity.

When Wilder and Brackett tied the cross-cultural encounter of the humans and their four-footed companions to questions of national identity, class, and racial purity, they exposed Austria's elite as ultimately morally corrupt and lauded the integrity of the US elite. Whereas the Austrian female is connected to prejudice and snobbery and to a group of people who consider themselves superior to Americans, the less pedigreed American counters with his simplicity, his flexibility, his defense of mixed blood, and his moral strength.

Figure 2.3. Suggested advertisement from the pressbook for *The Emperor Waltz*. © 1948 Paramount Pictures. Credit: Universal Studios Licensing LLC. Courtesy of the Margaret Herrick Library, Academy of Motion Picture Arts & Sciences.

In the screenplay, Wilder and Brackett included humorous commentary that criticized the Austrian elite, but which is not easily translated to the screen. After a description of the ballroom in the opening scene, they make mild fun of those dancing. "It's the cream of the cream of the cream of European society, and whatever their sociological shortcomings, they really can waltz. The women have other talents as well; they know how to dress, how to carry themselves[,] how to wear their hair and present their jewels."[25] They view this society as one that lacks substance, concerned only with appearances.

By introducing the ordinary American to this resplendent scene, they set up a humorous visual contrast between the two nationalities:

> A figure is climbing up the quoins of the end column. It is a man, an American, to tell you the truth, name of VIRGIL HOMER SMITH. There is nothing extraordinary about him. If you met him in Kansas City or Passaic, New Jersey or Malone, New York, you'd never give him a second look. Against this resplendent milieu he stands out like a wad of chewing gum among the crown jewels. He's dressed the American way (1900 style): galoshes, a good warm topcoat, muffler, a soft hat, woollen [*sic*] gloves and black velvet ear muffs.[26]

Virgil Smith, just a regular guy, is an interloper, an irritant in the foreign surroundings whose presence brings Austrian prejudices to the surface. If Austrians and Americans are initially contrasted superficially by dress, Austrian attitudes and behaviors toward the American salesperson and his dog soon expose them as prejudiced.

The opening scene humorously presents Austrian disdain for Americans, when one of the guests asks to be filled in on the gossip of Smith and Stolzenberg-Stolzenberg's scandalous romance. Two of the Austrians sitting in the gallery characterize Smith as "most vulgar, obnoxious, ill-mannered." For them these characteristics are synonymous with his nationality. "In one word he's an American." And he is not just any American, but as the cleric among the group states, "And low even among Americans, he's what they call a traveling salesman." This elite gathering can find nothing good to say about this or any American.

In this initial scene the Austrian characters articulate attitudes not uncommon among the postwar Austrian population. Anti-American attitudes reaching back to the interwar debates and exacerbated by National Socialist ideology persisted across a significant swath of the population. "Even in renowned cultural journals, the United States was again depicted as 'the nation of greed and success . . ., the thundering America, the new world of inexperience.'"[27] Viewed as "a soulless, exclusively materialistic nation," the United States was the home of the modernist Moloch.[28] Certainly, there is truth to the critique of American materialism. However, in the context of the film, America's economic strength is viewed positively. Moreover, from the very beginning, the American audience is bound to be skeptical of any criticism directed at Virgil Smith and by extension Americans. Even if audiences do not know anything else about Smith, they cannot take these negative comments seriously with Bing Crosby cast in the role of the "impossible" American. Crosby, "the longest-serving and most successful star in Paramount history," was popular as the sympathetic all-American he played in lightweight comedies.[29]

Tapping into contemporary American sentiments about the material and moral superiority of capitalism, Wilder and Brackett lauded the United States' economic prowess without using the defeated country's position to do this.[30] In the scene when Virgil asks the emperor for Johanna's hand, Emperor Franz Josef argues that class differences would probably ruin Virgil and Johanna's chances for a happy marriage and that Johanna would have to try to forget her aristocratic background. Here, Virgil snaps back, "Where she came from! Because you're better than we are?" At this point, the emperor concedes American superiority. "I don't say we're better. As a matter of fact, I think you're better. You are simpler, you are stronger. Ultimately, the world will be yours." What began as a discussion concerning a match or mismatch between Johanna and Virgil evolves into one of the economic superiority of the United States. The film argues that a people unburdened by tradition will have the edge, which reflected the country's dominance in emerging world markets after World War II.[31]

In comparison with Wilder's *A Foreign Affair*, set in a postwar bombed out German capital and released in the same year, the positive assessment of the American may seem surprising. According to Georg Schmundt-Thomas, the love triangle set in occupied Berlin among an American army officer (John Lund), a German cabaret singer and former lover of a high Nazi official (Marlene Dietrich), and a strait-laced American congresswoman (Jean Arthur) "caricatures the ideological anxieties over American foreign involvement and the dangers of the new global hegemonic role as the trials and tribulations in the war between the sexes."[32] Although released in 1948, *The Emperor Waltz* was completed in the summer of 1946. Consequently, *The Emperor Waltz* was much more a comment on the Europeans' behavior during the Nazi era, praise for American democracy, and a prediction of the place of the United States in world markets. By contrast, *A Foreign Affair*, with its "realistic" background in occupied Germany, presents a more ambivalent picture of Americans and postwar politics.

In the film narrative of *The Emperor Waltz* the superiority of the United States, deriving from its economic strength, its diversity, and flexibility, is used to reject essentialist theories of national identity and to condemn racism. While the Austrians find the American's sales techniques duplicitous and proof of his lowly societal status, the facility with which

Virgil assumes multiple identities to sell his wares implies that national identities are social constructions. A modern bard peddling entertainment in his efforts to sell the phonograph, the American knows how to work his diverse public. Aware of the court protocol, he presents himself as a potentate when he seeks an audience with the emperor. Later he admits he stretched the truth a bit, but does declare that he is an officer in the Shriners. Through his musical ability and his Austrian dress, he unwittingly fools Johanna into believing he is Austrian. When the chauffeur stops the overheated car as Johanna, her father, and her dog approach the emperor's castle in the Tyrol, she sees and hears someone in a Tyrolean outfit singing. She remarks to her father, "Listen to that yodel. It's the voice of Austria, isn't it? Mountain-born, deep-rooted, eternal." The belief in national identity based on in-born qualities is soon debunked. The audience knows, of course, that the singer is neither Austrian nor mountain-born, and his voice is certainly not deep-rooted or eternal. Minutes later, after the dogs are entangled in another fight, Johanna is outraged upon her discovery that her authentic Austrian is only "the same objectionable American." When she demands to know why he is wearing the Alpine outfit, he quickly answers, "Well, if I wanted to make a deal with the Sultan of Morocco, I'd come dressed as a Dervish." Not only can the American yodel and even get the mountains to respond, he has an acute business sense and realizes the importance of adapting to the foreign culture to sell his wares. Wilder and Brackett nonetheless poke fun at this as Virgil initially has his hat on backwards, which he adjusts to imitate the Tyrolean men who pass him. However, after his confrontation with Johanna, he reverses the hat to its original backwards state as a sign of mild protest.

Wilder and Brackett conflate humans and canines throughout, not just for laughs or as double entendres that might pass the censors, but to take a stand against racism. The discourse on blood lines starts out rather innocently and humorously when Johanna has been summoned to court along with her father, the general Baron Holenia, and her poodle Scheherazade. The emperor wonders why they are so gloomy, asking, "Don't you approve of the alliance?" At this point father and daughter (and audience members surely) think that he is talking about a marriage for Johanna. "This match means a great deal to me. I've given it infinite thought. I've looked up the bloodlines on both sides. Fine, fine, one couldn't ask for better." He continues, "What pleases me most, both lines are very prolific. A little embarrassing to talk about this." Johanna becomes more and more uncomfortable. He wants the union to take place as soon as possible as he explains, "You see, spry as he is, he's a rather elderly gentleman." Johanna hesitantly asks how old. Only when the emperor gives the age of the bridegroom as twelve is Johanna relieved, realizing he is talking about the dogs.

When Virgil and Buttons enter the picture, the discussion of blood lines becomes attached to nationality. The aristocratic Austrian Johanna connects the notion of "pure blood" to national superiority, while the American Smith rejects this. After Buttons is bitten and left bleeding by Scheherazade, Virgil carts the dog over to the Stolzenberg-Stolzenberg Palace on Stolzenberg-Stolzenberg Way to demand an apology. At this point he and the countess argue about pedigree and each dog's contribution to society. She goes on haughtily, asking rhetorically, "Have you ever heard of blood lines?" then elaborating, "Hers go back to the eighteenth century." Virgil counters, maintaining his dog has a much older lineage, "His go back to as far as they've been having dogs." Johanna retorts with a list of Scheherazade's relatives. "Perhaps you've heard of one of her ancestors, Papillion, the poodle of Marie Antoinette. They were both guillotined in the French Revolution.... Her father belongs to Czar Nicolas of Russia.... Her mother to the Infant of Spain.... Her twin brothers belong to a cardinal and live in the Vatican. As for Scheherazade herself, she's just become engaged to the dog of his Majesty Francis Joseph the First." Although all illustrious personalities, the Austrian aristocratic dog is associated with European despots and the Vatican, which did not receive high marks for its actions or lack thereof in the Holocaust. Somewhat unsure of his dog's parentage Virgil is nonetheless quick to respond, convinced that Button's relatives have contributed to society. "Well, his mother belongs to a milkman in Springfield, Illinois, and his father, his father [clearing his throat], well, you've got me there.... Button's brother helps a kid named Stinky O'Hara deliver newspapers and his sister was making an honest living as a watchdog until she was hit by the Baltimore and Ohio." Although the American dog does not have the same pedigree, he does have an honorable history.

The dog/people parallel takes a serious turn at the end of the film, when Scheherazade has puppies, tying Austria to the genocide of the Nazi era. The scene begins humorously as the emperor and Johanna's father pace back and forth in anticipation of the impending arrival of newborns. Then, if only for a few minutes, the film alludes to the Jewish genocide. Johanna's father, seeing that the puppies were sired by Buttons and not Louis XIV, tells the emperor they were born dead and orders the veterinarian to kill them. When Virgil catches him in the act, the animal doctor defends his actions, stating "Orders have been given." The allusion to the National Socialists is repeated when the Haydn melody or *Kaiserhymne* announces the emperor's entrance to the ball. The tune of the anthems of the Habsburg monarchy and of Nazi Germany ("Deutschland, Deutschland über alles") ties Germany's crimes to Austria. The originally humorous comparisons between dogs and humans reaches a very serious climax when Virgil, pups in hand, confronts the emperor:

You're not going to kill them! You're not going to, do you understand? Because I'm not going to let you. I don't care how many of you there are. As a matter of fact, it's probably a good thing there are so many of you. Maybe all of you together can scrape up enough decency to lay off these little duffers who've just begun to breathe. They're not pure enough for you, huh? Not quite your sort. Freaks. Little mongrels you wouldn't have around. So what are you gonna do? You're gonna shake 'em off that great big noble family tree of yours and let them rot as if nothing had happened?

This passionate speech with the use of dogs to point to and condemn the Nazi genocide stands out in contrast to the overall lighter tone of the film.

Certainly, Wilder's knowledge of Austria would have made him skeptical of the victim narrative. Hired by the Office of War Information, Wilder traveled to Germany, viewed documentary footage from the death camps, and conversed with the native population in 1945. At the same time, he sought to find out what had happened to his mother and other family members.[33] If postwar Austrians were looking at their imperial past as a way to establish a national identity distanced from Nazi Germany, Wilder and Brackett exposed this myth with a tongue-in-cheek portrayal of Austria-Hungary.

Although neither film scholars nor Wilder's biographers discussing *The Emperor Waltz* fail to mention the serious subtext and its connection to the Jewish genocide, contemporary reviewers did not see it.[34] Most reviewers declared the film with a domestic box-office take of over $4 million as fun light entertainment with some occasional remarks on lapses of good taste.[35] The sexual innuendos that some reviewers found more or less sophomoric disturbed outspoken audience members greatly.[36] Both the formal reviews and the "fan" letters suggest that the American audiences were looking forward, not back, inward, not outward.

The cross-cultural romance carries with it many messages. In the union between Johanna and Virgil, Johanna has learned much. She rejects the ideology of her society wedded to pure blood lines. Virgil wins his countess, sells his phonograph, makes a mint of money, and exposes the society for what it is. In his confrontation with Austria and Austrians, the American entrepreneur demonstrates the economic and moral strength of his nation and praises its supposed disregard of pedigrees.

Even though *A Breath of Scandal* shares Ferenc Molnár's 1928 play *Olympia* as its source, the emphasis is shifted.[37] By 1957, when Paramount considered the project that would become *A Breath of Scandal*, the Cold War had cast its pall over many aspects of life in the United States, among others the debates concerning sexuality and national identity set off by the publication of the Kinsey reports in 1948 and 1953. With the appearance of the bestselling Kinsey report *Sexual Behavior in the Human Female* in 1953, the discussion on female sexuality and national identity gained new urgency.[38] The health of the nation was thought to be tied to the sexual health of its citizens and particularly to that of women. According to the historian Miriam G. Reumann, "Virtually all authorities who commented on female sexuality believed that women's behavior indicated the state of the nation's morality and culture and offered valuable clues to its future."[39] Many found the public revelations that women had a sex life before and outside of marriage worrisome and viewed it as a clear sign of the deterioration of American society.

Set in 1907 Austria-Hungary, *A Breath of Scandal* engages with contemporary debates on female sexuality and ties them to the nation's health, echoing Cold War rhetoric. In Paramount's last cross-cultural romance, a modest American engineer (John Gavin), hoping to buy bauxite from Emperor Franz Josef, falls in love with the hot-blooded, haughty Princess Olympia (Sophia Loren). In this scenario the Austrian aristocratic woman learns that love, sex, and marriage are a holy triumvirate and the healthy alternative to a decadent life with pre- and extramarital affairs.

When the Italian co-producers Marcello Girosi and Carlo Ponti (Sophia Loren's husband) signed an agreement on January 2, 1958, with Paramount to co-produce multiple pictures with Loren, *Olympia* was on the list.[40] More than any of the other Austrian-American romances, the casting of the female protagonist shaped the direction of the film. Sophia Loren's own sexual presence coupled with debates on female sexuality and the censors' demands forced those making the film to walk a tightrope between the desire to "sex it up" and the need to avoid censure from the Production Code Administration.

Girosi and Ponti had a particular interest in molding the character of Olympia. In a seven-page memorandum dated March 3, 1959, Girosi argued that the part needed to be rewritten to better suit the actress's personality. According to him, Olympia should have a "dual personality," "an exterior cold and extremely well-behaved Princess, and the other one of a turbulent and occasionally very passionate woman."[41] Loren's character should "give a more intimate and secret aspect to her real personality, which is that of a passionate and rather turbulent nature."[42] As an Italian actress playing an Austrian princess, her unbridled sexuality could be seen as foreign; at the same time she resembled the untamed female sexuality that Kinsey had recently described.

When Girosi argued that the motivation for Olympia's fear of the emperor's disfavor needed to be strengthened for contemporary audiences, he tied marriage practices to nationalities. The promise of being a lady-in-waiting hardly seemed a convincing enough reason to limit her sexual exploits. Girosi called for "a more modern, direct and understandable 'goal' for Olympia and her parents."[43] He suggested a marriage that would also be a political alliance with "Prince Rupert, who not only bears one of the great names of Austria, but is notoriously known as the illegitimate son of the Emperor himself." He argued that Olympia's parents would go for it, because they would "want to see her married to one of the great names of Europe, and secondly because they feel that only in the protective security of a marriage will the strange, impulsive character of their daughter best be kept in check."[44] The "strange, impulsive character" is a direct expression of her sexuality, and Girosi thought her parents would feel it needs to be "kept in check" or in Cold War parlance "contained." As the historian Elaine Tyler May argues, "In the domestic version of containment, the 'sphere of influence' was the home. Within its walls, potentially dangerous social forces of the new age might be tamed, where they could contribute to the secure and fulfilling life to which postwar women and men aspired."[45] In line with this thinking, marriage is only a partial solution, for it cannot be just any marriage. To be truly "contained," Olympia's sexuality must be within a democratic marriage based on love and not an arranged marriage.

In response to Girosi's suggestions, in the "1st Preliminary Green Script," dated May 15, 1959, one of the scriptwriters, Walter Bernstein, introduced Princess Olympia as the sexual aggressor consistent with her role in the film. Olympia lives in a sick society in which marriage has little to do with love, and extramarital affairs are the status quo. Exiled from court to her deceased husband's castle in the country because of an earlier peccadillo, Princess Olympia is bored and jumps at the chance of a possible tryst when the unsuspecting American appears on the scene. Having caused her to be thrown from her horse when he loses control of his car, Charlie Foster sets out to help the damsel in distress. Olympia feigns being hurt so that the American must carry her to a nearby deserted hunting lodge that, unbeknownst to him, happens to belong to her. The "injured" princess, who has presented herself as a peasant, does her best to get Charlie into bed.

In the Austrian-American configuration, Charlie Foster represents the American male who has a healthy relationship to sex. Unaware of Olympia's ulterior motives for having him take her to the hunting lodge, the upstanding American remarks on their "unconventional" situation of having to spend the night together. "I could be the kind of man to take advantage of a situation like this."[46] Out of respect, not lack of desire, he will not take advantage of her, which he makes sure she knows. "Now listen, don't get me wrong. Men are men everywhere."

Even when mistreated and "infected" by the society's duplicitousness, the American male is able to overcome his baser instincts. The court's immorality appears contagious when Charlie blackmails Olympia into spending a weekend with him, promising to leave Austria to avoid being interviewed by an agent of the emperor. However, alone with her at the scene of their first meeting, he foils his own sexual urges by taking a sleeping potion, which he does as much out of a sense of decency as out of love. Expecting that he would exact his revenge by sleeping with her, she is puzzled by his restraint, and even more so when he releases her from her obligation of spending the entire weekend with him. At this point, Olympia declares her love for him and immediately plots their future. He should have "two aluminum plants, one in Berlin and one in Vienna" so she can have easy access to him after she marries Prince Rupert. As soon as he realizes she expects him to become her lover, he takes her back to Vienna, disgusted. Whereas love and marriage go together for the healthy American, the decadent Austrian is still wedded to an "outdated" version of marriage.

To underscore love as an essential component of marriage in the healthy American world view, the cultural divide concerning marriage is repeatedly articulated. Olympia is called back to court because the emperor has arranged her marriage to the Prussian Prince Rupert, which he touts as an "instrument of history," in which "two great states [are] welded together." Later, when Charles asks Countess Lina (Angela Lansbury) whether Princess Olympia loves her intended, she responds, "What an adorable question, Mr. Foster. This is a marriage not a love affair. I don't think their feelings enter into it one way or the other." This attitude is incomprehensible to the American. When he convinces Olympia to meet with him after her formal engagement, he poses a question that reiterates the clash of marriage cultures:

> CHARLIE: And this marriage you're planning, it's being arranged for you?
> OLYMPIA: According to custom.
> CHARLIE: You really think you can live without love?
> OLYMPIA: Certainly not. What a ridiculous idea.
> CHARLIE: Then you do care for this Prince Rupert?
> OLYMPIA: I scarcely know him.

Olympia offers an explanation to the perplexed young man in metaphorical terms:

> CHARLIE: You're getting me mixed up.
> OLYMPIA: It's quite simple, Mr. Foster. I like to listen to music.
> CHARLIE: What does that have to do with it?
> OLYMPIA: It doesn't mean I have to marry a musician.

By engaging in extramarital affairs, as seems customary in this society, she can have her status and pleasure, too. Although the citizens' sexual lives must be above reproach before a royal marriage, there seems to be a tacit agreement that extramarital affairs are where love and sexual gratification meet.

In all versions of the script, Princess Olympia gives Charlie his walking papers, underscoring the clash between the Old and New World values. However, in the "1st Preliminary Green Script" from May 15, 1959, Charlie's response to her rejection and the preempting of his intended marriage proposal explicitly connects a society's mores to the surroundings and by extension to a political system:

> I was going to offer to take you out of all this . . . mess, this rottenness. You're too good for it, Olympia. You deserve a chance at a decent life, among honest, respectable people. It doesn't matter where a person was born or what kind of a stinking background she grew up in. You're a nice person underneath . . . the muck and the filth haven't rubbed off on you.[47]

In this passage and the discussion of its removal following the censor's objections, the national debates prompted by the Kinsey Report shine through. Ring Lardner Jr. who was working with Walter Bernstein on the script, was dismayed by subsequent revisions, which cut "out various bits and pieces reflecting the curious moral standards of the imperial aristocracy."[48] Lardner wanted to link tropes of Austrian decadence to sexual profligacy, as he explained in a communication to Girosi: "Now I felt strongly that what made Charlie different and a more engaging fellow was for him, instead of humbly begging her to consider his suit, to offer her a healthy, sane life in place of her rotten, decadent one."[49] The blacklisted writer unwittingly echoed Cold War anti-Communist sentiment, particularly if Austria-Hungary with its secret police and dictatorial emperor could be imagined as a stand-in for the Soviet Union.[50] According to Elaine Tyler May, "The Soviet Union loomed in the distance as an abstract symbol of what Americans might become if they became 'soft.' Anticommunist crusaders called on Americans to strengthen their moral fiber so they might preserve their freedom and their security."[51] With his proposal of marriage, the American presents the European with a healthy outlet for her sexuality and an escape from a hypocritical society weakened by luxury and decadence.[52]

When Olympia decides to abandon the arranged marriage, leave Austria and go to the United States, she opts for an American-style marriage, which is explicitly tied to democratic values and considered a proper outlet for her sexual urges. After the emperor forgives her a second time, Princess Olympia is free to marry Prince Rupert. Wishing only her happiness, her father inquires whether that is what she really wants. When she mournfully responds, "I will meet my responsibilities," he suggests she reconsider her priorities. To offer her a model, he turns to his own marriage. She learns that for her father having a mistress was only a ruse, "for appearances' sake only" to preserve his social standing. In contrast to society's expectations, his union with her mother was based on love and sexual fidelity. "I will now shock you even more. Your mother and I have been faithful to each other for thirty-six years." He humorously suggests, however, that their love and fidelity must remain a secret: "People would think we were undermining the government." When he emphasizes that "you choose love or you don't," he implies that Olympia can choose love over her loyalty to her family and Austria-Hungary. Once he knows that she will choose Charlie over a loveless marriage, he links her choice of a mate to American democracy in his parting words. "You will find America a most peculiar place. Everyone thinks he's equal to everyone else. They even write it into their laws." The familiar and congenial Frenchman, Maurice Chevalier, playing an Austrian prince pronounces that American individualism and democracy go hand in hand with choice in marriage. As presented in the film, "The postwar imperative for Americans to embrace the freedoms of individualism and democracy, along with a related emphasis on egalitarian marriage, lent a cold-war twist to the idea that modern women were entitled to—even expected to—enjoy sexual pleasure."[53] Olympia's unabashed sexuality within a marriage based on love points away from past models and toward a new American future that views "contained" female sexuality as an essential part of such a union.

Billy Wilder's *A Foreign Affair*, which saw the GIs in danger of being contaminated by the German Fräulein, offers a valuable point of comparison. By contrast, *A Breath of Scandal* shows that the healthy American can withstand temptation and even tame the impetuous foreigner. For Olympia's sexuality to be "contained" in a loving marriage, she must leave her past behind, not unlike women in the fifties. As Reumann maintains, "the discourse on modern American women's sense of sexual entitlement also mirrored social and cultural demands made *of* many postwar women—that they disaffiliate from their origins to create new nuclear families, leave behind ethnic and religious ties to the past, and trade old attitudes and behaviors for middle-class norms."[54] By choosing to run off with Charlie Foster, Olympia rejects the decadent European ways. In the United States, she will be introduced to the middle-class "democratic" American marriage and her sexuality will be safely contained.

Conclusion: Lessons Learned from Austrian-American Encounters

With Austria as the locus for the cross-cultural romances, Paramount's filmmakers placed their American protagonists in surroundings that were at once foreign and familiar. Although set in Vienna, *Evenings for Sale* sends multiple messages addressing domestic challenges arising in the early years of the Depression. Jenny Kent thinks she has found her romantic ideal and an escape from mundane life when she meets Franz Degenthal in Vienna. However, Jenny abandons her dream to accept the less romantic role of grandmother, and Lela, Franz's true love, is criticized for her harsh judgement of his work as a gigolo. Although the American leaves Vienna, she does not leave it untouched, but aids the count's entrance into the middle-class. *Champagne Waltz* revives the debates from the twenties on the Americanization of Europe, ultimately to argue for the contribution of those fleeing Europe. When the jazz musician learns the value of an endangered Austrian tradition, the film demonstrates its compatibility with American idioms as well as its market potential. While in Austria the two musical idioms appear antithetical, but the promise of the diversity of the United States provides a new home for the endangered tradition and its musicians. The film also suggests indirectly that those arriving from Europe can support themselves and will not become public charges.

The personal insight, love, and friendship the American protagonists gained during their stays in Vienna and from their relationships with the Austrians are no longer possible after the country's involvement in World War II, knowledge of the murder of millions by the Nazis, and the anticommunist hysteria of the Cold War. In *The Emperor Waltz* and *A Breath of Scandal*, both set in turn-of-the-century Austria, the Austrians have valuable lessons to learn from the visiting Americans. In *The Emperor Waltz*, the Austrian countess falls for the less sophisticated American and abandons the defense of pure blood lines. Debates on female sexuality in the shadow of the Cold War made their mark on *A Breath of Scandal*. The Austrian princess rejects decadent mores for a healthy sexual relationship within the confines of marriage in a democratic society.

3: The Empire Strikes Back: Imperial Austria Fights Nazis, 1938–41

BEFORE THE UNITED STATES declared war on Germany in December 1941, Hollywood was reluctant to produce anti-Nazi films. Studios feared alienating the German market after the National Socialists came to power in 1933, and producing films openly critical of the Third Reich also posed numerous domestic challenges. Moviegoers seemed particularly skeptical of an industry that had painted the Germans in stark black and white terms during World War I.[1] Consequently, a large portion of the population found the reported brutality of the Germans and the Nazi regime hard to believe. According to the historian Michaela Hoenicke Moore, "Americans had to be convinced by those who identified Nazi Germany as a threat to the United States that there was something newly ominous about that nation."[2] Homegrown anti-Semitism proved another hurdle. Moore notes, "It was pre-existing attitudes toward Germans and Jews that in many cases prevented the news of discrimination, persecution, and, eventually, mass murder from being taken seriously."[3] Widespread isolationist sentiment in Congress and among the American population must have also discouraged politically-minded anti-fascist filmmakers. The United States' involvement in World War I and the disintegration of hope for peace had fed the desire among Americans of all political stripes to stay out of Europe's affairs.[4] Before the United States entered World War II, film industry executives were also concerned that expressly political movies might run counter to the United States' policy of neutrality.[5]

Little changed after Austria became a part of the German Reich in March 1938. Republican Senator William E. Borah of Idaho captured the sentiment of a sizeable number of Americans, when he "discounted the political significance of Hitler's seizure of Austria and called those who stressed Austria's plight actors."[6] By contrast, members of the Hollywood community involved in activities to inform the public of the dangers of fascism must have viewed the Anschluss as yet another indication of Hitler's inhumanity and his threat to world peace.[7] Representatives from Universal, MGM, RKO, and Twentieth Century-Fox working in Vienna experienced the Anschluss and the brutality of the Nazis first hand. Universal's Austrian representative William Satori closed up shop and escaped to the United States. When MGM's Jewish sales manager Felix Bernstein was removed from his position, he also moved to the United

States. The RKO representative was transferred to Rome. The fate of Twentieth Century-Fox's legal representative in Vienna, Dr. Paul Koretz, was unknown for a short time.[8] Moreover, in the wake of the Anschluss, a new wave of refugees, who had worked in the film industry in Europe, arrived in Hollywood.[9] Considering the political climate in the United States, anti-fascists in Hollywood turned to roundabout ways of attacking Germany on screen. For example, a group at Warner Brothers made a series of films that "depicted famous non-American individuals whose life stories highlight significant parallels between the times in which they lived . . . and contemporary Europe and America."[10] This included films on Louis Pasteur, Florence Nightingale, and Emile Zola. Others saw possibilities in Austrian stories.

Plotting Austrian Stories

Stories set in imperial Austria provided the opportunity to attack Germany's politics by proxy, while ideally attracting diverse audiences in the United States and abroad.[11] Although many of the émigrés and exiles working on these films may have had ambivalent attitudes toward Austria and Austrians, according to Jan-Christopher Horak, they reckoned with the fact that "the myth of an Imperial Austria still held sway over the collective psyche of most Americans, reenforced by countless films, Viennese operettas, and Strauss waltzes."[12] At three different historical junctures—late fall 1938, summer 1940, and late summer 1941, filmmakers in Hollywood implicitly attacked Hitler's policies with stories set in imperial Austria. In November 1938, a little more than half a year after the Anschluss, MGM released a Johann Strauss Jr. biopic, *The Great Waltz*, with roots in the *pasticcio*-operetta *Walzer aus Wien* from 1930.[13] The Hollywood incarnation of the Strauss story ties Vienna's fate in 1938 to the world through Strauss and his waltzes and through the patriotism of Strauss and Emperor Franz Josef. If the Anschluss prompted a nostalgic foray to Johann Strauss's Vienna and distanced Austria from its German neighbor, the German takeover of Czechoslovakia, its attack on Poland in September 1939, and Germany's subsequent conquests sent some Hollywood producers back to imperial Austria for stories that could double as comments on Germany's politics. In 1940 MGM turned to a popular novel by the Jewish-Austrian and author of *Bambi*, Felix Salten, as a means both to entertain and comment on the current situation.[14] In *Florian* the fate of a royal Lipizzaner and his human companions before, during, and after World War I points to the fate of refugees from Nazi Germany. In 1941, when the situation of European Jewry and others persecuted by the National Socialists grew even more desperate, the long-time film producer, Jewish-Hungarian William Szekely, then of Gloria Pictures Corp., turned to a Franz Schubert story with roots in the

Viennese musical pastiche *Das Dreimäderlhaus* by Heinrich Berté from 1916.[15] *New Wine* focuses on the tragic figure of Franz Schubert during the rule of an unnamed and unseen tyrannical Habsburg emperor in the early part of the nineteenth century, and ties the genesis of Schubert's music to love gained and lost, sacrifice, and the comfort one finds in religion.[16]

Hollywood was not alone in packaging contemporary messages in films set in pre-1918 Austria. Sabine Hake maintains that after the Anschluss the Viennese film company Wien-Film "continued to offer musical entertainment, but from the German viewpoint of Vienna as a variation on, if not alternative to, true Germanness."[17] Wien-Film's Mozart biographies took on a new political emphasis and, according to Hake, "appropriated the image of Vienna as the world capital of music in order to depict artistic genius as a manifestation of racial superiority."[18] At the same time, Hake notes the disappearance of "all references to Austria as a *Kulturgroßmacht* (cultural empire), whether they [the films] included emotional tributes to the Habsburg dynasty as the perfect union between church and state or nostalgic reminiscences about the multi-ethnic culture of the late Austro-Hungarian Empire."[19] If Wien-Film showed how Austrians and Germans were complementary or how Austrians embodied "true Germanness," Hollywood's post-Anschluss films, set in imperial Austria, presented decidedly different narratives adapted for and shaped by the American context.

By reworking Austrian stories and fictionalizing the history of Habsburg Austria in *The Great Waltz*, *Florian*, and *New Wine*, the filmmakers draw analogies between the distant past and the contemporary situation. In *The Great Waltz* and *New Wine* they specifically use the music of Johann Strauss Jr. and Franz Schubert to construct a distinct Austrian identity. When its patriotic protagonists leave Austria after the demise of the monarchy and exchange Europe for the United States, *Florian* engages with domestic debates on immigration, countering isolationist concerns and public resistance to the immigration of European refugees.

Hollywood's Imperial Austria versus German Fascism

Moviegoers would have to wait until early 1941 for a feature film set in Austria at the time of the Anschluss.[20] However, many must have seen the *March of Time* featurette "Nazi Conquest Nr. 1," which was shown in theaters beginning in April 1938. Three years old in 1938, *March of Time*, with its curious mix of reenactments and commentary, "reached a monthly theatrical audience of between 20 and 26 million people in between 9000 and 10,000 theaters within the United States alone."[21] A month after Nazi Germany officially annexed Austria, a sonorous voice on the "newsreel" proclaimed "the Austria, which Adolf Hitler despised was the Austria-Hungary of doddering old Emperor Franz Josef, the twentieth consecutive Habsburg to rule what had once been the Holy Roman Empire." As the emperor salutes his entourage, climbs into his open carriage, and waves to the cheering populace lining the streets, the narrator reminds viewers of the Habsburgs' importance for the survival of Western, Christian civilization in Europe. "For nearly ten centuries the Habsburgs have maintained the proud port of Europe. For it had been Habsburgs who ruled in the name of his Holiness, the Pope at Rome, Habsburgs who had driven the Turks from Europe." The "doddering" emperor advanced in years is greeted with affection by his people, and as a representative of the Habsburg dynasty, he is viewed as the inheritor of a great legacy. Moreover, the Habsburg Monarchy stands as a Christian bulwark against the East and Emperor Franz Josef as head of an empire with a long and rich history.

If Hitler despised the Austria-Hungary of Emperor Franz Josef, this was the Austria and the ruler that Hollywood loved. While Emperor Franz Josef was portrayed as a taciturn taskmaster and a representative of a hollow tradition in *Merry-Go-Round* and *The Wedding March*, this changed in the thirties. Two MGM films—*Reunion in Vienna* and *The Night Is Young*—and one Columbia production—*The King Steps Out*—are exemplary of the shift. In Sidney Franklin's *Reunion in Vienna* (1932) a gathering of former aristocrats pays tribute to the dead monarch in honor of his one hundredth birthday. In Dudley Murphy's *The Night Is Young* (1935) Emperor Franz Josef is a benevolent, avuncular figure who gently reminds his nephew of the importance of duty. The young, likable, yet-to-be-married emperor defies his mother for love in Josef von Sternberg's *The King Steps Out* (1936).[22] Building on this tradition, filmmakers portrayed Franz Josef sympathetically in *The Great Waltz* and *Florian* and drew parallels between Austria-Hungary and the United States to address contemporary audiences.[23]

Unlike earlier stage and film presentations of the composer's life, the dramatic conflict between father and son is eliminated in *The Great Waltz* in favor of an expressly historical context. The American version of the composer's life fictionalizes the mid-century revolution and Franz Josef's ascent to the throne in an attempt to entertain and elicit sympathy from American audiences for the fate of Austria and its citizens. On the face of it these events do not seem particularly suited for a comparison with the United States. What began as a peaceful protest on March 13, 1848, turned violent "when troops fired on the crowd, killing five and setting off mass rioting. By nightfall Metternich had been dismissed and on the 15th a constitution promised."[24] In the months following there were revolts throughout Europe and another in Vienna at the end of November that was crushed. When Emperor Ferdinand abdicated on December 2 and his eighteen-year-old nephew ascended the throne, this was viewed "as Habsburg recognition of the need for modernization."[25] Franz Josef would eventually dismiss the sitting parliament and reject the constitution as an era of neoabsolutism began; he was hardly a suitable figure to represent democratic principles.[26]

The filmmakers took great liberties with historical reality. However, their version of the events is more than simply Hollywood's disregard for historical accuracy, because it drew parallels with the contemporary situation. Although originally on opposing sides of the revolution, Johann Strauss Jr. and Franz Josef, two icons of Austrian identity, both supported its goals in their own way. The émigré writers Vicki Baum and Gottfried Reinhardt, who were the first to revise the handed-down story, offer some parenthetical information on the Austrian revolution for the Americans. "This revolution of 1848 was not so much one of the working classes but a more intellectual movement, mostly led by students and the young idealistic representants [*sic*] of the new democratic ideas."[27] Their short description distances the Austrian revolution from the bloody Bolshevik and French Revolutions and compares it to the American fight for liberty. In this revolution, the citizens desire the right to govern themselves in a democratic system, thus presenting a counter-narrative to the enthusiastic crowds welcoming Hitler in 1938.

In the early versions by Baum and Reinhardt, Strauss's involvement in the revolution was tied to his need to escape the confines of his bourgeois marriage. However, in the final version the Austrian émigré Walter Reisch and Russian émigré Samuel Hoffenstein ascribed other motivations to Strauss's revolutionary ardor. In the film a short text announces the revolution and Strauss's participation in it. "Vienna loved Strauss waltzes—and listened to new ideas. It clamored for the right of man to govern himself, and so one day—Strauss wrote a march." Responding to his public's demands, Strauss composes the "Revolutionary March" complete with lyrics:

> Ev'ry man has a right that he lives for,
> That he fights for, that he gives for—
> We are ready to fight and we're marching,
> For the time to march is now.
>
> The march goes on, it must go on
> Till more men and more men come by and have gone—
> There is work to do that must be done,
> We'll stay in the fight till the fight is done.

The lyrics complement the placards calling for freedom of the press, an end to tyranny, a constitution, arms for students, and exiling the tyrant

Metternich. The song also implies that Austria's (male) citizens are ready to fight tyranny and that more will be joining the cause, suggesting that there is hope for resistance in 1938.

When Johann Strauss and Franz Josef first meet, the two men represent different sides in the upheaval; however, as exemplary Austrians they ultimately both oppose tyranny.[28] After Strauss rallies the crowd to ransack Count Hohenfried's palace, obviously for no other reason than revenge for the earlier humiliation he suffered there, he has a chance meeting with a not yet identified nobleman. Only addressed as "Your Majesty" by Hohenfried, he turns out to be Archduke Franz Josef, who engages Strauss in a short conversation. When he asks why the musician is rebelling, Strauss hesitates as he searches for an answer and then replies defiantly "Why, [chuckle], why because, [hesitation] because tyranny, oppression, it's written on those banners out there. Can't you read?" Strauss can do little more than parrot the demands of the revolution. When asked directly, "And how are you oppressed, Mr. Strauss?" he cannot come up with anything concrete and merely responds, "Oh, never mind that. And if you all know what's good for you, you'll sneak out the back way." After this the archduke responds quickly, calling him impertinent and ordering his arrest.

Although he challenges Strauss's motives for revolting, the archduke is ultimately viewed as supporting the demands of the revolution, just not the looting and ransacking. In his conversation with Strauss, he is shown as fair and truly curious as to the composer's demands. While Strauss's position as a revolutionary is somewhat weakened, Franz Josef's qualities as a leader are strengthened by his deep concern with the health of the empire. When Count Hohenfried asks to be excused so he can rescue his lover, Carla Donner, the archduke refuses, responding that Austria is an "empire in distress" and suggesting that personal matters must take a back seat to matters of state. The morning after the short revolution, the coachman, who carried Strauss and Carla Donner through the Vienna Woods after their escape from the police, announces joyously, "The revolution is over. We've got a new emperor. Franz Josef, a young wonderful new emperor. We've got a constitution." When a banner with a picture of the new emperor is unfurled, Strauss realizes he had tweaked the new sovereign's nose and even called him a stuffed shirt when they met at Count Hohenfried's.

By presenting Johann Strauss as a revolutionary not able to articulate his oppressed position and Franz Josef as one with the new constitution and somewhat illogically a hero of the revolution, the stage is set for the reconciliation scene between the emperor and the waltz king. At the end of a long sequence showing the genesis and proliferation of the "Blue Danube Waltz," the screen places the audience in front of Schönbrunn in 1888, some forty-three years after the revolution. The elderly Strauss has been called to court to meet with the aged emperor.[29] A much humbler Strauss meets the emperor, who pooh-poohs the composer's formality and reminds him of their earlier meeting, admitting that he was indeed a stuffed shirt. During the audience Emperor Franz Josef names Strauss the "King of Vienna" and presents him to crowds of cheering Austrians when he leads him onto the balcony.

Viewed against the background of the historical events of 1938, the reconciliation of these two icons of Austrian identity takes on contemporary significance. When the balcony reunion was introduced in the 1934 Baum-Reinhardt treatment, Hitler had been in power over a year and a half. At that time the reunion may have served as visual counterweight to the pull of Hitler's rallies. In November 1938 when *The Great Waltz* was released, the visual import of the scene takes on an even greater significance. The imaginary meeting of the venerated Emperor Franz Josef and the celebrated composer Johann Strauss Jr. on the balcony of Schönbrunn with cheering crowds of Austrians serves as a counter-image to crowds that welcomed Hitler at the Hofburg in March 1938. Moreover, it points to the hope of a political reconciliation between the left and right in Austria and suggests the belief that the people's love for Austria will win out.

In *Florian*, not a revolution, but the cataclysmic events surrounding World War I and the demise of the monarchy provide multiple opportunities to weigh in on the events of the day. The film, very loosely based on Felix Salten's eponymous novel, follows the fate of a prized Lipizzaner and his two-legged and four-legged companions during the last days of the empire, the war, and the transition from monarchy to republic. By contrast, the film weaves the stallion's tale together with the love between a duchess and a commoner, who emigrate to the United States after the demise of the monarchy.

Despite the extensive participation of European émigrés in the adaptation of Salten's story for the Hollywood screen, the American producer Winfield Sheehan played the greatest role in shaping the subtexts that address contemporary issues.[30] A member of the Hollywood Anti-Nazi League, Sheehan also had a personal Austrian connection through his wife, the opera singer Maria Jeritza,[31] and the white stallions with which she had been presented in honor of her contributions to the Vienna State Opera.

Although Sheehan emphasized that the film should avoid political topics in a memorandum from October 3, 1938, by September 1939 he was very concerned that Austrians and Germans be differentiated in viewers' minds. In a four-page document to Sheehan dated September 14, 1939, Nicholas Gyory responded to concerns that the producer must have voiced in an earlier communication: "I have searched the various books in an effort to find material which could be used to show the difference

Figure 3.1. Adolf Hitler giving a speech on the balcony of the Imperial Palace, Vienna, March 1938. Reproduced with permission of the Österreichische Nationalbibliothek.

Figure 3.2. Emperor Franz Josef and Johann Strauss Jr. on the balcony at Schönbrunn in *The Great Waltz*. Screen capture.

between the Austrian and the German peoples."[32] This exchange also implies that there had even been some discussion of using Emperor Franz Josef as a mouthpiece to express anti-German sentiment, but Gyory rejected this avenue and concluded, "Since any words that we may put into the Emperor's mouth will, of necessity, be hearsay, it occurred to me that your paragraph regarding the basic difference in the German and Austrian peoples might be the best way of reaching your objective."[33] As a guide, Gyory employed a single volume, Guido Zernatto's *Die Wahrheit über Österreich* (The Truth About Austria), published in 1939. The book's author, a cabinet member under Christian Social Chancellor Kurt Schuschnigg and one-time General Secretary of the Fatherland Front, a supra-political organization in fascist Austria, wrote in the introduction that the volume was an attempt "to portray the events in Austria objectively." He highlighted his situation as an exile and a patriotic Austrian. "I wrote this book—with the many deficiencies it may have—with a bleeding heart, filled with an irrepressible love of my fatherland from which I was driven and that I will never stop loving, loving, loving."[34] While Zernatto's narrative was shaped by his love of country and his experience as an exile, his conservative worldview and approval of the fascist Corporate State (Ständestaat) are also unmistakable.

Whittling 300 pages down to less than four pages, Gyory highlights a variety of contrasts between Germans and Austrians that helped shaped the portrayal of Austria-Hungary, Emperor Franz Josef, and the Austrians in *Florian*. According to Zernatto, Austrians were devoted to their country and its landscape and not to "a fuehrer."[35] Gyory also cites Zernatto's contrast between the Austrian and Prussian in their opposing approaches to duty. "To the Austrian, duty means service; to the Prussian, obedience to orders. In Austria there was room for the individual, and his work for the general good was acknowledged. But the Nazis destroyed the individual."[36] He highlights Zernatto's praise of the monarchy's multi-ethnic influence on contemporary Austrians. "In the Austro-Hungarian monarchy dwelt more than ten racial entities. Their culture and mentality affected and left its imprint on the Austrian type. This type has something of all of these races and is individual and distinctive."[37] Extrapolating from Zernatto's analysis, Gyory points to a commonality between Austria-Hungary and the United States. "As time went on and the Austro-Hungarian Empire became a fact, it approached, in concept and, to some extent in actuality, our own United States."[38] With these differences between Germans and Austrians and the alleged similarities between Austria and the United States, Gyory concludes, "I believe that if we create in dialogue and individuals the real, kindly Austrian type, the objective you have in mind, will be entirely encompassed, and that there will be no chance for anyone to confuse these people with the present Nazi regime."[39] The characteristics Gyory culled from his reading of Zernatto worked their way into the film both in the construction of the "Austrian Empire" and in its kindly, industrious, and conservative citizens.

Differences between Austrians and Germans had to be implied since no Germans actually appear on screen. Indeed, Germany is mentioned only once during the entire film. Yet, given the constant presence of German aggression in the news in 1939, and the film's explicit critique of the warlike Germans of 1914, old Austria compared favorably to contemporary Germany. The film explicitly depicted Emperor Franz Josef's sincere dedication to serving his people and to upholding tradition. This portrayal may have contrasted in viewers' minds with what they knew of Adolf Hitler and his bellicose dictatorial regime. Similarly, the Habsburg Empire is presented as resembling a melting pot, remarkably similar to the United States.

A pro-Austrian stance is established at the very beginning of the film, and by the end of the first scene elements of Gyory's message to Sheehan are evident. *Florian* opens with credits passing over a still shot of a pristine Alpine village with orchestral music playing in the background. The musical accompaniment changes to the *Kaiserhymne*, the anthem of the monarchy. At the same time the introductory text situates the action in late imperial Austria-Hungary: "OUR STORY BEGINS IN THE DAYS WHEN THE AUSTRIAN EMPIRE WAS A GREAT AND DIGNIFIED NATION . . . THIRTEEN DIFFERENT RACES AND LANGUAGES, UNITED BY ADROIT STATESMANSHIP, A POWERFUL ARMY, AND ONE COMMON LOVE . . . WINE, WOMEN, AND SONG." Whereas the initial image transports viewers to some unspecified Alpine location and the music temporally connects the story to the time of Emperor Franz Josef, the text appeals to nostalgia for a lost empire with its hedonistic tradition. Rather than situating the initial action in an existing location, the filmmaker sets his viewers down in Glucksberg (Glück = luck or happiness and Berg = mountain), a fictitious village whose name further associates Habsburg Austria with good fortune and happiness.[40] While the still photograph of the village is on screen, the patriotic hymn changes abruptly to a waltz, an additional marker of Austrian identity and its joie de vivre in countless films. Both the opening images and the introductory text set Austria apart from clichés of a stern, disciplined, and bellicose Germany.

The film also draws a line between the two German-speaking countries more subtly by aligning Austria with the United States. In the introduction, Austria is contrasted with mono-ethnic Germany and appears to resemble the United States in its unthreatening brand of ethnic diversity. In the next scene Austria is further distanced from Germany and more explicitly aligned with the United States through a good-humored discussion on the essence of democracy. The camera pans up from the people at the entrance of the inn to a sign locating the action in the "Golden Crown Taverne." Inside men playing cards are involved in a lively argument. The newspaper editor decries over-taxation and bemoans the fact that, unlike Switzerland and the United States, the monarchy is not democratic. The veterinarian Dr. Hofer, a major protagonist, criticizes his colleague's lack of national pride, after which he is called upon to suggest a solution to Austria's lack of democracy, pontificating, "Dealing as I do with the elemental secrets of life, birth and death, I've devised this remedy. Czechs shall marry Austrians, Serbs shall marry Mohammedans, Slovaks Hungarians, Bosnians Croatians—and in a hundred years who would know whether his grandmother was a Serb or Czech, Hungarian, Mohammedan, Bosnian or care. Unity. And what is democracy but unity."[41] Hofer's democracy is not only based on blindness to ethnic and religious differences, but also bound to the eradication of such distinctions through marriage. With a twinkle in his eye, the veterinarian conflates unity based on intermarriage across ethnic and religious lines with a political system. In doing so, he draws a powerful parallel with the United States at the time when "many American opinion molders equated totalitarianism with enforced homogeneity and came to see diversity as a defining feature of democracy."[42] He simultaneously invokes a utopian ideal antithetical to Hitler's goal of racial purity. This discussion of democracy facilitates the later immigration of the main protagonists to the idealized United States, where the potential of the one-time Habsburg Monarchy can be realized and where love across class boundaries does not provoke scandal.

Just as this distances Austria from its northern neighbor, an exchange between the emperor and the heir-apparent Archduke Franz Ferdinand provides a thinly veiled commentary on the situation in Austria before the Anschluss. Although Gyory may have advised against putting anti-German sentiments in the mouth of Franz Josef, the emperor's conversation with the heir apparent provides a useful juncture for positioning Germany as aggressor. If the earlier section stressed differences between Germany and Austria and similarities between Austria and the United States, this conversation goes one step further and positions Austria as an adversary of its northern neighbor. Immediately after the successful performance of the Lipizzaner stallion Florian before the emperor, and on the eve of Archduke Franz Ferdinand's departure for Sarajevo, Emperor Franz Josef stresses the importance of the trip. "A great deal depends on you, Franz," the emperor states. "Berlin grows more restless every day, searching for excuses to dominate. Every diplomatic move we make must be towards good will, respect, and understanding."

By casting Germany in the role of aggressor and specifically as an opponent of Austria, the emperor's farewell remarks reflect the urgency of his mission and the threat Germany posed to contemporary Europe.[43] By early June 1940, when the film premiered, Germany had already annexed Austria and Czechoslovakia, invaded Poland and divided it with the

Soviet Union, and attacked the Low Countries and France. The emperor's explicit link of Germany with war could remind the audience of the ways in which contemporary Austria's fate was tied to German aggression at the time of the film's release. Moreover, the emperor's expressed desire for "good will, respect, and understanding" seems to echo values espoused by the United States that contradict German bellicosity. Finally, the scene may also have raised the question of how effective contemporary diplomacy had been in containing German expansionism. By this point British Minister Neville Chamberlain's appeasement policies had proven ineffective, and some Americans believed that the neutrality of the United States bordered on moral bankruptcy. While diplomatic measures may have appeared desirable and even noble at one time, taken against the backdrop of current events in Europe, many believed that action was more appropriate.[44]

The film's simplification of Austrian history, even more extreme in its portrayal of the revolutionary changes at the end of World War I, implicitly rallies support for refugees from Hitler. The scenes depicting the assassination of Franz Ferdinand during his trip to Sarajevo are followed by a brief scene with Dr. Hofer and his compatriots back at the Golden Crown Taverne, and then a shot of the emperor's mournful face, suggesting his reluctance to declare war. His proclamation of war is followed by a sequence that shows documentary-like footage through a kaleidoscope. The shots of soldiers going off to war flanked by jubilant bystanders are replaced by scenes of battle. These are interrupted occasionally by individual shots showing the fates of the main characters—Archduke Oliver, Duchess Diana's erstwhile fiancé, dies in battle; Diana works as a nurse; and Anton is wounded during an enemy bombing and saved by his faithful horse Florian. The long war sequence closes with a series of shots of soldiers marching home with the superimposed title: "THE WAR OVER. A CRUSHED AND DEMORALIZED ARMY RETURNS HOME TO A FUTURE OF HOPELESS UNCERTAINTY." The next shot shows defeated soldiers, then a dissolve to close-ups of radicals rioting with "REVOLUTION" superimposed over these images. This is followed by a dissolve to a series of shots—a lone mounted policeman is pulled off his horse by an angry mob, a sailor demolishes a shop window as the crowd behind him rushes in to loot it, buildings are set afire, and mounted policemen try to break up angry mobs in the city and outside a palace that resembles Schönbrunn.[45]

In the film, revolutionary violence is directed generally against property owners and specifically against the Habsburgs and all those who may have opposed the alleged new communist regime. In reality, the situation in Vienna had deteriorated long before the end of the war, with widespread hunger among the entire population that had resulted in spontaneous protests.[46] Moreover, support for the political revolution or transition from monarchy to republic was shared among multiple parties, from the Socialists to the conservative Catholics.[47] While earlier versions of the screenplay made reference to the domestic food shortage, the final version omitted this, suggesting that the violence was the sole product of the dissatisfaction of the returning soldiers stirred up by Bolshevik revolutionaries.

The revolutionary violence in the film can be read in multiple ways. On the surface it is a simplified version of the transition from monarchy to republic. The use of words like "revolution" and "comrade" by one of the new officials as well as their attack on Anton specifically as a "royalist" mark the revolutionaries as communists. Through their demeanor and appearance, they are coded as lower-class thugs. By emphasizing left-wing violence through images and language, the film plays on anti-communist and anti-Soviet sentiment in an effort to stir up sympathy for the refugees to the United States. The Bolsheviks and their brutality toward the Romanovs had been a favorite target on the Hollywood screen, supporting anti-communist sentiment in the United States.[48]

The screen violence and persecution of former aristocrats can also be interpreted as a veiled presentation of the political situation in 1938. The images of the burning buildings suggest a brutal takeover of Austria with the Habsburgs standing in for the unnamed persecuted. Some viewers might possibly have recalled the destruction of the synagogues and other Jewish property during the November Pogrom of 1938. Spliced into the rioting, Hofer appears first alone and then with Diana outside the walls of a castle, where he declares, "I'm glad the old emperor didn't live to see this. I'll have to get you out of Vienna at once." Not only does the end of the war result in social upheaval, but it brings new challenges for the female royal. Her life is threatened by the revolutionary violence that has erupted in Vienna. In a conversation with Anton, the doctor alerts him to the seriousness of the situation, "Listen, there's not much time to lose. The revolution's broken out in Vienna. They're fighting in the streets. The Habsburgs are in hiding. Nobody knows how much blood will be spilt. If the mob gets the upper hand the old order will be smashed forever. It's only a question of weeks, maybe days. There's no hope, no hope at all." A minor aristocrat such as Diana was unlikely to have been in any grave danger from the Austrian revolution in 1918. Moreover, nobles did not lose their titles until the Law on the Abolition of Nobility (Adelsaufhebungsgesetz) was passed in 1919, and with the exception of the emperor's heirs, they were able to retain their property. In the film, however, the congenial Habsburgs and Duchess Diana become stand-ins for all those persecuted in Austria because of their birthright.

The parallels to 1938 and the plight of the refugees become even more transparent in Diana's escape from Austria. Advising Anton on helping the duchess flee, Hofer remarks, "You wouldn't get two miles in daylight. They'll begin to block the roads to the border as soon as they're organized." Just as members of the Habsburg Monarchy and royalists are in danger in the film, "undesirables" and opponents of the National Socialists found themselves in a veritable prison after the Anschluss. Smuggled over the Swiss border by Anton, Diana faces possible deportation to Austria. Acting as her spokesperson, Anton explains to the Swiss official, "She fled for her life. What time was there for papers? The mob's loose over there. Nobody knows yet how it will turn out. You must have seen for yourself. You know what will happen if you turn her back." Again, the lines are much more applicable to the post-Anschluss circumstances than those after World War I.

If Diana is a stand-in for those persecuted because of their birth and emigration is a matter of life and death, Anton's situation lends itself to multiple commentaries on the contemporary situation of non-Jewish opponents of the Nazi regime. According to the Swiss official, Anton could seek asylum in Switzerland, but as an Austrian patriot he refuses. When Diana pleads with him, even orders him to stay with her in Switzerland, he responds, "There must be a first time for everything, even disobedience. Over there is Austria, mixed up in a family fight. Whether I like it or not I belong in it. There's nothing to worry about. It isn't permanent. It's only a fuss of today." Against the backdrop of 1940, it was unclear whether the feud was "permanent" or not. In any case, the "family fight" was certainly more than a "fuss of today." Anton is captured by revolutionaries and spends a stint in prison, making it clear that leaving Austria is the only alternative. The demise of the positively portrayed multi-ethnic empire was certainly made as a contrast to National Socialist Germany to elicit sympathy for those fortunate enough to escape.

The worsening of the situation in Europe and talk of the United States entering the war made Franz Josef's empire less practical for comment on the contemporary situation. While the new Austria of *Florian* becomes untenable for those loyal to the emperor and unsafe for others because of their birth, in Reinhold Schunzel's *New Wine* (September 1941) the regime is openly repressive from the beginning. Set during the rule of Franz I, a time unfamiliar to Americans who knew Austria only from the screen, this Austria is explicitly compared with 1941 through the frame story, a Schubert concert at Carnegie Hall. When the camera peers over the shoulder of someone at the concert, it focuses on the program notes, which set the stage for the main story within the frame story. "Nearly one hundred thirteen years ago, Franz Schubert, from his lonely soul, poured out melodies that have lived. In Vienna of those days it was the best of times and the worst of times.... As Dickens said, the season of light and of darkness ... a period much like our own."[49] The immediate fade from the program to a close-up of a drum beating transports viewers to the late 1820s. A voice proclaims, "In the name of his Imperial Majesty, mercenary regiments are to be formed at once. All single, unemployed men are ordered to report to recruiting stations immediately." Set in prerevolutionary times, the film provides little information on the ruling class. The Habsburg emperor goes unnamed and never appears. However, he is represented by the military, which is rounding up men to force them to serve as mercenaries for the King of Naples.[50] The order demanding that all single, unemployed men "report to recruiting stations immediately" is repeated before viewers are then taken inside a café, where the recently fired Schubert joins a group of friends. All single and unemployed, they discuss their precarious situation when Schubert's landlord comes to alert him that the authorities are looking for him. When the soldiers enter the café and demand the men's papers, Schubert escapes after one of his friends creates a diversion. Later, when the composer returns to Vienna, Poldi, his landlord, informs him of the fate of his friends—one stayed in Italy, one is in jail, and one is dead.

For moviegoers, who had witnessed the revolution in the Strauss film or those more informed about Biedermeier Vienna, the immediate fade from the program to the call for conscription may have led viewers to tie the events to Metternich's Austria. Such associations evoke comparisons to the "New Germany" and imply that the citizens of Vienna and by extension those of the entire *Ostmark* were forced to serve in Hitler's army unwillingly. Those who protest face death or jail and the lucky ones avoid service by fleeing into exile. In this Schubert "fantasy," the fate of Europe's refugees is not far below the surface. Just after Schubert is fired from the Hungarian farm, where he sought refuge after entering the country illegally, Hungarian soldiers come searching for him. Because he has no passport, he is to be deported. Fortunately for Schubert, the emperor is no longer hiring out mercenaries to the King of Naples. By contrast, in 1941 those without passports fleeing Hitler found themselves in precarious life-or-death situations.

In *The Great Waltz*, *Florian*, and *New Wine* audiences are transported to three different periods of Austrian history with parallels to the contemporary situation. In 1938, when the real Austria had been absorbed by Germany, they witnessed the nineteenth-century revolution, resulting in a constitutional monarchy in *The Great Waltz*. Two years later, Austria-Hungary was compared favorably with the United States and viewers were encouraged to identify and sympathize with those forced to leave the Old World in *Florian*. In *New Wine* the frame story draws parallels between Schubert's time and contemporary political upheavals. Sacrifices, similar to those that Schubert had to face, may be demanded in order to fight such a regime at home and abroad.

Strauss and Schubert versus Hitler

Long before Austria appeared on screen, Vienna had often been labeled the capital of music and music had been viewed as an essential part of Austrian identity. Reporting on his visit to Austria in the mid-1840s in a published travelogue, the American physician-author John W. Corson declared, "Vienna is, perhaps, the most musical city in the world."[51] He elaborated further: "I have heard nearly the whole assembly in one of their Catholic churches join with the organ in chanting a beautiful and difficult anthem; and the leading attraction in Vienna for years has been Strauss's famous band."[52] In addition to singing or listening to works of Johann Strauss Sr., Corson described how the Viennese expressed themselves in dance: "The whole population, too, appear to let off their exuberant spirits through their heels. More than one half of the placards you see in the streets are of music and dancing."[53] Music, Corson reported, be it sacred or profane, is something that animates all classes, and in summer citizens even "waltz in the open air."[54] Ninety years later in the days following the Anschluss, G. E. R. Gedye, the *New York Times* correspondent in Vienna, drew on the city's close associations with the waltz to argue the plight of the Austrians and the seriousness of the situation. The seasoned reporter, well aware that the waltz had long served as a marker of Austrian identity, declares, "The swaying lilt of the Blue Danube has been drowned in the martial strains of the Horst Wessel song and Adolf Hitler's favorite Badenweiler march," and on the radio "German military marches have ousted Viennese waltzes."[55] In the nineteenth and twentieth centuries, the waltz has been seen as inextricably bound with Austrian national identity.[56]

Filmmakers in Austria and abroad built on Austrian musical traditions. Austrian biopics of the silent era "focused on the musicians and composers so integral to Austria's national identity."[57] In Hollywood, the introduction of sound cemented the association of music to Austrian identity. Hollywood films set in Austria used popular waltzes and marches to locate the setting and as part of the backdrop for their share of struggling composers, musicians, and singing citizens. Maurice Chevalier plays a musical Austrian officer in Ernst Lubitsch's *The Smiling Lieutenant* (1931); James Tinling directed the first Hollywood Schubert biopic *Love Time* (1934) with Nils Asther as Schubert; Ramon Navarro plays the warbling romantic lead in MGM's *The Night Is Young* (1935); and opera singer Gladys Swarthout assumes the role of a descendent of Johann Strauss Jr. in *Champagne Waltz* (1937).

In Julien Duvivier's *The Great Waltz* and Reinhold Schunzel's *New Wine*, the connection between the compositions of Johann Strauss Jr. and Franz Schubert and national identity takes on an ideological dimension determined by the impact of the worsening political situation in Europe.

Hollywood could turn Austria's musical heritage into a vehicle to convey humanitarian and political messages.[58] In 1938, months after the Anschluss, Strauss's music evokes Viennese citizens' deep love for their city, their revolutionary spirit, and the country's musical connection to the free world. Three years later, Schubert's music, supposedly composed in the shadow of exile and out of love and loss, relates the precarious position of the Austrians as well as the sacrifice demanded of contemporaries and the comfort they can find in the spiritual world.

The opening to *The Great Waltz* makes no bones about the film's historical inaccuracies:

> In Vienna in 1844 "nice people" neither danced the waltz . . . nor kissed their wives in public . . . nor listened to new ideas . . .
> In 1845 came Johann Strauss II and his immortal melodies . . .
> We have dramatized the spirit rather than the facts of his [Strauss's] life, because it is his spirit that has lived—in his music.

From beginning to end, the film puts the biography of Strauss II on its head. Absent is the rivalry between him and his composer father, the tension arising from the father's abandonment of the family for another woman, and Strauss Jr.'s three marriages. The drama or "truth" of the film is not to be found in the facts of the waltz king's life, but in his music.

In *The Great Waltz* Strauss's compositions are viewed as organic, growing out of the composer's relationship to Vienna and appealing to all classes. At the same time his music transcends time and space. Although Strauss is identified as middle class through his failed profession as a clerk in a bank, his music is tied to Vienna and all its citizens. His debut at Dommayer's Casino appears headed for disappointment as the orchestra plays to an almost empty hall. When the opera singer Carla Donner appears with her entourage and requests he play, the proprietor, who was about to call it a night, throws open the windows, angrily inviting the neighborhood to listen. Upon hearing the lovely strains of Strauss's music, protesting students, families at home, lovers on a sidewalk bench, and tourists on a bus to Grinzing stream into the hall and fill the area around it. When Schiller, a member of the Vienna opera, moved by the music, jumps up and starts singing "I'm in love with Vienna," he captures the mood of the crowd and perhaps that of many who fled the city after the Anschluss. Later that evening, upon the invitation of Carla Donner to the palace of Count Hohenfried, her benefactor and lover, Strauss plays a waltz that at first shakes up and then moves the stodgy Viennese aristocracy.

Long sequences link the inspiration of two of Strauss's most famous waltzes to Vienna. The first sequence recounts the "birth" of "Tales from the Vienna Woods," which is naturally set in the lovely wooded outskirts of the city (actually Chico, California). After escaping from the authorities with Carla Donner, who has unwillingly been drawn into the revolution, the revolutionary composer jumps into a horse-drawn cab with her. The driver takes them to the Vienna Woods, the only place not barricaded. The "birth" sequence begins on the following morning with a long shot of the carriage on the side of a lake as birds chirp. The two feuding parties, Strauss and Donner, having fallen asleep, are leaning on each other. The next close-up shows them being revived by the cheery coachman, who also informs them of the early hour and that they have a long and beautiful day ahead of them. The driver sets out at a leisurely pace through the woods, passing sheep and shepherds along with way. The antagonism between the composer and the opera singer slowly wears off as a tune emerges from the surroundings. The horses' clopping provides the beat; "the conversation" between shepherds' horns establishes the first phrase in a melody. The driver suddenly plays the harmonica and the atmosphere becomes even more relaxed. A bird's chirping sets Strauss off whistling and mimicking the feathered creature. The composer then begins singing the wordless tune and embellishing it. When he gets stuck, Carla cannot resist helping him out despite lingering antipathy. A horn from a post coach fills in the remainder of the melody. At this point, Strauss and Donner rise from their seats and sing as the driver accompanies them on his harmonica. The finale comes when Donner sings breathless trills and the two fall into and then out of each other's arms. "Tales from the Vienna Woods" is born out of a collaborative effort in the eponymous forest.

The second long musical sequence relates the genesis of Strauss's "The Blue Danube Waltz," connecting the composer and his music once again to Vienna and ultimately to the world.[59] Shortly after the singer and the composer break off their affair, as Carla Donner sails for Budapest, Strauss is shown in a close-up looking plaintive. The camera dissolves from his face to sparkles on water as Donner's voice slowly fades away. The glistening water fades out over a shot of Strauss walking slowly, then sitting down on a set of steps next to the Danube. A foghorn in the background reminds viewers that the river is not far. A close-up of Strauss dissolves to a sunrise with the first strains of "The Blue Danube Waltz." Then as the melody continues there is a long-shot with Strauss as laughing maidens skip past him to do their wash. A cut to a close-up of Strauss with a pensive look suggests he hears the music emanate from the surroundings. From him the picture fades to a series of shots taken along the Danube in Austria as the waltz continues. Unlike "Tales of the Vienna Woods," where the composition resulted from a collaborative effort, "The Blue Danube Waltz" comes from Strauss's renewed attachment to the city and the countryside. It also is a nostalgic gesture, suggesting what has been lost by those fortunate enough to have escaped.

As the music plays on, the audience is privy to its dissemination when the camera fades back to Strauss superimposed over sheet music, followed by a dissolve to "The Blue Danube Waltz" coming off the printing press. The camera then draws back from the press to a room of employees whistling the waltz, one dancing with a broom, and one conducting the whistlers with a feather. As the printers work in time with the music, sheet music in a variety of languages flies off the press—first in Spanish, then Russian, followed by German, French, and finally English. The last two title pages of the sheet music are superimposed over a large string orchestra playing the waltz. The camera then fades to a second orchestra, to a third, and even a fourth. The entire time there is a type of mysterious fog floating among the string players in each cut. Kaleidoscopic shots of the harpists and then of hands on a keyboard follow. This dissolves to horns superimposed on horns. The horns fade to a flag flying over a globe which dissolves quickly from one close-up to another of dancers, whose nationalities are first identified by their dress and then by the flags superimposed over the dancing couples. Included in the group of about ten couples are young and old, dancers from warm and cold climes, and from north and south. The music is tied very much to its "birthplace" Austria, but the music appeals to a worldwide audience. The multiple language editions of the piece, the huge orchestras, and the dancing pairs from around the world unite Strauss with international audiences and distance Austria from its German aggressor. The lush musical orchestration and the extravagant waltz scenes tie the composer and his music—and by extension Austrians—to the world, distancing them from the ideology of the country's "occupier."

Three years after *The Great Waltz* was released, the boisterous waltz music of Strauss and the jolly musical Austrians seemed unsuitable for commentary on the worsening situation in Europe. Narratives surrounding the life of Franz Schubert (1797–1828), another nineteenth-century composer, better fit the mood. Having died at the age of 31, known in lore as unsuccessful in love and supposedly unrecognized during his lifetime, he could serve as a useful symbol for expressing Austria's plight.[60] Moreover, his music has an emotional depth and breadth lacking in Strauss's compositions.

Whereas Strauss's story is presented as fictional from the outset, Schubert's biopic *New Wine*, although equally invented, is staged as factual.[61] The frame story places viewers at a Schubert concert in Carnegie Hall. When a concertgoer opens the program notes that contain information on Schubert and his times, audience members can read, "Franz Schubert learned the lessons of sorrow, transmuting bitter experience into immortal beauty, finding his true self through emotional depths, touching the harmonies of romance with a rare grace and charm." The musical biography is a story of the power of love, the necessity of sacrifice, the impact of loss on creative genius, and the comfort of and inspiration from faith, all of which serve as possible models for audiences in 1941.

In *New Wine*, Schubert's music is not so much tied to a specific place, but to stages in the composer's tragic life. The program claims that Schubert "from his lonely soul poured out melodies that have lived." While pastiches of Schubert's music are woven throughout the film, the creation of Schubert's "Serenade," the "Unfinished Symphony," and "Ave Maria" are explained and connected to Schubert's alleged exile in Hungary and his love for and loss of someone he meets during that exile.[62] Having narrowly escaped being conscripted into a mercenary force, the struggling composer finds himself hungry and penniless in rural Hungary where he seeks employment as a sheep shearer. Hired for work he is obviously incapable of doing, he is fired by the competent and beautiful manager, Anna, who orders him given food and a night's lodging. As a parting gift, he composes "Serenade" for Anna. Upon playing and singing it, she describes it as having "grace and charm and gentle magic." She declares it is "wings to another world." Schubert's music has the power to offer listeners temporary relief from the uncertainties of this world.

While "Serenade" was inspired by his precarious situation in exile and Anna's generosity, his failure to finish his Symphony in B Minor (aka "The Unfinished Symphony") and the inspiration for "Ave Maria" are attributed to the loss of love. When Schubert is eventually allowed to return to Vienna, Anna accompanies him. Realizing with the help of the friendly landlord that the composer will forsake his music if they marry, she returns to Hungary. Because she did not remain, he left the symphony unfinished. The loss of love leads to a religious turn which is dramatized through the creation of "Ave Maria." Schubert, broken-hearted, states, "A man must turn his face to God." At this point, he and the camera focus on a picture of the Virgin Mary with Ave Maria written under it, cuing the music to begin. The camera fades from the picture to Anna at an outdoor service with the people reciting, "Hail Mary full of grace." As the group disperses, Anna remains, walks up to the crucifix, and crosses herself. Then the picture fades back to Schubert, looking at the picture of Maria, and then to him composing, all while the chorus in the concert hall 100 years later is heard singing in the background. The consecutive dissolves set up a psychic, almost religious connection between Franz and Anna as she is transformed into a virginal figure and the choir in the present suggests the strength that might be found in religion. The importance given to religion contrasts with the Nazis' treatment of the church and the persecution of religious opponents.

The Great Waltz and *New Wine* tell audiences two different musical stories from nineteenth-century Austria with contemporary echoes. In *The Great Waltz* Strauss's music, which inspired social and political revolutions, draws from clichés of supposed happier times in "gay" Vienna.

Although Austria had officially ceased to exist as a state when the film was made, its spirit lived on in Strauss's music on the Hollywood screen. Tied to the contemporary world through the Carnegie Hall concert in *New Wine*, Schubert's compositions are not revolutionary, but nonetheless for the people. Composed during a repressive time in a world that did not appreciate it, Schubert's music is presented as relevant in troubled times.

Hollywood's Austrians Becoming Americans

Both sympathy with the plight of refugees fleeing the Nazis and criticism of nativist attitudes in the United States work their way into *Florian*. In its portrayal of the demise and immediate aftermath of the monarchy and fates of the protagonists, the film suggests the futility of resisting a tyrannical post–World War I system and argues instead for the necessity of emigration. At the same time, the film urges "Old World" immigrants to leave Europe behind, to assimilate fully into US society, and thus become productive citizens in their new home.

The story of the patriotic equestrian Anton and the avuncular veterinarian Dr. Hofer is that of the pain of leaving home and the necessity of forgetting the past. During the post–World War I revolution that threatens Duchess Diana's safety, Anton smuggles her out of Austria over the Swiss border on Florian's back. As Anton reenters Austria after leaving Diana in Switzerland, a shot from a rebel pursuing him rings out. Diana is led to believe he is dead, but he has merely been knocked unconscious and is captured by the revolutionaries and imprisoned, where he is reunited with Hofer. Later, after Anton and Hofer are released from prison, because "the new government is tired of feeding political prisoners," they return to Lipizza, only to find the stable empty and in shambles.[63] Anton realizes that the conflict between revolutionaries and royalists has made his situation in postwar Austria untenable. With Hofer's encouragement, he decides that his only hope for a meaningful life lies in emigration.

The interactions between Hofer and Anton after their reunion introduce lessons to be learned by both Americans and the new immigrants to the United States. Americans should become aware of the devastating emotional effects of loss of home on the immigrants and the challenges in leaving one's past behind. The film attempts to make Americans aware of the potential contribution refugees can make in the New World. Simultaneously, the film points the newcomers in the "right" direction on the path to becoming Americans. The refugees in the audience are reminded of the necessity of leaving the Old World behind and the importance of shedding their European identity quickly and assimilating productively into the New World.

After the war, Hofer assumes the role of Anton's advisor, teacher, and guide in his transition from Austrian to refugee to American. Without him Anton might never have left Austria, let alone made the voyage across the ocean. While Hofer suggests the ease with which one can become an American, Anton shows that leaving "home" is not easy. There are both emotional and financial considerations. Recalling Florian's birth and great promise in the empty stall at Lipizza, Hofer remarks, "So ends an old civilization," and Anton replies, "And a dream." Although it is clear that Anton is still mourning the loss of Diana, Hofer seizes the moment as an opportunity to move on in life, exclaiming, "I don't want you chasing for something still out of reach. She's gone. All that's gone. You have a new world to organize for yourself, out of new things, people, and conditions." The new world is not to be found in the new Austria, but ultimately in the United States. However, as Anton prepares to move on, new worries about practical matters arise. Anton brings up the topic of finances: "It isn't easy to organize a new world [brief pause] without any money." The pause is accompanied by a change in expression. Anton appears ready to move on, but at the same time he reminds the audience that in addition to good will money is necessary. Like many refugees after the Anschluss, Anton has not only lost his world, but his means. Like Anton, many refugees had little or no money. Unlike the exiles, the knowledgeable Hofer has stowed away money in a Dutch bank and is willing to share it with Anton. And yet Anton's attachment to Austria makes him hesitate:

> ANTON: You want to leave Austria?
> HOFER: We must, but we must both go to look for a new world. Not to go on longing for the old.
> ANTON: I suppose you're right, but it isn't easy, throwing away every memory and every loyalty.
> HOFER: You had other loyalties.
> ANTON: Florian. (hesitation) Do you think we could find him?
> HOFER: He's a part of the old order that will fit into the new world we're going to make. It is for Florian that we must search.

Moving on—but with Florian—offers the protagonists the possibility of retaining elements of the Old World, something refugees might find comforting, even as they accept the need to adapt to the values of the New World. Hofer and Anton ultimately set off for the United States in search of the white stallion, who had been auctioned off to a Coney Island showman, who then sold him to a junk salesman, who had in turn sold him to be exported from the United States. Physically abused by both American owners, a treasure like Florian needed someone from the Old World to appreciate and cultivate his qualities, to make him truly useful in the New World. Consequently, the film, like *Champagne Waltz*, argues that these newcomers should not be seen as a threat; rather they bring unique and worthy traditions to their new homeland.

To garner further sympathy for the refugees, the film dwells on the pain of departure. Anton's initial lethargy suggests the traumatic nature of "throwing away every memory and every loyalty." Even after he agrees to search for Florian, he remains at first apathetic. In their search for the Lipizzaner, the two return to the Hofreitschule (Spanish Riding School) to examine the sales records. While Hofer enquires about Florian's whereabouts, Anton relives his performance with the stallion before the emperor in a flashback, a memory that both saddens him and strengthens his resolve to find Florian.

The first step toward a "cure" for Anton's melancholy is saying good-bye to the Riding School; the second step is taking leave of his European identity. Standing at the railing of a steamer headed for the United States, Anton asks his traveling companion Hofer, "Where does the ocean stop being European and become American?" Hofer glibly replies, "For a European never, but for us Americans it's all America until the very last wave." This scene captures Anton's misgivings about leaving Austria and his apprehension about a new life in the United States. Just as there are no national boundary markers in the ocean, he is unsure how to make the transition from being European to American. By contrast, Hofer, who already identifies as an American, suggests it is easy to transfer loyalties.[64] Furthermore, he implies both the impossibility and undesirability of hyphenated identities—one is either European or American. At the same time, he indirectly criticizes new arrivals who refuse to shed their former identities and echoes the rhetoric that viewed hyphenated Americans with disdain and suspicion.[65]

With his optimism and new-found American patriotism, Hofer wants to infect Anton with his enthusiasm, and he initiates him into the New World, appropriately, by explaining American money:

ANTON: So you've become an American already.
HOFER: Uhum. And having achieved that distinction before you I'll now attend to your education. First, the matter of money. . . . A five cent piece is called a nickel.
ANTON: And you'd give away every last nickel to a friend without asking why he wanted it.
HOFER: Ten cents is called a dime.
ANTON: But I'm going to work hard. This new life is going to be good. I'll pay you back everything and more.

Not only does Anton express his gratitude, but he shows himself eager to contribute to the New World through hard work. The process of

Americanization begun on board is well underway by the time Anton arrives in the United States. As he disembarks, he carries a book with a picture of Abraham Lincoln on the cover. During the voyage Anton has embraced two pillars of American society—capitalism and democracy, which he lives out in the film's dénouement. Anton proves himself financially responsible, giving riding lessons at a high-class stable after he finds Florian. Moreover, he is able to realize America's democratic promise when he is reunited with Diana, who finds him after reading an article announcing his performance with Florian. The best of the Old World has been combined with the best of the New.

Yet, as much as the film sets out to plead the case for the refugees and to counter nativism and anti-Semitism, it fails to confront them directly. As the historian David H. Kennedy points out, "American society in the 1930s was not free of the stain of anti-Semitism, but most Americans, Jews and gentiles alike, generally condemned Nazi racialism."[66] However, a *Fortune* poll from mid-1939 revealed Americans' reluctance to increase the numbers of refugees allowed to enter the country legally. When asked the question, "'If you were a member of Congress, would you vote yes or no on a bill to open the doors . . . to a larger number of European refugees?'" the answers fell along the following lines, "Eighty-five percent of Protestants, 84 percent of Catholics, and an astonishing 25.8 percent of Jews answered no."[67] In this atmosphere, placing Austria in a good light and implicitly attacking Germany would not have been a hard sell. By the same token, raising sympathy for new arrivals was a greater challenge. In this case the film's makers adopted a strategy that played down or effaced differences between Americans and the new arrivals.

By portraying Austria-Hungary as similar to the United States, the film suggested that the newcomers embodied traits that made them potentially model citizens of the United States. Even their speech habits must make them seem native. While many involved in making the film were European and Jewish, the major "Austrian" protagonists were played by very Anglo-Saxon sounding actors. Robert Young starred as Anton, Charles Coburn played Hofer, and Helen Gilbert assumed the role of the Duchess Diana. Even those Austrians who died in Europe were played by American or British actors with Reginald Owen as Emperor Franz Josef and Lee Bowman as Archduke Oliver. The only person who spoke with a foreign accent was the court ballet dancer played by the Russian dancer Irina Barnova. By contrast, the Hungarian-born actor S. Z. Sakall (Szöke Szakáll), a waiter in the film, had no lines whatsoever.

While this may seem like a coincidence, MGM documents on the film suggest otherwise. An early screenplay dated September 1, 1938, includes the following instructions for the director: "No hand kissing, no courtly bows, no extreme, formal etiquette, and avoid burlesque impression in all parts of the picture story. We want it to be completely acceptable and easily understood by American and English audiences. Dialects in any language to be avoided. We should not cast foreign speaking actors who will give audiences an awful mixture of speech as well as distract and confuse."[68] While on-screen authenticity was disregarded, the promise of easy assimilation was not.

Concerned with the depiction of Austrians destined to immigrate to the United States, Winfield Sheehan wanted them to be portrayed as hardworking, productive, and adaptable. In a memorandum from October 3, 1938, Sheehan emphasized, "It is important to pick up Anton if possible in each scene performing some useful work. It would be well to have Elizabeth [later renamed Diana] performing some task or girl's duty whenever possible, so as to remove any feeling that she may be an idler or lazy."[69] His concerns reflect the spirit of the Immigration Act of 1917, according to which those "likely to become a public charge" could be barred from entering the United States. While the clause had only been loosely enforced up until the 1930s, the burgeoning numbers of unemployed and fear that foreigners would take away jobs from Americans most likely led to its stricter interpretation.[70]

The professions chosen for the new screen immigrants should not pose a threat to those held by "real" Americans. Because the United States had been plagued by unemployment since 1929, many Americans felt the market could not accommodate new job seekers and ethnic and political refugees were hardly welcomed. "Through 1938 and much of 1939 unemployment stood at between eight and ten million. The economy did not again reach the level attained in mid-1937 before World War II. Against this background restrictionists had little difficulty making credible their allegation that every refugee who entered the United States and found employment put an American out of work."[71] In early versions of the screenplay, Anton worked in a mine in the United States before he found Florian, and Diana was slated to work as a waitress and later as a governess. In the final version, however, Anton is employed as a riding instructor in a New York City stable. How Diana has survived is not clear, and Hofer appears to be independently wealthy.

With the story of the human fates and parallel story of the rise, fall, and rehabilitation of the Lipizzaner Florian, Winfield Sheehan wanted to appeal to as broad an audience as possible. As refugees, both Anton and Diana must be seen as productive members of society and not future wards of the state. The protagonists who immigrate to the United States—Anton, Diana, Hofer, and even the Lipizzaner Florian—embody apolitical characteristics that the American public would deem admirable, allowing for an easy transformation from Austrian to American.

Conclusion: A Losing Battle

The highly fictionalized historical events and composer biographies in the films set in imperial Austria with their embedded messages reflect on the ever-changing political situation in Europe. In 1938 the makers of *The Great Waltz* engaged with nostalgia and music, distancing Austria from its pugilistic German cousin. With its revolution and the peoples' demands, the film argues that Austria shared traits with the democratic United States. In *Florian* the diversity of the multi-ethnic empire compares favorably with the United States, while the fate of the aristocracy and patriotic Austrians during the short-lived revolution after World War I echoes the events of March 1938. In the 1941 film *New Wine*, Schubert's struggles are conveyed in his music and serve as comfort and inspiration in troubled times. Moreover, the repressive regime of Schubert's time was designed to parallel the contemporary situation in Austria.

Despite these efforts, the reviewers in *The New York Times* failed to see or acknowledge the films' political and humanitarian subtexts, nor did they mention the situation in contemporary Vienna. Just weeks after the November Pogrom, Frank Nugent called *The Great Waltz* "a confectioner's delight among extravaganzas—ornamental, artificial, inclined to the pompous," but nonetheless "a bore." A month after the Germans invaded France, Bosley Crowther made no mention of the situation in Europe in his review of *Florian*. But for the film, which received little praise, he notes that the humans acted "with such solemn reticence that you might think they were afraid of stealing the picture from the horse, if that were possible." In 1942 the reviewer of *New Wine*, too, saw no connection between the contemporary situation and Schubert's life. For him, "Its costumed capers are empty; Its 'New Wine' has been poured from an old bottle."[72] That the reviewers concentrated on the critical merits or lack thereof is understandable, but that none mentioned the situation in Vienna suggests that filmmakers needed stronger ammunition. In 1941, the same year imperial Austria disappeared from the screen, filmmakers turned to depictions of the Anschluss and its aftermath in *So Ends Our Night* and *They Dare Not Love*, which will be discussed in the next chapter. When imperial Austria reappeared in films made after World War II, the Old World was usually shown in a critical light.

4: Reflections and Refractions of the Anschluss on the Hollywood Screen, 1941–42

AFTER THE LAST HOLLYWOOD HOLD-OUTS, Twentieth Century-Fox, MGM, and Paramount, had been expelled from Germany by fall 1940, alienating the German market was no longer an issue.[1] By that time Hitler had swallowed up much of Europe and was engaged in the Battle of Britain. Yet, anti-Nazi films still made up a very small part of Hollywood's total output in 1941. With much of the European market eliminated, domestic concerns dominated.[2] In response to the slump in business in Detroit in May 1941, a reporter for *Variety* speculated that "too many pictures and too many newsreels with a militant 'cause' or propaganda slant have cooled the public, particularly in the isolationist mid-West, on the pictures."[3] No matter what the politics of those in Hollywood might be, American audiences seemed reluctant to attend pictures dealing with the National Socialist threat here or abroad.

Moreover, directly addressing the European situation in Hollywood entertainment could turn out to be more than just a poor investment. In August 1941, Senators Gerald Nye and Bennett Champ Clark introduced Senate Resolution 152, which called for "a thorough and complete investigation of any propaganda disseminated by motion pictures and radio or any other activity of the motion-picture industry to influence public sentiment in the direction of participation by the United States in the present European war."[4] *So Ends Our Night* and *They Dare Not Love*, two films in which the Anschluss finally appeared as more than just a passing reference, were included among seventeen films that caught the subcommittee's attention during the September hearings.[5] Although short-lived, the hearings nonetheless underscored the scrutiny Hollywood faced from vocal isolationists for such a small percentage of its production.[6] However, even when the United States declared war on Germany in December 1941, filmmakers rarely turned to Austria to attack German politics.[7]

Although the demise of Austria as a sovereign state did not lack drama, translating its political significance for Americans three years after the fact would not be an easy task.[8] At the time of the Anschluss, Americans may have read about it in newspapers, heard the live radio reports from foreign correspondents such as Edward Murrow, or seen newsreel footage. Even then the variety of opinions circulating in the

United States on the relevance of the events of March 1938 domestically and internationally reflects the split between interventionists and anti-interventionists.[9] Although the United States had officially recognized the annexation, the country was divided. Senator William E. Borah of Idaho captured the sentiment of isolationists in and outside Congress as reported in the *Washington Post*, when he declared in late March that the events in Austria were "not of the slightest moment to the United States as a Government," concluding that the Anschluss was "natural, logical, and inevitable."[10] By contrast, Roosevelt had originally wanted Congress to pass a bill to raise immigration quotas in the wake of the Anschluss.[11] Discouraged by his advisors, Roosevelt withdrew the latter request for fear that the isolationist Congress would actually reduce quotas or eliminate immigration all together. Instead, he bypassed Congress and "combined the small immigration quota for Austria with the much larger German quota for a single annual quota of 27,370."[12]

Those who argued that the Anschluss was not legitimate believed Germany's aggression would eventually reach beyond Europe. For example, in 1938 Dorothy Thompson, one of the most outspoken journalists on the dangers of Nazism, took up the question in her introduction to *My Austria*, the memoir of the recently deposed Austrian Chancellor Kurt Schuschnigg. She pointed out that "it is unique that a friendly power offers an ultimatum to another friendly and sovereign power threatening armed invasion." However, for Thompson, threatening a sovereign country was only the first outrage: "that invasion should follow the acceptance of the ultimatum; and that the man who entirely correctly served and represented his country should then be arrested, and threatened with the charge of High Treason by the invader" was unthinkable.[13] In order to tie Austria's distant fate with that of the United States, she expounded on what she called "the Austrian idea." She concluded that "the Austrian idea is the western idea—from Rome, through the Middle Ages universalized by the Christian Church, through the Renaissance universalized by a common source of art and inspiration, to the very dream of the United States of America: the idea of mankind of many origins finding a common language and a common home: a Realm of the Spirit."[14] She connected the fight against National Socialism to the fight for civilization and the fate of Europeans to that of Americans. "If that spirit wins through, Europe lives. If it perishes Europe dies . . . and we, too, children of Europe, men and women of the western world."[15] Despite the surfeit of opinions, the Anschluss remained a distant event for many Americans.

In his article on Austria in Hollywood's anti-Nazi films Jan-Christopher Horak provides possible reasons for the country's on-screen scarcity. He argues that since anti-Nazi films demanded unambiguous plots shaped by US war propaganda, the Anschluss had to be seen as the "prelude to the Second World War, the Austrians as the first victims of the Nazi terror, Vienna as a beleaguered city under the yoke of fascism."[16] Because of the gap between these claims and the cheering crowds seen welcoming Hitler in newsreels as well as the more intimate knowledge of Austria by many in the film industry, he notes that a certain uneasiness was expressed when Austria or Austrians appeared on screen.[17] According to Horak, it was not clear whether they were friend or foe. "It might just be because of this uncertainty that Austria rarely appears in Hollywood's anti-Nazi-films—particularly by those from German-speaking immigrants—and then usually only marginally."[18] The portrayal of Austria and its citizens at the time of the Anschluss in *So Ends Our Night* and *They Dare Not Love*, both made before the United States entered the conflict, and in *Once upon a Honeymoon*, released roughly a year after war was declared on Germany, invites a refinement and expansion of this argument.

If the seizure of Austria was of little consequence to the majority of US citizens in 1938, filmmakers sought to make it meaningful for American audiences in these three films. Although they all deal with the same reality, the films fracture Austrian history in unique ways to advance specific narrative agendas. *So Ends Our Night* mirrors the lives of German refugees before and after the Anschluss. Their already precarious status worsens with the Anschluss, when Austrians cheerfully greet the Germans and the story ultimately challenges the inhumanity of US immigration policies and isolationist stances. The distortions in *They Dare Not Love* claim Austria as Germany's first victim and hail the British entrance into the war as essential in resisting the Nazis. Moreover, the film implicitly supports Otto von Habsburg as emperor of a reestablished multi-ethnic empire. Coming after the United States declared war on Germany, *Once upon a Honeymoon* shifts the emphasis and inserts two Americans into the mix. Showing the Anschluss as an attack on democracy and the prelude to the war, it criticizes those Americans who chose to ignore the news. At the same time, it offers reasons for the United States' involvement in the conflict.

Despite different takes on the events of March 1938, the three films share certain features. Rather than present stories that delve into the reasons for the Anschluss and connect it to the political and social upheaval in Austria since 1918, the filmmakers divorce the events of March 1938 from Austria's internal politics. None show the persecution of Austrian Jews, and the country's socialists and communists are totally absent from the screen. To ground their presentation in "reality" and bring the events closer to Americans, the filmmakers all weave in documentary and pseudo-documentary material, and they align acknowledged clichés of Vienna with their anti-Nazi messages.

Another Unfriendly Door Closes in
So Ends Our Night (February 1941)

Produced independently and distributed by United Artists, John Cromwell's *So Ends Our Night* weaves stories of love and personal sacrifice together with the fates of three German refugees. With Erich Maria Remarque's *Flotsam* as its source, the film follows in a tradition established by United Artists that had come "to be identified most closely with the well-crafted, well-acted and prestigious literary adaptation which was popular in the 1930s."[19] Josef Steiner (Fredric March) flees Germany after his escape from Dachau, and he is forced to leave his beloved wife (Frances Dee) behind; Ludwig Kern (Glenn Ford) a half-Jewish nineteen-year-old German refugee is on his own after his parents die; and Ruth Holland (Margaret Sullavan), a young German-Jewish chemistry student betrayed by her Nazi fiancé, has also fled Germany. As the film follows the refugees from Vienna to Prague, back to Vienna, then to Switzerland, France, and Germany, the European tour offers no glamor, but soberly presents the exiles' precarious situation.

In an effort to stir up interest for a potentially unpopular topic, the promotional materials for *So Ends Our Night* promise audiences a dramatic story of love and adventure, leaving out the circumstances and the European backdrop.[20] One advertisement hits multiple bases, first highlighting drama: "LIVING EVERY STOLEN MOMENT TO THE HILT! . . GRASPING AT THE PLEASURES OF LIFE!! Hounded And Driven To Cover!!" Further in the advertisement the dramatic claims change to a more general pitch to the emotions and the promise of identification with the characters: "Womans' and Mans' Emotional Passion, Filmed In All Of Its' Tempestuous Ardor! . . . It Will Stir Your Heart!, Your Every Emotion, You Will Live Every Moment Of It! . . You'll Never Forget It!, . You'll Be Calling It Great!"[21] If they were lured in by an advertisement such as this, moviegoers might have been surprised by the evening's fare.

While the advertisements are purposefully vague, *So Ends Our Night* is immediately introduced as "the story of the people without passports" that "begins in Vienna in 1937, before the German occupation of Austria." The text over the silhouette of a mass of fleeing refugees on the horizon reads: "When the present rulers of Germany came into power, thousands of people, compelled to take refuge in neighboring countries found themselves in the most fantastic dilemma of our times. For they had no passports, those all-important papers which enable a person to enter and remain in a country other than his own." Cromwell then paints a stark picture that does not stray far from the literary source, Remarque's *Flotsam*.

So Ends Our Night introduces a Vienna to the screen that moviegoers who were used to seeing it as the capital of lilting waltzes and suave nobles might find alienating. The four episodes in Vienna—totaling about 26 out of 117 minutes—are just that, episodes along the route of the refugees fleeing Hitler with the Anschluss sequence as the last Viennese vignette. The pre-Anschluss episodes show a seedy, unwelcoming side of Vienna, from the shabby hostel where the refugees are staying to the ill treatment they receive from the police, who cooperate with German agents. In this Vienna, forgers profit from the untenable situations of refugees without papers. Moreover, the German-Jewish refugees are not shielded from anti-Semitic attacks and the post-Anschluss scene captures throngs of Austrians gleefully welcoming the arriving "conquerors."

The film's composer, Louis Gruenberg, who had studied in Vienna, uses music both to underscore the tense situation and to cast a critical eye on the Austrian capital. When the film opens, strings are playing an unsettling, repetitive phrase. As the camera begins its travels over Vienna's rooftops, a few bars of waltz music are heard. Then dissonant strings overwhelm the musical cliché associated with a happier time in Vienna. A figurative storm is brewing as the camera nears the window of a shabby hostel where refugees without proper documents are lodged and soon to be arrested. Later, when Steiner is shown making money as a card sharp in a bar-café, a second musical commentary is inserted. Here, the film composer mixes aural and visual clichés from Hollywood Westerns with an Austrian idiom to underscore the refugee's desperate situation. Seated in a café in a pose reminiscent of that popular American genre, men are involved in a high-stakes card game, while a tune is playing in the background on what sounds like a saloon piano. When the music morphs briefly into a Strauss waltz, it sounds equally tinny. The waltz does not bring lovers together as in so many other Hollywood Austria films, but the hollow sound signals the emptiness of the clichés. Pre-Anschluss Vienna resembles the Wild West where justice is left up to the individual.

In the four-minute Anschluss segment—approximately sixty-nine minutes into the film—newsreel footage and studio enactments underscore the danger confronting Josef Steiner, the only refugee of the threesome left in Vienna. The sequence shows both the enthusiasm with which many Austrians met Hitler and the dangers it posed for opponents of the regime. Accompanied by ominous music, the Anschluss is announced through the placard "Nazis invade Austria!" attached to a brick wall in an unknown location. The suggestion of victimhood claimed in the poster is contrasted with the shots of crowds greeting the "invaders." The visual announcement of the Anschluss is followed by thirty-five seconds of staged dramatizations spliced into newsreel footage. A brief series of medium shots show Steiner in a crowd enthusiastically greeting the arriving Nazis. Through shot and counter shot, the political refugee is shown recognizing the Nazi, Brenner (Erich von Stroheim), who has been pursuing him since the beginning of the film.[22] The claustrophobic mise-en-scène, in which Steiner is surrounded by flag-waving Austrians, mirrors his situation. His already restricted freedom of movement turns into a deadly prison, and it becomes clear that he must flee.

The Vienna portrayed in the four episodes is not the welcoming city of Strauss waltzes known to many moviegoers; it is unmasked as anti-Semitic and unwelcoming of refugees. Through it and the refugees' other stops in Europe, the film invites audience members to reflect on the desperate situation of the continent's dispossessed people. More particularly, they can consider the hurdles refugees face when trying to escape to the United States, a place that Ruth and Ludwig mention wistfully in the closing lines.

They Dare Not Love (May 1941) and the Death of Imperial Austria?

An unhappy combination of love story, thriller, and drama, Columbia's *They Dare Not Love* begins with a fractured dramatization of the Anschluss.[23] It is almost as though a film set in imperial Austria had been spliced together with a thriller on the Nazi take-over and a cross-class love story. Thrown together by circumstance on the night of the clandestine German invasion, the Austrian Prince Kurt (George Brent), the Austrian patriot Professor Keller (Egon Brecher), and his daughter Marta Keller (Martha Scott) flee Vienna together. When Kurt and Marta meet again on the same steamer bound for New York, they fall in love. After Marta's father reminds her that Kurt is a prince and she only a commoner and asks reproachfully whether she has forgotten her fiancé Wilhelm, she avoids Kurt after they disembark in New York. Through a series of convoluted events, Kurt and Marta find themselves prisoners on a German ship headed back to the Reich and free to love each other, as they head for a certain death trap. The two are saved when the sympathetic German captain knowingly ignores a coded message ordering him to avoid a British ship after that country's declaration of war on Germany.

As with *So Ends Our Night*, the promotional materials make no mention of the specific backdrop. One suggested hyperbolic advertisement promises a thrilling love story. Addressing the potential audience and referring to the two lovers pictured, the text reads: "YOU . . . who dare to take your beloved in your arms tonight . . . gasp at the heart-terrifying story of these two . . . of who it was whispered . . . THEY DARE NOT LOVE." Smaller type suggests the film offers something for a variety of viewers: "Heroic lovers in a drama of breath-taking power . . . of blood-tingling adventure . . . of hair-raising suspense . . . of eye-misting tenderness . . . of heart-stabbing gallantry!" Some might go for the drama, others for the suspense, yet still others for the heart-wrenching story. The image of a sinking ship on one ad might lead moviegoers to suspect the film had something to do with the conflict in Europe, while the dramatic title implies a forbidden romance. In an effort to attract a diverse public and allow speculation as to the film story, the advertisements remain purposefully vague.

The distortions in *They Dare Not Love*, this most unique and indeed bizarre portrayal of the Anschluss, arise from the "melding" of multiple mirrors. The story of Austria's demise and its refugees appears to understand itself in the tradition of Hollywood's imperial Austria with the royal protagonist and a cross-class romance. The odd slant is perhaps not so surprising given that the Hungarian-born scriptwriter Ernst (Ernö) Vajda was involved; he had worked with Ernst Lubitsch (among others) on numerous films set in a gay Austria.[24] Moreover, although the rendering of events woefully misses the mark, the events echo aspects of a fractured Austrian history shown in a *March of Time* featurette on the Anschluss from April 1938 and in newspaper articles reporting on Otto von Habsburg in 1941. With the ultimate goal of arguing the necessity of war, the filmmakers draw on and reproduce filmic clichés from previous imperial Austria movies. Moreover, Austria's claim of victim status is repeatedly substantiated.

After the not-so-subtle suggestion that the story takes place in Austria-Hungary when the credits roll over the backdrop of the Habsburg double-headed eagle, the film is introduced in a documentary style. When the credits disappear, the screen goes black briefly and then text appears that zeroes in more specifically on the place and time:

Vienna
On that tragic day that saw fury unleashed—a fury that was to crush peoples and nations in its ruthless drive to conquer the world—Austria was the first.

The date "March 11th 1938" is then splashed dramatically across the screen, temporally locating the action even more exactly.

This is followed by a curious reenactment of the Anschluss with an even stranger presentation of its public announcement to a group of Austrians in the first eleven minutes. In order to eliminate any sign of public acceptance of the Anschluss, *They Dare Not Love* includes no newsreel footage. Rather, it presents the annexation of Austria as a clandestine takeover by the Germans. After the date disappears from the screen, the camera focuses on feet and torsos. The first set of feet meets up with a second set, and after some mysterious hand signals, the pairs of feet separate, and the action is repeated as some secret message is spread among Hitler's followers. During one of the exchanges, a suitcase falls open, revealing Nazi paraphernalia. After a shot of a clock showing the hour of 7:00, the camera follows several sets of feet shuffling through a door. When the camera pans up to the writing on the door—"German Travel Agency Vienna"—it points the finger directly at Germany as the instigator of the takeover. In several subsequent shots, men are seen donning Nazi uniforms as others arrive with suitcases with the requisite trappings. The camera then cuts to a map of Europe and zooms in on a hand that aggressively covers Austria. This scenario documents the Nazi takeover as a German assault with no welcoming crowds.

Although the filmmaker forgoes using newsreel material in the introduction, documentary material is manipulated in the scene when the German takeover is publicly announced to substantiate Austria's victim status further. At the café where Prince Kurt stops on his way out of the country, he joins a group of acquaintances who appear totally unaware of the German machinations. An employee interrupts the orchestra playing, couples dancing, and lively conversations, and solemnly announces, "Ladies and gentlemen, a message of great importance is being broadcast." What follows is a truncated version of Chancellor Kurt Schuschnigg's real resignation speech, broadcast on March 11, 1938, at 7:45 p.m.:

> People of Austria. Today we are faced with a critical situation. The government of the German Reich has presented an ultimatum with a fixed time limit demanding our immediate surrender. In the event of refusal it is intended that German troops shall march into Austria within the hour. I state before the world we bend to violence. In the face of invasion we have ordered our army to withdraw without resistance. And so I take my leave of the Austrian people with the heartfelt wish, God help Austria.

The speech in the film was abridged and slightly but significantly reworked to shore up the claim of victimhood and to make the events more understandable for American audiences. The italicized portions of the translation of the full speech as reported in the *Los Angeles Times* on March 12 coincide roughly with the film's speech:

> *Today we have been confronted with a difficult and decisive situation.*
> I am authorized to report to the Austrian people on the events of the day.
> *The German government presented* the Federal (Austrian) President with *an ultimatum with a time limit* according to which he had to appoint as Chancellor a candidate who would be proposed to him and appoint a government according to the dictates of the German Reich.
> *Otherwise German troops would march into Austria at the hour named.*

> *I declare before the world* that reports which were spread in Austria that there have been labor disputes, that streams of blood were flowing, that the government was not master of the situation and could not keep order, were invented from A to Z.
> The Federal President authorizes me to inform the Austrian people *that we yield to force.*
> Because even in this grave hour we are not minded at any price to shed German blood, *we have given our armed forces an order that in case invasion is carried out they are to withdraw without resistance* and await decisions on [*sic*] the hours which are to come.
> The President has intrusted [*sic*] Gen. S. Schilhawsky, inspector-general of troops, with command of armed forces. Through him further instructions will be given to the armed forces.
> *So, in this hour, I say good-by with the heartfelt wish that God will protect Austria.*[25]

While the speech in the film captures much of the original, the omissions and revisions gloss over Austria's internal political strife and strengthen the film's repeated implications that Austria was still a monarchy and claim that it was an unwitting victim. The speech contains no mention of the federal president, ignoring the fact that Austria was no longer a monarchy. The dropped reference to German blood glosses over the tie between German Germans and ethnic Germans in Austria as well as the long-held desire of many to become a part of Germany. The reaction of those listening to the speech and the fact that the speaker is left unidentified are also significant. As the speech is delivered, the entire crowd at the café stands solemnly at attention. Among the group is Professor Keller, whom Prince Kurt congratulated earlier for his book that has "proven more forcefully" than ever before that Austrians are not German. Keller, a composite of the Austro-fascist cabinet member Guido Zernatto, author of *Die Wahrheit über Österreich* (The Truth about Austria, 1939), and Kurt Schuschnigg, Austria's last chancellor and author of *My Austria*, has the final word. At the end of the broadcast, he mournfully pronounces, "Austria is dead, our Austria." However, Keller does not elaborate any further and audience members may perhaps wonder, which Austria is dead? They do not have to wait long for an answer. When the Emperor's Hymn (Kaiserhymne) is played over the radio immediately after the speech, this unofficial national anthem implies that Austria is still a monarchy and audiences may believe the emperor is bidding his country farewell and not Schuschnigg.

Audiences are further invited to infer that Austria was a monarchy, since the fictional Prince Kurt von Rothenberg is the Nazi's prime target. Refusing to leave even after having received a warning, the prince is reminded by his loyal servant that he is not just an individual, but a symbol. "As long as you're alive, Austria has a hope." In the New York sequence the audience is reminded of the aristocrat's symbolic importance for a large portion of the Austrian population. Encouraging Barbara Murdock (Kay Linaker), an American socialite, to marry Kurt, the German agent Baron von Helsing (Paul Lukas) explains, "I'm going to be very frank with you, Barbara. Here, in America, Kurt is known only as a playboy. But, in Austria he's almost a legend. Up in the mountains of the Tyrol, there are peasants who never think of sleeping at night without first uttering a prayer which includes his name." Von Helsing goes on to suggest the presence of potential resistance to the National Socialist regime in Austria. "There are men and women in Vienna, all over Austria, who whisper together in dark corners, praying for the day when they can rise up against the Reich." They lack a figurehead that Germany fears. "It isn't what Kurt is, but what he stands for which counts. Kurt von Rothenberg, the rallying point, the banner, which men would fall behind. You see, Germany can't afford to let Austria rise up and stick a knife in her back." Naming Tyrol and Vienna as strongholds of Austrian patriotism was surely not accidental. The two areas would have been familiar to Americans, the Tyrol, because of the recreational opportunities the mountains offer, and Vienna, as the former capital and home of the Habsburg residence. The more informed might identify Tyrol as the home of deposed Chancellor Schuschnigg or Andreas Hofer, the nineteenth-century freedom fighter who challenged Napoleon.[26] Moreover, since the Tyrol was known as one of the most Catholic and monarchist regions in Austria before the Anschluss, the focus on the province could imply that there was strong anti-Nazi sentiment and possible resistance there.

Being an Austrian patriot in Hollywood movies is rarely expressed through attachment to a particular party or entity, and Kurt is no exception. His Austrian identity is conveyed through associations known to the movie-going public from Hollywood's earlier films set in Austria and through his attachment to his people. As he is being driven to the border in an open vehicle, he hears Strauss's "Tales from the Vienna Woods" broadcast from the Café Wienergarten, a spot popular with the well-heeled. The shot serves two functions. On the one hand, it is reminiscent of the scene in *The Great Waltz* when Johann Strauss Jr. and Carla Donner compose the tune in the open carriage and, on the other, it shows that Kurt cannot resist the magnetism of the waltz as it draws him to the café. A short time after avoiding capture by the Nazis when they storm the café, Prince Kurt solemnly declares his allegiance to Austria in front of Professor Keller and his daughter and over the dead body of his chauffeur. "I swear by all that I hold holy, by laughter and gaiety and sorrow, by everything I have ever wanted out of life, to bring back my Austria—one day, one day." In a conversation with Barbara Murdock, Kurt informs the socialite that there are "about seven million" Austrians giving him "seven million reasons to do something" for Austria's freedom. The seven million Austrians are not viewed as fellow travelers or Nazis, but faithful subjects living under the yoke of the National Socialists waiting for a rallying point. The viewers are offered proof of Kurt's love of Austria, which is rooted in a vague notion of the country's cultural heritage and the prince's paternalistic tie to his people as their sovereign.

Though the reenactment of history and the portrayal of Prince Kurt as the country's savior appear absurd, particularly from a distance of more than seventy years, it was not far removed from the presentation of the Anschluss in the *March of Time* featurette that screened in theaters for the first time on April 15, 1938. Staged as serious commentary, the ten minute forty-six-second-long "Nazi Conquest No. 1" combines text, pictures, reenactments, and narrative to present a fractured version of Austrian history as fact.[27] According to Raymond Fielding, "Although the *March of Time* was professedly nonpartisan, a clear and persistent antifascist tone was becoming apparent in its analysis of world politics and rising militarism."[28] "Nazi Conquest No. 1" is undoubtedly anti-Nazi, but it is neither accurate nor non-partisan. With its view of Austrian history, the film argues for the restoration of the monarchy. After the narrator introduces Emperor Franz Josef as the bulwark of Western, Christian civilization, he launches into a scurrilous history of post–World War I Austria that suggests that the country is entirely Catholic, totally anti-Nazi, and monarchist if not a monarchy. After the narrator pronounces "the world now knows that the treaties that left Germany demoralized and Austria dismembered set the stage for Adolf Hitler," a map of Austria-Hungary fades to a post–World War I map of Europe with its many nation states. The narrator then proceeds to give a fractured overview of Austria's postwar history. "Through the next 15 years impoverished and leaderless with its Habsburgs in exile, Austria was to move first toward socialism. Then after bloody revolt, it was to look once more toward its old rulers." Three unidentified pictures follow: the State Opera, a symbol of high culture; the Parliament, a symbol of democracy; and a communal apartment, a symbol of "Red Vienna." However, without additional commentary, it is left to the viewers to decipher the meaning of these images as well as the subsequent series of shots of the military on the street, people lined up, a close-up of a soldier, and soldiers marching. The narrator then suggests that the thirties witnessed the widespread desire for a return to monarchy. "In 1933, devout Austrians prayed for the safe return of the thousand year inheritance of their race, the Catholic monarchy of the Habsburgs." The accompanying images highlight the ties between the Catholic Church, the monarchy, and the military. The following series of images includes a shot of a church service, women dressed in black, a close-up of a hand holding a rosary, an officiating priest, a woman crossing herself with rosary in her hand, then an old man crossing himself, followed by soldiers and then the priest again. The narrator repeatedly insists that Austrians, devoutly Catholic, persistently looked to their former monarchs for salvation, painting a one-sided picture of Austrian politics and society. "But by 1933, Adolf Hitler was a power in Europe. And when Austria's Chancellor, little Engelbert Dollfuss, moved toward Habsburgs' restoration, Hitler waited no longer." The audience sees an orating Dollfuss followed by the iconic picture of Dollfuss's dead body on the couch after his assassination and a series of shots of his funeral. The narration also suggests that Dollfuss's successor, Kurt Schuschnigg, worked actively to reinstall the monarchy. "And as all Austria mourned the death of its chancellor, martyred by Nazi assassins, Hitler realized that the act by which he had hoped to gain Austria had failed for under the government of Kurt Schuschnigg, Dollfuss' chosen successor, Austria turned even more strongly toward its old leaders. Throughout Europe, there was talk that young Otto, exiled son of Karl, the last Habsburg emperor would soon be on the throne." The featurette underscores the Habsburg connection by showing someone hanging a picture of Emperor Karl, followed by a shot of his son, Otto von Habsburg, and then a cut to a picture of the heir apparent on the wall.[29] In this unique view of Austrian history, Hitler was kept in check for so long by the Christian Socials' desire to reinstate the Habsburgs as Austria's rulers. By the same token, the film suggests it was the exact same move that ultimately led to the "invasion" and not the threat of the plebiscite announced by Schuschnigg in February 1938.

Fact finders would have had a field day with this so-called newsreel. Although the Treaty of Versailles and the Treaty of Saint Germain did impact Austria negatively, foiling the attempts of the postwar socialist government to become part of Germany, Austria was anything but leaderless from 1918 to 1933. The Social Democrats, who had envisioned becoming part of a larger Germany, headed a coalition government until 1920, when they went into the opposition. From then until the Anschluss, the position of chancellor was filled from the ranks of the conservative Christian Socials. The narrator refers to a "bloody revolt," but provides no context or date of the brief civil war of February 1934. He fails to mention that 1933 witnessed the end of democracy in Austria and the establishment of the so-called fascist corporate state. Nor does he reveal that government troops made the first move on housing units of socialists under the pretense of searching for weapons in 1934. Schuschnigg's actions are also portrayed in a somewhat strange light. Rather than turning to the pretender to the throne or trying to repair relationships with the left, Schuschnigg first turned to Mussolini for help and then made concessions with Hitler. When Schuschnigg met with Hitler at his headquarters in Berchtesgaden in February 1938, Hitler demanded the inclusion of Nazis or Nazi sympathizers in the cabinet and an amnesty for many imprisoned National Socialists in exchange for Austria's continued sovereignty. After agreeing to these terms, Schuschnigg then announced on March 9 that a plebiscite would take place on Sunday, March 13, by which the Austrian people would be called upon to vote yes or no to the question: "Are you for a free, German, independent and social, Christian and united Austria, for peace and work, for the equality of all those who affirm themselves for the people and Fatherland?" Hitler answered swiftly and severely, presenting Schuschnigg with an ultimatum: He could resign and appoint Arthur Seyss-Inquart chancellor or face an invasion of the German army.[30]

Multiple aspects of the *March of Time*'s fractured presentation of history resurface in *They Dare Not Love* and suggest the sway that certain narratives and images of Austria had in the United States. This is particularly true when the narrator of "Nazi Conquest No. 1" contrasts Vienna's imperial heritage with the ominous take-over. According to the featurette, the Anschluss transformed the once "proud old capital" into "a new outpost in the ruthless Nazi realm." A "loss of its land" is accompanied by "the surrender of its [Austria's] oldest and most cherished traditions." The narrator elaborates, "As the old Habsburg capital, which was happy and tolerant only yesterday, takes on a strange new face, thousands already know that for them the dread day has come." Although the narrator never openly claims that Austria was a monarchy at the time, it appears that imperial Austria is being mourned. As numerous shots of a ball are shown, the narrator declares: "To all the world comes the realization that the gay days of old Vienna of Habsburg and of Strauss are gone forever and the carefree spirit that survived both war and revolution is today but a forbidden memory."[31] Along with the narrative, viewers see a shot of the town hall and hear a Strauss waltz, followed by a shot of an elegant staircase and multiple shots of a ball. *They Dare Not Love* implies a similar pre-Anschluss world with the scene at the Café Wintergarten.

Similarly, the report on Otto von Habsburg in the *March of Time* featurette and the more detailed articles on Otto von Habsburg in national papers in the year preceding the film's release find faint reflections in the character of Prince Kurt. In 1940, newspapers were full of articles on the pretender to the throne, who had traveled to the United States. The *Los Angeles Times* article "Prince Otto Seen as Ruler," from February 1, 1940, tied the royal's activities to a desired restoration of the throne: "Prince Otto of Habsburg and perhaps the future Emperor of a resurrected Austria, who for the last 15 years has led a life of seclusion in a quiet and unpretentious chateau not far from Brussels, is slowly coming into the limelight again." A *New York Times* article from March 5, 1940 announced Otto von Habsburg's visit to the United States with the subtitle "Habsburg Archduke to Study Our Democracy as Model for a Federated Europe." His democratic aspirations for a future Europe are connected to his hopes of restoring his title and the Habsburg claim.

Audiences might have unconsciously or consciously connected Prince Kurt to Otto von Habsburg.

Building on the tradition of earlier Hollywood imperial films and greatly stretching the truth, *They Dare Not Love* depicts Austria as Germany's first victim and directly ties the fate of the Austrians to Great Britain's entrance into the war. Austrian royalty, those identified as Austrian patriots, and seven million Austrians are seen as the victims of the Nazis. Shades of the film's refracted version of history with its narrow focus on the country's non-Jewish victims resurface later in *The Sound of Music*.

Once upon a Honeymoon (November 1942), or Democracy in Danger

In contrast to the two prewar dramas, director Leo McCarey chose a romantic comedy to tie the events in Europe to the United States and show Americans why they are fighting in this European war. RKO's *Once upon a Honeymoon* includes two American protagonists and follows their misadventures from the Anschluss to the German takeover of Paris. On the day of the Anschluss the Brooklyn-born daughter of Irish immigrants, Katie O'Hara (Ginger Rogers), alias Philadelphia socialite Katherine Butt-Smith, is in Vienna preparing for her marriage to an Austrian baron (Walter Slezak). Ignorant that her future husband is Hitler's "secret finger-man" and not the Austrian patriot he claims to be, she brushes off the American journalist Patrick O'Toole (Cary Grant), when he tries to expose the baron. In the course of the film, Katie undergoes a transformation from a naïve gold digger to an outspoken patriot, while falling in love with O'Toole, as he follows her across Europe.[32]

After the United States declared war on Germany, films dealing with the situation were much more open about their efforts to combine entertainment with a political pitch. Consequently, the promotional campaign for *Once upon a Honeymoon* called for different tactics than those used in *So Ends Our Night* and *They Dare Not Love*. The proposed posters and newspaper ads explicitly refer to the war in Europe and the Nazi threat. One poster for *Once upon a Honeymoon* features Ginger Rogers and Cary Grant, smiling while running across a map of Europe with explosions emanating from Poland and France.

Audiences might be more prepared for a war backdrop, but not necessarily the film's mixture of comedy and tragedy.[33] The copy on one poster directly addresses the "'impossible' blending of war at its worst and riotous romantic comedy at its best." Another invites potential viewers to "laugh at it all in the one big picture that sweeps you over a world at war on a tidal wave of romantic comedy!" The comedy that deals seriously with the events in Europe aims at showing Americans what they are fighting for and against.

If the Anschluss was a four-minute episode in the middle of the narrative in *So Ends Our Night* and eleven minutes at the beginning of *They Dare Not Love*, McCarey devotes twenty of 117 minutes to the Anschluss episode in *Once upon a Honeymoon*. Its length and position at the beginning of the film underscore its importance. In this comedic sequence, the director weaves in radio broadcasts and newsreel footage to situate the action temporally and frame the multiple commentaries on the Anschluss. The two Americans in this sequence present two diametrically opposed stances toward foreign affairs. Katie O'Hara, the naïve American gold-digger occupied with her own personal interests, is uninterested in foreign affairs and consequently fails to see the Anschluss's relevance for the United States. By contrast, Patrick O'Toole understands it as an assault on democracy.[34] Moreover, as an outspoken anti-Nazi radio commentator, he highlights the growing role foreign correspondents played in informing a public that was somewhat resistant to such reports.[35]

With hindsight, the film highlights the threat that Hitler poses for Europe and the world.[36] The credits dissolve to an image reading "Timetable of A. Hitler," underneath which is written "Calendar." This background morphs into a map of Europe, with a clock-like swastika-shaped dial rotating, a shot that is repeated each time Hitler swallows up more territory. After the camera zooms in on the word "Calendar," the page gets torn off to expose a close-up of the map of Austria. This dissolves to a picture of a Viennese skyline and waltz music, recalling a romantic vision of the city. As ominous music replaces the waltz, newsreel images appear. Crowds gather in front of the parliament and town hall; the camera cuts to the Opera with people milling about and a Nazi flag on the building; this is followed by a shot of marching soldiers flanked by onlookers. The last two newsreel shots reveal someone hanging a swastika pennant from a building and a medium close-up of a building with three swastika banners hanging down and a curious crowd in front. At this point, the Austrian position vis-à-vis the Anschluss is left open. The quick sequence does not dwell on Austrians enthusiastically greeting Hitler or reveal anyone being persecuted by the invaders. Rather it shows curious onlookers and a place in disarray with an uncertain future.

The external hullabaloo contrasts greatly with the interior scenes of Katherine Butt-Smith/Katie O'Hara's preparations for her upcoming marriage to the Austrian baron. Her lack of concern for the political upheaval despite her proximity to the events sets the stage for the commentary. With a good portion of humor, the film criticizes the failure of many Americans to view the Anschluss as a threat to world peace. Unaware that her future husband is a Nazi, Katie looks forward to becoming a baroness. Hoping to find out information about the baron, the journalist Patrick O'Toole pretends to be the tailor for the future bride, for whom she has impatiently been waiting. As he fumbles at taking her measurements, a radio broadcast of Arthur Seyss-Inquart, the interim Nazi Chancellor of Austria, comes on. When the broadcast begins, the inept tailor-impersonator turns up the volume and provides a condensed translation and commentary of the German. Katie, not the least bit interested, protests, "But we're not finished." He quickly responds, "But I'm afraid Austria is," as a voice in German continues. He then explains, "There's a new Austrian premier, Seyss-Inquart," to which she chirps happily, "Oh, Seyss-Inquart." O'Toole then tries to convey the seriousness of the situation. "He's saying Austria has decided to go with the Reich, without even a vote from the people." Rather than mention that there had not been democratic elections for the past five years or consider the impact that the German takeover will have on the country's Jewish citizens and other opponents of National Socialism, O'Toole highlights the undemocratic nature of the takeover. Katie shows her ignorance when she responds to the reporter's rundown of Seyss-Inquart: "Oh, my fiancé is terribly fond of him." Had she been paying attention to the news, she would know that Seyss-Inquart was at best a Nazi sympathizer and could have made the connection that her future husband was only masquerading as an Austrian patriot. O'Toole tries to point out her faulty logic: "He hates Hitler, he likes this fellow? You know this fellow is giving away his country without even asking his people." The camera then shows a shot of her looking very indifferent, saying, "Tsk, tsk, tsk, can't we have some music?" Just as she has managed to shut out the events unfolding before her eyes, she is blind to the obvious facts of her future husband's political leanings. Upon her request O'Toole switches to another radio station with waltzes. Katie then begins swaying to the music and says, "Ah, that's what I adore about Vienna." Here, she represents those Americans who hold on to an uncomplicated romantic vision of Austria and value entertainment over information at a time of crisis.

McCarey continues to use Katie's self-interest and ignorance to humorously expose America's love affair with Austria, when her fiancé appears at her apartment. Because "Hitler's already here," the baron announces they must leave for Czechoslovakia immediately, postposing their wedding. Visibly annoyed, she agrees that the change of plans is indeed an emergency, not because she commiserates with the Austrian situation, but because it inconveniences her. "Well, it most certainly is when I'm forced to leave without clothes." Worried that he might be postponing or even cancelling the wedding, she grouses, "Now see here, Liebling, I'm not quite sure I approve of this. Merely because Austria has fallen or Hitler is here or whatever it is." Like many Americans in 1938, Katie does not view the Anschluss as a serious international threat. Moreover, like other Americans before her, she is too busy with her own affairs and repeatedly ignores the call to pay attention to Hitler's machinations. When O'Toole, hiding in a backroom to avoid the baron, announces Hitler's arrival to Kate, she responds, "Well, I can't see him now. I'm dressing." Her blindness is topped off when Katie emerges from the backrooms of her apartment at the exact moment her husband and his Nazi cronies toast Hitler's arrival. When they turn to her with raised glasses, she thinks they are toasting her. "Oh, how charming. Thank you gentlemen, ever so much. How sweet." Only concerned with her egotistical desires, she is ignorant of the truth behind this gesture. Her future marriage to a Nazi baron and her subsequent disillusionment parallel both Hollywood's slow break with Germany as well as the awakening of the American public.

The Anschluss sequence ends when a map of Austria is torn off the calendar, and the camera cuts to a map of Czechoslovakia, panning up to the swastika clock "ticking away." Austria may have been the Nazis' first conquest, but it will not to be the last. The turning of the clock repeats itself when the Germans take over Poland, Norway, the Netherlands, Belgium, and finally France. The American viewers are given a context for their involvement in the war. Moreover, had Americans realized the significance of the Anschluss and listened to the reports coming from Europe, they would not have ignored the seriousness of Hitler's conquests for the world.

Conclusion: Bringing the Anschluss Closer to Home

Even if Americans had read about the incorporation of Austria into the German *Reich* in newspapers, heard about it on the radio, and in its aftermath seen newsreel footage of the jubilant crowds greeting the German army and Adolf Hitler in Austria in March 1938, the goings-on in Austria must have seemed distant to most Americans in 1941 and 1942. In response to varying positions in the United States concerning the situation in Europe, the filmmakers in *So Ends Our Night*, *They Dare Not Love*, and *Once upon a Honeymoon* use different mirrors to stage the events. In *So Ends Our Night* Austria serves as an important station in the flight of refugees before and after the Anschluss. Despite the distorted if not fractured view of history presented in *They Dare Not Love*, it is a logical sequel to the industry's imperial Austria films. At the same time that it draws from earlier screen portrayals to claim Austria's victim status, it aligns the American public more firmly with England against Germany. The US participation in the war brought with it a shift in emphasis in Hollywood's Austria. *Once upon a Honeymoon* presented the Anschluss as Hitler's first move to eliminate the "democracy" of another country and it is used to justify the United States' involvement in the war. The Anschluss scene emphasizes the importance of questioning the romantic images of the city and stresses the importance of keeping abreast of the news. Although largely forgotten today, *So Ends Our Night*, *They Dare Not Love*, and *Once upon a Honeymoon* illustrate how the Anschluss could be used to convey the seriousness of the European situation. While *They Dare Not Love* clearly portrays Austria as the victim of "Hitlerite Aggression," both *So Ends Our Night* and *Once upon a Honeymoon* offered a bit more nuanced presentation for their messages.

5: Confronting and Escaping History: *The Cardinal* (1963) and *The Sound of Music* (1965)

WHEN OTTO PREMINGER AND ROBERT WISE resurrected Austria at the time of the Anschluss in *The Cardinal* (1963) and *The Sound of Music* (1965) respectively, they had vastly different takes on this period of history, both from each other and from the makers of *So Ends Our Night*, *They Dare Not Love*, and *Once upon a Honeymoon*. Except for wanting to make a successful film, their motives could not have been more divergent. Shortly before the film's premiere Preminger stated in a *New York Times* article from December 8, 1963, that he liked "'to make pictures about the interesting themes and topics of the day.'"[1] In this film he dealt openly with abortion, mixed marriage (Jewish-Catholic), and racism, all burning issues in the sixties. By contrast, in a *Times* article from November 20, 1966, Wise maintained that he "'wasn't trying to say a damn thing in "Music".'"[2] Rather, he was offering movie goers a respite from controversy. Unlike the films discussed in the previous chapter, *The Cardinal* and *The Sound of Music* were neither a call to arms nor justification for US involvement in the war.

If the makers of *So Ends Our Night*, *They Dare Not Love*, and *Once upon a Honeymoon* shared a common enemy in the National Socialists, Otto Preminger's and Robert Wise's mutual foe was television. In their divergent takes on Austrian history, the filmmakers engaged in similar techniques and strategies to motivate viewers off their couches and entice them into movie theaters. Preminger and Wise both turned to an age-old practice and worked with source material that had been proven successful. *The Cardinal* was based on Henry Morton Robinson's 1950s bestselling novel of the same name. Before it was turned into a Hollywood film, the Broadway musical *The Sound of Music* had enjoyed a three-and-a-half-year run.[3] In addition, both directors employed strategies typical of the sixties.[4] Shot in color with wide-screen technology, *The Cardinal* and *The Sound of Music* were among many Hollywood movies filmed at European locations in the sixties.[5] At a time when more Americans were living and traveling in Europe than ever before, such films could prime visitors for a European adventure or provide them with a virtual (return) visit.[6] Travel articles on Austria peppered the *New York Times*, suggesting the country's desirability.[7] In addition to the forays abroad, *The Cardinal* and *The*

Sound of Music were also both marketed as so-called "roadshows." After the premiere, they were not released in multiple theaters in each major city, but initially shown in just one select theater.[8] To create an "event," they had a limited number of showings per day with reserved seats, programs, and an intermission. These two films, both clocking in at over 170 minutes, were ideally suited for this marketing ploy.

The filmmakers' interest in a story set in Austria around the time of the Anschluss may seem surprising given that the situation in the United States and Europe was light years away from that facing the earlier filmmakers. The relative domestic peace and prosperity of the fifties were followed by a decade characterized by domestic political and social upheaval.[9] As the United States' involvement in Vietnam increased and casualties escalated, the peace movement grew in response. At the same time, as brutal acts of murder were carried out against African Americans, the Civil Rights movement was gaining momentum. The second wave women's movement was also underway, challenging traditional gender roles. The election of the first Catholic president in 1960 was surrounded by (Protestant) fears over the extent to which the Catholic Church and the pope might influence affairs of the state. The Cold War was becoming more heated with the building of the Berlin Wall in August 1961 and the Cuban Missile Crisis in October 1962. Interest in Nazi Germany and the Holocaust was refueled by the telecasting of the Eichmann trial in 1961.[10] A month before *The Cardinal* premiered the nation witnessed the assassination of its president.

Although Preminger and Wise resorted to similar strategies to attract audiences, they painted very different pictures of the Anschluss and the reactions of the citizenry. Nonetheless, both films were equally shaped by contemporary contexts. In the Anschluss episode of *The Cardinal* Preminger inserts fact into a fictional story and attempts to present the reasons for the reaction of Austria's Catholic leadership to the Nazi takeover. At the same time he ties the episode to the film's larger reflections on the responsibility of institutions such as the Church in challenging racism, fighting totalitarian regimes, and preserving democracy. The screenplay for *The Sound of Music* drew on earlier fictionalizations of the story of the von Trapp family, who left Austria in 1938 because of their Catholic convictions. Rather than a historically accurate rendition of the events, Wise constructs Austria as a place outside of history. The way in which he inserts the historical event ultimately portrays Austria as a victim of history. While Wise claimed that he had no message in mind when he made the film of the equally escapist musical, it most certainly contains multiple messages on conservative values that spoke to viewers in 1965 and continue to resonate even today. An examination of the two films demonstrates how the same historical episode can be used as a means to comment critically on the past and present or as a distraction from conflict. Preminger confronts Austrian history at the same time that he takes a stand on contemporary issues. By contrast, Wise uses the story of the von Trapp family to provide audiences with an escape from contemporaneous controversies.

Confronting the Present through the Past in *The Cardinal*

The producer/director Otto Preminger took advantage of the episodic globe-trotting nature of Henry Morton Robinson's *The Cardinal*, in which the author follows the rise of Stephen Fermoyle, the son of Irish immigrants in Boston, from parish priest to cardinal. In addition to the forays from Boston, to Rome, to a rural parish in Vermont, and to the racist south, Preminger introduced two long segments located in Austria that do not appear in Robinson's tome.

Clocking in at seventeen minutes, the first Austrian segment finds Fermoyle (Tom Tryon) in 1924 Vienna, after he took a leave of absence as a result of a crisis of faith. Working as an English teacher, the young priest meets Anne-Marie, a young Austrian (Romy Schneider), whom Preminger substitutes for the Italian countess in the book version. Although he falls in love with Anne-Marie, Stephen returns to the priesthood at the end of the episode. In the second Austria segment, Preminger replaced Robinson's discourse on the relationship between the Vatican and Italian fascist regime with the conflict between the Vatican and Austria's Church leadership. This second Austria segment, thirty-five minutes in length, takes place in the days shortly after the Anschluss and explores the controversial role that Austrian Cardinal Innitzer (1875–1955) played after he initially welcomed the Nazi takeover.

In his autobiography, Otto Preminger explained, "The shooting of *The Cardinal* offered me an opportunity to put on film something that concerned me deeply: the behavior of the Catholic Church during the Nazi occupation of Austria."[11] Born in 1905 in Wiznitz, located in the eastern part of Austria-Hungary (now Ukraine), Preminger was almost ten when his family settled in Vienna, where his father worked as a government lawyer. In his autobiography Preminger writes of the anti-Semitism that his father and family faced in Austria.[12] Among other things, he describes his own conflict in the Catholic country when he was offered the position of director-manager of the Burgtheater, if he converted to Catholicism. Although he did not consider himself a religious follower of Judaism, he refused to convert and retained the position of managing director of the Theater in der Josefstadt, until he left Austria for Hollywood in 1935. Not particularly an innovator, the final play he staged in Vienna was *The First Legion* by the American playwright

Emmett Lavery, "in which a priest regains his faith after a crippled boy who believes in miracles is healed."[13] In his 2007 Preminger biography, Foster Hirsch speculates that this might have been "a placatory gesture toward the staunchly Catholic regime."[14] In any case, the premiere was attended by numerous Catholic dignitaries, among others Cardinal Innitzer. Perhaps, Preminger revisited his conciliatory attitude toward the Catholic Church under the Austro-fascist regime because of the Austrian Catholic leadership's approval of the Anschluss.

The framing of the film and the placement of the Vienna episode point to readings that engage with the past as well as contemporary issues. The film begins and ends on the day of Fermoyle's investiture as cardinal sometime after April 1938 and before September 1, 1939. As the credits roll, the camera follows an as yet unidentified Fermoyle, as he walks toward some unknown goal.[15] At one point, he passes by a wall with a reference to Mussolini in the form of graffiti stating "Viva il Duce." Leaving out the novel's attention to the relationship between fascist Italy and the Vatican and substituting the Anschluss in Austria, Preminger can make the Church's stance against authoritarian regimes stronger. He reinforces this by removing the events from a larger Austrian context and not touching on the close relationship of the Austrian Catholic Church to the Austro-fascist government. At the same time, by targeting Innitzer and his approval of the Nazis, Preminger can contribute to contemporary discussions on this past.

In the first conversation in the film, when a former Papal superior greets Fermoyle, he relates that he is unable to come to the ceremony, because he has to go to Poland at a time when the country "seems to be Hitler's next target." By mentioning Poland before the German invasion, the relative time of the frame story is established. The use of the imminent invasion of Poland may serve a double function here. In the early sixties the fight between the communist government and the leaders of the Catholic Church, particularly the courage of Polish Cardinal Wyszyński, were frequent news items. In contrast to Innitzer's cooperation with the "outside" powers, this hints at the possibilities of a different response in opposing a totalitarian regime.

For the Anschluss segment Preminger condenses the events of about seven months into a couple of days in which he tracks Innitzer's change from his initial approval of the Anschluss and his belief that he could negotiate for Catholic rights with Hitler to his disillusionment and opposition to Hitler. The director introduces the Anschluss segment with documentary material in a type of mini-history lesson for contemporary audiences. Placed around fifty minutes after the intermission, the segment begins with a German-language newsreel of Hitler arriving in Austria. As the camera pulls back from the newsreel, viewers see Fermoyle with other clerics in Rome as he begins translating, "March 13, 1938 Hitler enters

Vienna at 5:30 p.m., welcomed by enthusiastic crowds." This real footage is then followed by staged newsreel footage with documentary material woven in. The narrator announces, "Cardinal Innitzer, archbishop from Vienna, reads a letter signed by him and all other Austrian bishops, welcoming Hitler to Austria." The camera then focuses on Innitzer (Josef Meinrad), as he reads essential parts of the actual letter that had been delivered from all Austrian Catholic pulpits on March 27, 1938. "We acknowledge happily that the National Socialist movement has for the German Reich and especially for the underprivileged classes achieved outstanding progress. The bishops are extending their blessings and their best wishes for the future of these efforts. On the day of the plebiscite it is for us bishops a natural national obligation to declare ourselves as Germans and as part of the German Reich. We expect of all faithful Catholics that they will know what they owe to their people."[16] Although readers of the *New York Times* in the thirties would have been familiar with Innitzer and the consequences of his actions, this is no doubt new information for many viewers in the sixties. With this truncated version of a factual letter the Austrian bishops had read from the pulpit and which was published in *Völkischer Beobachter* (the official newspaper of the National Socialist Party), Preminger includes the essential parts of Innitzer's stance that prompted an immediate reaction from the Vatican. However, he leaves off a significant statement on the perceived threat of communism, which proclaims, "We are also convinced that through the actions of the National Socialist movement the danger of godless Bolshevism which destroys all will be averted."[17] By omitting this, he does not place communism and fascism in opposition to each other, but he sets up the stage for connecting them together under the term totalitarianism.

To weave the fictional character into a historical episode, Preminger does not have Innitzer travel to Rome and recant in the Papal newspaper, nor does he have the Papal Nuncio to Berlin travel to Vienna to shut down the Nunciature, as was reported in the *New York Times*. Rather he simplifies the exchanges between the Austrian Catholic Church and the Vatican and has the American go to Vienna as an emissary, who has the official function of shutting down the Nunciature. However, according to his mentor at the Vatican, he has a more important albeit unofficial role to play, which "will be an educational one, instructing a prince of the church in the realities of the modern world." Coming from a member of an ancient institution that is slow to embrace change, this seems rather odd. What are the realities of the modern world? What insight does the Vatican have into these realities that Innitzer does not? If the contemporary audience considers the "realities of the modern world" and the need to oppose them, the film points them to domestic racism and the threat of totalitarianism.

In his first meeting with Fermoyle, the cardinal explains himself to the representative of the Vatican and by extension to an American audience. Preminger's Innitzer, whose treatment of the American is bound to make him unsympathetic, is condescending and arrogant. Not taking the Vatican's concerns seriously, he is quite confident that what he did was in the best interest of Austrian Catholics. He maintains, "Hitler wants Austria, a great many Austrians want Hitler. If the Church presides at the marriage we'll get better treatment than if we didn't." He suggests that Rome is ignorant of the brutality of the Nazis. "Does Rome have any idea how Hitler responds to criticism? Would you like to see Catholic men and women scrubbing the sidewalks like so many Jews?" At this juncture, the film makes one of its few references to Jewish persecution, alluding to those citizens who were forced to scrub the symbols of the former regime off the sidewalks with toothbrushes in the days following the Anschluss. While acknowledging one example of the Nazis' treatment of the Jewish population, it appears the Church has made no effort to condemn it. Instead, Preminger has Innitzer explain Austrians' desire to become a part of Germany. "The joining together of all German people is what we have been dreaming of for a thousand years. The Germans and we are different in many ways, yes, but our blood is the same." The cardinal states that the connection between blood and national identity is particularly hard for an American to understand, one of the few points the two agree on. However, by placing this episode immediately after the sequence in which Fermoyle experiences the Ku Klux Klan in Georgia, the film suggests that there are limits to Americans' acceptance of diversity. The proximity of these episodes suggests that Preminger may also have been aware of news reports that connected activities of Austrian neo-Nazis with the Ku Klux Klan.[18]

In the second and third meetings between Fermoyle and Innitzer, Preminger reworks documented events further for dramatic purposes and because of time constraints. Rather than having the cardinal go to Rome and have his official recantation appear in the Vatican publication, the screen Innitzer tries to placate the Vatican, while not alienating the Germans. Although he casually delivers the corrections demanded of the Vatican to Fermoyle after an evening at the opera, it is ultimately an empty gesture. The Nazis would not allow any corrections to be published and he refuses to have the statement read at mass on the day of the plebiscite, unless he gets a direct order from the Vatican. On what appears to be the next day—in any case the day of the plebiscite—Fermoyle angrily confronts Innitzer for his early "yes" vote for the Anschluss and the fact he gave the Nazi salute. Innitzer retains his arrogant stance and maintains that his vote was a very personal one and not an appeal to Austrian Catholics. He admits that he said "Heil Hitler," with the explanation, "The words have become part of the German language, they are used instead of good morning or good evening, even, I regret to say, instead of God bless you." His arrogant stance sets him up for the humiliation to follow.

In Fermoyle's last sequence with Innitzer, Preminger rehabilitates the cardinal in record time, weaving together fictional and actual events that took place over a seven-month period. In a matter of narrative hours and narrated minutes, the cardinal goes from boasting that a non-Roman can successfully negotiate with Hitler, to being humiliated by Hitler, to recognizing his failure and taking limited action. This whirlwind turnabout prompted criticism from contemporary critics and more recent scholars. In his December 13, 1963, review the *New York Times* critic Bosley Crowther registered his skepticism: "Back in Rome and consecrated a Bishop, he [Fermoyle] is sent to Vienna in 1938 to persuade an ingenuous Cardinal Innitzer to avoid becoming involved with the Nazis. A flash of violence and the Cardinal is persuaded, and our hero returns to Rome to be elevated himself to the rank of Cardinal." Foster Hirsch writes, "Typical of the film's approach to 'difficult' subject matter is its vacillating treatment of Cardinal Innitzer, who at first is blind to the evils of fascism, but then undergoes a rapid, unconvincing change of heart. Despite his avowed animus toward Viennese collaboration with the Nazis, Preminger seems to be pulling his punches here."[19] Rather than "pulling his punches," the director condenses months into minutes, consequently making Innitzer's actual turnabout unbelievable. To make the transition more credible, Fermoyle witnesses Innitzer's humiliation and sudden change of heart. Innitzer invites Fermoyle along to his meeting with Hitler, confident that he will gain concessions from Hitler for the Church. Not only is he kept waiting and Fermoyle not allowed to accompany him, but Hitler verbally abuses the cardinal. Visibly shaken by his meeting with Hitler, Innitzer relates his "conversation" to Fermoyle. "He repudiated all his promises to me, every one of them. There's going to be a war, he says, and the Church must be drafted into the service of the Fatherland the same as the army. In Austria there must be even more control than in Germany because we have such a Catholic majority. Our schools are to be abolished, our youth groups dissolved, Catholic marriage will no longer have the force of law." The film paints the meeting with Hitler as the first step in Innitzer's transformation and screen rehabilitation. It also shows that his concerns are limited very much to the status of the Church and its members. When he emerges looking stunned, he relates to Fermoyle as they are leaving, "At the very end he started yelling and asked me if I didn't think Almighty God had chosen him to lead the German people to their destiny. He didn't wait for an answer. And I remembered myself at the plebiscite, raising my hand in a heathen salute and saying not, praised be the Lord, but Heil Hitler." Innitzer's personal humiliation leads to the realization and shame of how he compromised himself as a Catholic. Moreover, he failed to accomplish his goal of protecting the rights of the Church.

In portraying this episode, Preminger draws on a series of incidents from the fall of 1938. According to a report in the *New York Times*, by September 4 Cardinal Innitzer had protested the Nazi disregard for the Church's right to have religious marriage ceremonies recognized by the state as well as the disbanding of some Catholic institutions.[20] Then, as reported in the *Times* on October 9, Innitzer held a traditional celebration (*Rosenkranzfeier*) for Catholic youth that always coincided with the beginning of the school year. Because it could not be publicized in the usual manner, those in charge expected a small crowd, at most 2,500 youth. However, word got out and sources estimate the crowd between 7,000 and 10,000.[21] Although not known as an accomplished orator, Innitzer is reported as having given a stirring, well-planned sermon, parts of which were included in the film's homily.[22] According to reports of these events, some of the organizers became aware of the Nazi youth outside who were harassing believers. Instead of going home quietly as the Catholic leaders had requested, the fired-up youth poured out of the church and called for their leader, purposely reworking Nazi phrases, such as "We want our Führer" to "We want to see our Bishop" and "We greet our Bishop."[23] When Innitzer answered their calls and appeared at the window, it is reported that the youth below spontaneously began singing the "Herz-Jesu-Bundes-Lied," a song whose history goes back to Tyrol's struggles against Napoleon. According to the *New York Times*, Nazi youth stormed the bishop's palace as well as the *Churhaus*, an adjacent Church building, the next evening. The Nazis looted the premises and threw a priest out the window.[24]

In the film, Innitzer's public reversal is swift. Deeply troubled by his actions, Preminger's cardinal returns to his residence after meeting with Hitler, where a large group of Catholic youth greet him. Inspired by them, he holds a spontaneous homily. To suggest its documentary character, the sermon is held in German as subtitles appear. Innitzer acknowledges that the Catholic youth have lost much through the disbanding of their organizations, but he urges them to hold even more firmly to their belief in Christ, who he declares, "alone is our 'Fuehrer' and 'Savior.'" Before he retires to his residence, he states that only Christ can bring happiness. Innitzer's rousing speech is immediately followed by violence. While the Catholic youth are listening intently, a group of young Nazis is shown marching in their direction. While cutting back and forth from the Catholics gathered to marching Nazis, Preminger has a young Catholic woman (the Austrian operatic singer, Wilma Lipp), inspired by the cardinal's words, ascend what appears to be an outside pulpit and sing the "Hallelujah" from Mozart's *Exultate, jubilate*. The crowd of Catholic youth soon joins in. The camera continues to cut back and forth between the groups, building up to the violent confrontation. After fighting with the Catholic youth, the Nazis break into and loot the cardinal's palace and throw a member of the cardinal's staff out the window.

The cardinal's regret, his speech before the youth, and the anger and violence unleashed upon him both change Fermoyle's attitude toward him and give him a first-hand experience of Nazi methods. He realizes the danger the cardinal has put himself in by voicing dissatisfaction with the new regime. Now shown in the same frame, which has been rare up until now, they both express concern for the other's safety:

INNITZER: We must get you out of here. With the Vatican passport you are one of the few people who can leave the country. At least for the moment you can. You must tell the truth about Hitler's promises.
FERMOYLE: You can't stay here Your Eminence, you're not safe.
INNITZER: Safety, I am afraid, is among the illusions we can no longer depend on. Pray for me.

Fermoyle, who up to this point has been stymied by Innitzer's attitude, suddenly sees him as a vulnerable individual and urges him to seek safety. By refusing to leave, the cardinal reclaims a leadership role in the Church and provides a positive model for his flock. In the end his resistance appears to mirror that of Cardinal Wyszyński under the Communists in Poland. The *New York Times* ran several articles on the Polish cardinal who had been engaged in similar struggles. However, in contrast to Innitzer, Cardinal Wyszyński never gave the regime his official approval. After serving a prison term because of his refusal to agree to government orders, he continued to stand up for the rights of the Catholic population.[25]

In the parallel story focusing on the fate of Anne-Marie, the young woman Fermoyle had fallen in love with in the first Vienna segment, the word "totalitarian" is dropped for the first of two times. Parallel to Innitzer's transformation, Preminger has Anne-Marie recognize her own role in her husband's suicide. Having a Jewish grandmother and fearing arrest, her husband jumps out of their apartment window when the Gestapo comes to the door. Later, she seeks refuge with Fermoyle, as a representative of the Papal Nuncio, when Gestapo agents come after her for supposedly wanting to smuggle jewels out of the country. However, she gives herself up, not because she believes herself guilty of smuggling, but because of her failure to be there for her husband. When Fermoyle visits her in prison, she refuses his help and makes clear she will make no effort to fight. He protests, arguing, "The most important reason of all is for your sake, because of what you are, not an ant in a totalitarian anthill, but a human being, an individual with a God-given soul of your own." With the use of the term, Preminger ties the Nazi period to contemporary discussions on totalitarian regimes. The historian Benjamin L. Alpers writes of the relationship, "The idea of totalitarianism thus helped keep public interest in understanding Nazism alive; since totalitarianism suggested that Nazism and communism were essentially similar, understanding the former Nazi enemy became a way of grappling with the emerging Soviet foe."[26] Fermoyle suggests that whether fascist or communist, such regimes are bent on destroying individuality.

Fermoyle brings up "totalitarianism" again when he speaks of the "global crisis" facing the free world at the time of his investiture as cardinal, which immediately follows the scene with Anne-Marie. Thankful for the honor the Vatican has bestowed on him and the United States, he names "America's first bishop, John Carroll," who "was the brother of a signer of the Declaration of Independence and a living example of that loyalty to Church and State, to religion and to democracy that this moment in history demands from us all." Obviously recalling his recent experiences in Vienna, he states:

> I have seen at close range the hell on earth that awaits us all if totalitarianism prevails, if the world forgets that all men alike are the children of God endowed by their Creator with the unalienable right to life, liberty, and the pursuit of happiness. That is America's creed. That is the gospel of the Church. It is in danger at this moment from men and doctrines that are the enemies of all freedoms, political as well as religious. The defense of freedom calls for strong voices, strong hearts, strong hands. Pray for me that I may not falter and for the liberty and exaltation of our church and our beloved country.

Preminger brings the dangers of totalitarianism home in this final speech, which would have multiple echoes in the United States.[27] For one, the blacklisting during the McCarthy era in the United States still cast its shadow.[28] The terror promulgated by the Ku Klux Klan and the shame of racial discrimination continued to plague the United States, denying a large portion of its citizens their inalienable rights.

With *The Cardinal* Preminger provided viewers with a rare albeit limited window into an episode of Austrian history with Austrian Nazis, fellow travelers, and Catholic opponents, including a slight nod to Jewish persecution. He sought to show his audience that there is more to Austria than Apfelstrudel. By focusing on Innitzer, the director presented an Austrian who initially welcomed the Anschluss as did many of his countrymen, but ended as someone who regretted his actions and desired that the truth be known. By opening the door to the past, the director attempted to tell other "truths." With Preminger's return to Austria's past, he also addressed contemporary issues and warned of the dangers of totalitarianism and the responsibility of Americans and institutions, such as the Church, in the fight against it.

Denazifying Austria and Escaping Controversy in *The Sound of Music*[29]

Robert Wise approached this period of Austrian history much differently. He and his team were never interested in using the story of the von Trapp family for a truthful examination of Austria's past or as a stand-in for contemporary controversies.[30] Within the course of the love story between the widowed captain and the gregarious novice, Wise and his team distance Austria from its Nazi past and depict it as a victim of Nazi aggression.[31] Ironically, many viewers believe that the film conveys a reasonably realistic rendition of the events—and the von Trapp family. Indeed, the popularity of the film lies in the paradox of portraying a real family in a real place at a real time in history in ways that uncouple the place from the historical reality and root national identity in family values.

Even before the credits appear, the filmmakers use the Austrian countryside to distance the country from a social reality, taking full advantage of the possibilities that location shooting and the newly applied technology offer. Not at all interested in a realistic portrayal of the historical situation or the "true story" of the von Trapp family, the screenplay writer Ernest Lehman maps out an introduction that "goes beyond realism."[32] "I will not describe the specific locations. I will tell you the mood, the feeling, the effect that I would like to see. We are floating in UTTER SILENCE over a scene of spectacular and earthly beauty. . . . Isolated locales are selected by the camera and photographed with such stylized beauty that the world below, however real, will be seen as a lovely never-never land where stories such as ours can happen, and where people sometimes express their deepest emotions in song."[33] The cameraman Ted D. McCord translated Lehman's vision through dramatic aerial shots reminiscent of techniques developed in fifties travelogues.[34]

The spectacular opening and the accompanying sound set the stage for a dehistoricization of Austria while engaging viewers on a visceral level. The first shot captures clouds with no sounds other than the wind. The camera moves from the clouds over rugged mountains, to a view of a valley, then to a beautiful mountain lake. The next aerial shots pass over a river valley, a tiny village, and toy-size castles, providing a bird's eye view of a picturesque land untouched by strife. The wind sounds yield to a birdsong, which gradually evolves into an instrumental rendition of *The Sound of Music* theme. The camera then pauses on a hilltop meadow with mountains in the background as Maria (Julie Andrews) appears on the horizon. When she whirls into view she gives the mountains a voice, singing the landscape to mythical life with the lyrics "The hills are alive / With the sound of music, / With songs they have sung / For a thousand years." Hearing the convent bells calling the nuns and novices to Vespers, Maria interrupts her song, grabs her wimple from the ground, and runs back to the convent. As the overture plays, the credits roll over stills of more beautiful scenery in and around Salzburg, reminiscent of photographs from a tourist's album with its baroque cathedral, a quaint Austrian chapel situated on top of a rocky protrusion, and the town's carillon. Austria is introduced through an almost deserted landscape, creating Lehman's desired, enchanted, musical never-neverland. In this world, love of nature and song is tied to national identity.[35]

Lehman's screenplay sets up Austria as a country removed from political and social conflict, only to reintroduce a historical event, the Anschluss, into the vacuum created. It does this convincingly by establishing an inner logic in the film that results in the portrayal of Austrians unambiguously as victims. Wise locates this "never-neverland" temporally and geographically with a documentary gesture. The introductory "travelogue," the initial song, and credits close with the inscription: "Salzburg, Austria, in the last Golden Days of the Thirties" over a picture of the city of Salzburg. However, the thirties were anything but golden. The Salzburg historian Robert Hoffmann puts unemployment in the city at 26 percent in 1934.[36] In his memoirs, Bruno Kreisky, the former chancellor of Austria, aptly and concisely described this period of Austrian history: "Massive unemployment, chronic misery, and starvation wages shaped life in Austria and influenced political events."[37] However, in Hollywood's version of Austria, there is no mention of political dissent, no civil strife, and no Austro-fascist government.[38] This Austria is not threatened from within, but like Austria in *They Dare Not Love*, it will be overrun by Germans and betrayed by a few traitorous Austrians. By locating the action geographically and historically in "Salzburg, Austria, in the last Golden Days of the Thirties" and focusing on a family that the American public may have been well acquainted with either through the musical or reports on the family's musical summer camps, Wise primes viewer expectations and erroneously implies that the story reflects reality.

Through falsification of the historical events leading up to and including the Anschluss, as well as the composition of the scene depicting the Anschluss, Wise lends credence to Austria's victim status.[39] As in the musical, there is no mention in the film of the scheduled plebiscite for a free Austria nor of the negotiations between Austria's Chancellor Schuschnigg and Hitler. Neither Schuschnigg's famous radio broadcast nor Hitler's arrival in Austria are referenced. The annexation is signaled initially only by the bells after the lavish wedding of Maria and the Captain. As Lehman instructs, "a transition takes place in the sound of the bells. During a dissolve, the bell-music becomes harsh, discordant, mournful, something has happened, it is not joyful."[40] The Anschluss transpires with little warning, at an unspecified time in summer, rather than in March, when it actually occurred.

The combination of sound, color, and a carefully composed mise-en-scène in the Anschluss scene mark Austria as a defenseless target of German aggression. "We are CLOSE on the final bell-tower sequence. The bell is still tolling mournfully. Now it comes to a stop. At first there is a complete void of sound. And then we HEAR an ominous SOUND in the distance, the SOUND OF MARCHING FEET. The CAMERA PANS DOWN from the tower to the square below, and we know then what has happened to Austria. A detachment of Storm Troopers is marching across the square. *Anschluß* has come."[41] The sound of the joyful bells obliterated by mournful clanging signals the Anschluss and symbolizes its deeper meaning for the once golden Austria. The silence that follows immediately contrasts somber Germanness with Austrian musicality. The sound of music has been replaced by the sound of marching feet. The transformation is also underscored in the Anschluss scene through the use of color. The storm troopers march across the sterile square with only the Nazi flag adorning it. In addition, the composition of the scene conveys the threat that the new order poses to Austria and Austrians. The bird's-eye shot of the square with no citizens in sight is framed by tall buildings, creating a trapped feeling.

The reactions of the Austrians in the film also set Austria up as a victim of National Socialism. Contrary to historical fact, the film portrays no public display of enthusiasm after the Anschluss. The square remains ominously devoid of civilians, implying that most people are at home scared. Although the director and his crew were well aware of Austrian sentiments, they did not show Austrians greeting Nazis because this would ultimately have seemed out of place. There never appears to be any reason why the Austrians (other than a few renegades) would welcome the Germans. The identifiable Nazis are the von Trapp's butler, Rolf (the young admirer of the Captain's oldest daughter), Herr Zeller, and an unnamed person at the party hosted by von Trapp. Thus, the Austrians who wish to be German are outsiders—either someone from the lower class (the butler), an impressionable teenager (Rolf), or non-aristocratic Austrians who appear able to advance only through the help of the Nazis.

Other than a few Austrian Nazis, there is no overt Austrian support of Germans, and the Anschluss appears to be a German import. Moreover, other plot elements strengthen the logic of the Austrians as victims. Although the only family not flying the Nazi flag in the Salzburg area is the von Trapp family, the open display of patriotism at the music festival, when the Austrian audience joins the Captain in his rendition of the pseudo-Austrian folk song "Edelweiss," implies two things: the majority of Austrians did not support National Socialism, and they were powerless to resist because of the military power of German National Socialists. The Captain vehemently opposes the Anschluss as is made clear in the scene when he rebukes the flustered Rolf, who after delivering a telegraph raises his right arm and cries "Heil Hitler." However, the very fact that von Trapp leaves Austria for his honeymoon suggests that the danger of a takeover must not have seemed so imminent; otherwise, he would not have left.

Devoid of social and political strife, Austria is logically the victim of a German takeover. Consequently, the Anschluss appears to have been instigated by a few aberrant Austrians and Germans—an event that surprised citizens despite some warning signs. The lack of dynamic development in the film also signals that the Anschluss is not the center of conflict and dramatic activity; it is merely a secondary conflict in which true "Austrian" values provide the strength to oppose National Socialism.

Despite the inner logic, the portrayal of the Anschluss and the events leading up to it concerned Darryl Zanuck, one of the producers. He worried that the Nazi menace was not made clear enough and wrote a letter to his son Richard Zanuck, then president of Twentieth Century-Fox. He argued that if the threat of an invasion was not obvious, the logical end of the picture would be the wedding scene. In a handwritten note on the letter, Ernest Lehman commented years later, "I must say I agreed with Darryl. His instincts were always unfailing. And yet, at the time, we all decided to ignore his suggestions, and the movie triumphed despite flaws."[42] Lehman may have conceded a flaw in the screenplay, yet within the context of the film story the portrayal of the Anschluss after the wedding is not as illogical as it first appears.

The musical portion of the film does end with the wedding scene and at this juncture the Germans cut the film when it was first released in Germany.[43] However, Richard Dyer argues that the seemingly unmotivated continuation of the story is believable because it is tied to an ongoing opposition between freedom and order set up from the very beginning of the film and only temporarily resolved with the wedding.[44] In this context, the National Socialist threat is transformed into yet another "mountain" to be climbed and a reminder that life's challenges are never ending, but masterable within a family with a loving patriarchal father and a supportive and ultimately subservient wife.

Evidently, some of the town fathers protested the scene "where Nazis march across the Residenzplatz and take over Austria."[45] They did not want the Americans hanging up swastikas on the square, exclaiming: "'Oh no, you can't do that, because the people of Salzburg were not sympathizers.'"[46] Only when the Americans suggested that they could use newsreel showing Austrians welcoming Hitler did the Austrians budge. Maurice Zuberano, the sketch artist and second unit supervisor stated: "The only thing we still weren't allowed to do was to use a crowd cheering, but I think we made our point without it."[47] But what exactly *was* the point they were trying to make?

There is no evidence in or written on the screenplay indicating that the Americans ever intended to show Austrian approval. Indeed, it was the studio's lack of interest in the political reality, among other things, that led William Wyler, who was being wooed to direct the film before Wise, to drop the project.[48] Wyler's biographer writes of his attitude toward *The Sound of Music*. "Lehman kept telling Wyler that Nazism was not what *The Sound of Music* was about. Wyler agreed. 'I knew it wasn't really a political thing. I had a tendency to want to make it, if not an anti-Nazi movie, at least to say a few things.'"[49] From the logic of the screenplay itself and statements made by William Wyler, the threat to use newsreel footage can only be interpreted as a cynical ploy. The Americans seem merely to be letting the Austrians know that they were aware that the citizens of Salzburg were not so innocent. However, an overwhelmingly overt show of Austrian approval would have destroyed the logic of the screenplay.

In contrast to *The Cardinal*, Austrians are viewed as different from Germans. Rather than being expressed in political terms, however, an Austrian national identity is defined through personal traits and values. The "Austrian" traits are coded in such a way that would apply to almost any nationality, no doubt contributing to the film's popularity and appeal then and now.[50] Wise associates a series of "positive" traits related to the love of nature and music with the Captain, Maria, and the children, and pitted negative supposedly non-Austrian traits against these. Musicality is opposed to a lack of interest in music, the rural to the urban, naturalness to worldliness, unquestioned patriotism to either a resigned attitude toward the Anschluss or a pro-Anschluss attitude, and the traditional patriarchal family to female economic independence.

Throughout the film, Wise uses music and pseudofolk elements to form the nexus of the traits constituting a personal and "national" identity. Expressions of love for country, family, and mate are conveyed in song, or song serves as the catalyst for these emotions. Maria's appearance and song in the opening sequence binds her to Austria through her closeness to nature and the music of "nature." "Austrian" folk music brings the Captain back to his family. Immediately after he has told Maria she must leave the house and return to the convent, he hears his children singing "The Sound of Music." It draws him into the house and to his children, at what point he is visibly moved. The song breaks the spell the Captain appears to have been under since the death of his wife. He joins the children in song, and the number culminates in a very emotional "homecoming." In addition, the first time the Captain sings "Edelweiss," a song which has been mistaken for Austria's national anthem by some Americans, he is brought even closer to his children.[51] Although he is still the stern father, he now disciplines his children with a twinkle in his eye and not without good reason. If "Edelweiss" brings the Captain closer to his family, when he sings the song at the festival, he is brought closer to his Austrian compatriots, who join in at his and Maria's invitation. The "homeland" he sings about is associated with nature and devoid of any class distinctions or ideological conflict.[52]

The two female protagonists—the Baroness and Maria—embody two contrasting models of femininity and nationality—the decadent versus the natural Austrian. The Baroness's manner and dress mark her as a sophisticate with a lifestyle clearly in opposition to Maria's. Not only does she smoke—something no one else in the movie does—she wears dresses that label her as a sophisticated urbanite. The red sequined dress in her final scene with von Trapp, which contrasts with the light, airy natural-looking dress of Maria, further stamps her as a woman of worldly experience, someone estranged from her "Austrian" roots. Not only her outward appearance but also the Baroness's personal qualities tie her to a decadent Austria. The Captain describes her as "lovely, charming, witty, graceful, the perfect hostess." Because of her lack of a genuine connection to music, nature, and children, however, she does not share the characteristics of a "true Austrian" and for this reason is not a suitable mate for von Trapp. By contrast, Maria has all the fitting traits, from her love of nature and her faith, to her love of children. Originally presented as a free spirit who upsets the order of the abbey, she follows the conviction that children should be treated with respect. The adults are there to listen, to understand, and eventually to be wise older friends. When a parent disciplines, it should be for a good reason. After her marriage to the Captain she is no longer the free spirit, but the supportive wife to the kind, understanding, but firm patriarch.

By virtue of the fact that *The Sound of Music* is a musical, an American idiom, the story of the von Trapps had already been removed from its cultural context. In such a world there is no place for a national identity based on social, political, or historical reality. Consequently, Wise builds on the Captain's overt patriotic statements and Maria's connection to nature and music to construct his version of an "Austrian" identity based on the love of nature, "Austrian" music, and children. Wise ultimately presents a scenario in which obstacles are best overcome within the bounds of a loving patriarchal family.

At a time when US leaders were questioned for their wisdom in sending troops to Vietnam, when phrases like "Your country, Love it or Leave it" were making the rounds, when war protesters were calling soldiers "murderers," and when an increasing number of women were organizing and demanding more rights, *The Sound of Music* offered temporary escape and propagated a conservative domestic model. The intact, loving, patriarchal, patriotic family could "Climb Every Mountain" together.

The conservative values presented in the film, the casting, and the real von Trapp family who had left Austria as refugees and come to America and could boast of their success, all provide multiple possibilities for identification.

In contrast to *The Cardinal*, the film has had long-term and far-reaching impact, beginning with the tourist industry in Salzburg. In 1965 the number of American tourists shot up 20 percent from the previous year and the stream of American visitors to Salzburg has not stopped since.[53] Clever marketers help tourists who travel to Austria in their search for traces of the von Trapp family or at least the film family. Companies offer *The Sound of Music* tours, which hit sights from the film in and around Salzburg.[54] On one of the bus tours, the group is invited to sing songs from the film.[55] Other tie-ins to the film include dinner shows geared toward the tourist population. In 1992 the von Trapp villa was restored and opened in 2008 as a hotel.[56] The city museum had an exhibition "Trapp Familie—Realität und 'Sound of Music'" from November 4, 2011 to September 15, 2013.[57] On April 13, 2018 the Sound of Music World in the center of Salzburg opened an exhibition on the facts and fiction of the family and the film.[58] These various tie-ins, *The Sound of Music* sing-alongs, the popularity of the villa, the museum exhibits, and the special anniversary issues of the film are all proof of the film's long-term popularity.[59] Although audiences may be more aware of the country's checkered past, particularly after the Waldheim controversy in the nineties, the film continues to shape viewers' conceptions of the country as a kind of fairy kingdom.

Conclusion: Profiting from Austrian History

Both *The Cardinal* and *The Sound of Music* did well when released and both received industry recognition. According to Wikipedia, *The Cardinal* was the "18th highest grossing film of the year," garnering $11,170,588 domestically with a profit of $5.46 million.[60] *The Sound of Music* was also a resounding financial success: "By December 1965, just nine months after the movie opened, *The Sound of Music* had been number one 30 out of 43 weeks and had already amassed $50 million in worldwide box-office receipts—after taxes."[61] Both received Golden Globe awards. *The Cardinal* was nominated for six Academy Awards, including Preminger for Best Director. *The Sound of Music* earned ten Oscar nominations and won five, including Best Picture and Best Director. The success of the films with their opposing pictures of Austria suggests that they spoke to contemporary audiences. By drawing attention to the actions of Cardinal Innitzer, Preminger could argue for the importance of remembering this past as well as inviting audience members to see present-day parallels. By contrast, Wise offered viewers a respite from the turmoil of the day with the inspiring and highly fictionalized story of the von Trapp family. However, although *The Cardinal* was popular when released, it has lacked the staying power of *The Sound of Music*. The impact of the scenery in and around Salzburg, the appeal of the singing family, and the brief escape the film allows have all contributed to *The Sound of Music*'s lasting appeal. Wise's presentation of the von Trapp family has resonated with the American public for generations and many who have seen the film believe they have learned something about Austrian history.

Conclusion: Hollywood's Austria—Its Past, Present, Future

IN THIS BOOK I HAVE ARGUED that the US domestic film industry adapted characteristics and stereotypes associated with Austria in ways that were shaped by American contexts. The many and often competing forces involved in producing any one film in Hollywood have contributed to specifically American takes on Austrian stories. Even when Hollywood's Austria shared traits with European productions, Hollywood's Austria films would differ from those. Hollywood's Austria was also not static. In the decades following the introduction of Austria to the Hollywood screen, the nature of and the changes in the film industry, transformations in audience perceptions or assumed perceptions of Austrians, varying tastes, and ever changing historical contexts would shape and reshape stories set in Austria and Austria-Hungary.

Just as the screen incarnations of Austria were determined by contexts within the United States, so, too, were the ups and downs of the country's popularity on screen. If we look at the overall production of Austria films—both those where the Austrian backdrop serves a specific purpose and those were it appears merely incidental—Austria's screen popularity or lack thereof can be tied in part to the country's perceived box office potential. Hollywood's Austria experienced its "heyday" in the twenties and the thirties. In those two decades Vienna, along with other European locales, served as the backdrop for many "sophisticated" scenarios. However, Vienna had a different air than other European cities, such as Berlin or Budapest. In the source text of *The Marriage Circle*, the story was originally set in Berlin and the scenario of *The Firebird* was originally to take place in Budapest. However, they were relocated to Vienna, because the city was more readily associated as a hotbed for affairs than other cities. However, its reputation as the capital of glamor and gaiety, its association with the music of composers such as Mozart, Schubert, and Strauss, and its connection with the House of Habsburg were equally important in endowing the city with a specific personality. In comedies and dramas about love, marriage, and sexual relationships, the capital city often appeared as a center of romance, illicit or otherwise. The introduction of sound in the late twenties and early thirties also contributed to Austria's screen popularity. Vienna's association with the love of music and famous composers made the city a logical choice for introducing and developing the new technology. After the Nazi rise to power in Germany in 1933, Austria became an alternative "German" backdrop. For example, *Paradise for Three*, set in Germany in Erich Kästner's novel *Drei Männer im Schnee*, was transferred to Austria. In the 1920s and 1930s, when Hollywood's Austria films were most popular, they numbered around forty. By contrast, the Austria films in the following seven decades number less than thirty. Excepting a modest increase of Austria films in the sixties, when filming on European locations brought with it financial advantages, Austria as the major locale became rare.

Siegfried Kracauer's thoughts on "in-group" and "out-group" peoples in his essay "National Types as Hollywood Presents Them" are helpful in considering Austria's position in Hollywood. Comparing the portrayal of British and Russians in Hollywood, Kracauer argues that Americans distinguish between "in-group" and "out-group" people. He notes commonalities between the English and citizens of the United States rooted in "race, language, historical experience, and political outlook."[1] He maintains that the English are an "in-group" people for Americans. By contrast, he highlights "a pronounced lack of traditions common to both countries" and no "intermingling" between the citizens of the United States and Russia or the one-time Soviet Union. He also refers to the antagonisms between the regimes, which have shaped "all popular notions Americans and Russians hold of each other."[2] Consequently, the English have had a unique place in Hollywood as an in-group, just as the Russians have had as an out-group.[3]

Austria and Austrians have never been members of an "in-group" like the English nor part of an "out-group" like the Russians. In part this is reflected in the way immigrants from Austria and Austria-Hungary have been perceived in the United States. The nature of the multi-ethnic empire made it challenging for consular officials to classify those arriving in the United States.[4] In his book *The Quiet Invaders* E. Wilder Spaulding writes, "our immigration, naturalization, and census officials found so few 'confessed Austrians' in the long years before the creation of the Austrian Republic in 1919, and they were so confused by the multitude of nationalities that came to us from the Habsburg monarchy, that our statistics for Austrian immigrants and Austrian-born are almost useless."[5] And it appears that the German-speaking Austrian immigrants "were content to be counted with the Germans."[6] As a result, the Austrians, however they may have self-identified, do not share the same connections as between the British and American Anglo-Saxons. They also were never viewed through the same lens as the Russians.

The number of Americans traveling abroad also can provide insight into Austria's place on the Hollywood screen. Although popular with American tourists, the Alpine country does not rival England, France, or Germany as a European travel destination. In 2011 Great Britain held

24.1 percent of the market share of Americans visiting European countries with France, Italy, and Germany at 17.7 percent each. Austria was in ninth place with 4.4 percent of the European market share. In 2015 the ranking was similar. In overall foreign travel the United Kingdom ranked third after Mexico and Canada. France was in fifth place, Germany in seventh and Austria in twenty-seventh.[7] To some extent, the statistics mirror the popularity of France on the Hollywood screen, which has had a presence since the teens of the previous century.[8]

Although stories set in Austria have been few and far between in the last two decades, three directors have proven that the works of Arthur Schnitzler and Stefan Zweig still speak to contemporary audiences. Austrian literature from the early twentieth century has served as the inspiration in both Hollywood and non-Hollywood productions. When Stanley Kubrick turned to Arthur Schnitzler's *Traumnovelle* (Dream Novella, 1926) as the basis for *Eyes Wide Shut* (1999), he not only set it in contemporary times, but moved it from Vienna to Manhattan, making the story more immediate for present-day viewers. Brazilian director Fernando Meirelles was inspired by Arthur Schnitzler's *Reigen* (Round Dance, 1897) for his internationally staffed and financed film *360* (2011). He takes Schnitzler's idea of a round-robin of sexual encounters and sets the story in the present. In his circle of sexual and non-sexual encounters, he takes viewers around the globe and includes a wide variety of characters, among others an Austrian pimp, a Slovakian prostitute and her bookish sister, a high-powered British businessman, members of the Russian mafia, an Algerian-French dentist, and an Englishman in search of his run-away daughter. Wes Anderson's 2014 *The Grand Budapest Hotel*, which was inspired by the writings of Stefan Zweig, is but a mild nod to Austria-Hungary and parallels some of the nostalgic longings expressed in earlier Hollywood Austria films. Set largely in and around a hotel in an imaginary kingdom that ends up on the east side of the Iron Curtain, the story revolves around a legendary concierge who represents a lost world of grace and beauty.

Two films geared toward the art-house crowd offer differentiated takes on Austria. Jem Cohen's *Museum Hours* (2012), set in contemporary Austria, focuses on the story of a quiet friendship between a Canadian woman visiting Vienna and a guard at the Kunsthistorisches Museum.[9] The BBC production *Woman in Gold* (2015) is the story of the restitution of the Klimt painting of Adele Bloch-Bauer to the rightful heir. It looks honestly at the country's troubled relationship to its Nazi past as well as the emergence of more enlightened oppositional voices in Austria in the twenty-first century. In conjunction with the film, the new home of the painting, the *Neue Galerie* in New York, sponsored an exhibit "Gustav Klimt and Adele Bloch-Bauer: The Woman in Gold" from April 2 to September 7, 2015.[10] With its focus on Austrian and

German art of the fin-de-siècle and the first decades of the twentieth century, the museum houses art from a period that, as one that garners the most interest in the United States, complements the content of the films.

Despite their virtual disappearance from the current Hollywood screen, Vienna and Austrian stories continue to attract audiences. From February 27 to April 20, 2014, The Museum of Modern Art (MoMA) in New York celebrated "the 50th anniversary of the Austrian Film Museum, Vienna, with a major collaborative exhibition exploring Vienna as a city both real and mythic in the history of cinema." It was entitled "Vienna Unveiled: A City in Cinema." The film festival included movies made in Austria, Great Britain, and France, with the majority from Hollywood studios. It presented films by "Austrian and German Jewish émigrés—including Max Ophuls, Erich von Stroheim, and Billy Wilder—as they look back on the city they left behind." It also included "an international array of contemporary filmmakers and artists—including Jem Cohen, VALIE EXPORT, Michael Haneke, Kurt Kren, Stanley Kubrick, and Richard Linklater," and claimed that "visions of Vienna reveal the powerful hold the city continues to exert over our collective unconscious."[11] Whether the city continues to exert its power over "our collective unconscious" is debatable, but the series certainly documents the variety of visions of the same city.

Although only a small portion of the film metropolis's total output, Hollywood's Austria films nonetheless provide insight into the interplay between the public's perceptions of a place and its screen incarnations. If asked to name a Hollywood film set in Austria, the average movie viewer today would most likely reply *"The Sound of Music."*[12] Over fifty years after its release it continues to influence the ways Americans view Austria. In the discussion after his talk "Beyond the Edelweiss: Austrian Image and Public Diplomacy Abroad" at the German Studies Association meeting in 2012, Hannes Richter of the Austrian Press and Information Service in Washington confirmed that *The Sound of Music* continues its hold on the American imagination. Although successful films have both preceded and followed *The Sound of Music*, its impact has yet to be displaced.

The factors that have contributed to the screen incarnations of Austria or Austria-Hungary as well as its presence or absence on the Hollywood screen have varied greatly. Many of the original factors that made Austrian stories attractive for the big screen have evaporated. As mores shifted, Vienna lost its cachet as the place for racy stories long ago. The Habsburg monarchy as the locus for displaced nostalgia or critique of undemocratic societies appears limited and contemporary audiences have little use for the old clichés and stereotypes. The German-Austrian-Hungarian presence in Hollywood of directors, readers, and writers familiar with Austrian literature, films, and operettas, has shrunk. Indeed, the two most famous Austrians in Hollywood in recent history—Arnold Schwarzenegger and

Christoph Waltz—have played Germans rather than Austrians. Subsidies, which could make Austria an attractive place to film, have become sparse. Finally, with a shift in global concerns, stories from and about the Republic of Austria appear of little import. Although Austria is not likely to disappear totally from the popular screen, its continued presence appears to depend on serendipity, such as a filmmaker's chance reading of a piece of literature set in Austria. In any case, the Austria that is projected will continue to be filtered through multiple eyes and resemble projections on a fun-house mirror.

Appendix: Hollywood Films Set in Austria

THE SILENT FILMS WITH ASTERISKS are presently unavailable, making it difficult for me to say with total conviction that the categorization is correct. Materials related to these films are noted in the bibliography under "Archival Material." With the exception of these and *Escapade*, I have viewed the remaining films or seen extant parts of them. They were available at University of Southern California, UCLA-Los Angeles, the British Film Museum, and the Library of Congress, or I purchased them on video or DVD.

Table A.1. Films set entirely or for a significant portion in an identifiable Austria

Film	Date	Director
Merry-Go-Round	1923	Erich von Stroheim/ Julian Rupert
*The Crimson Runner**	1925	Tom Forman
*The Greater Glory**	1926	Curt Rehfeld
The Enemy	1927	Fred Niblo
Hotel Imperial	1927	Mauritz Stiller
*Night Life**	1927	George Archainbaud
The Blue Danube	1928	Paul Sloane
The Woman Disputed	1928	Henry King/Sam Taylor
Love Me and the World is Mine	1928	E. A. Dupont
The Mysterious Lady	1928	Fred Niblo
The Wedding March	1928	Erich von Stroheim
The Case of Lena Smith	1929	Josef von Sternberg
His Glorious Night	1929	Lionel Barrymore
Daybreak	1931	Jacques Feyder
A Woman of Experience	1931	Harry Joe Brown
Dishonored	1931	Josef von Sternberg
Evenings for Sale	1932	Stuart Walker
Reunion in Vienna	1933	Sidney Franklin

(continued)

Table A.1.—*(concluded)*

Film	Date	Director
Love Time	1934	James Tinling
Fugitive Road	1934	Frank R. Strayer
Escapade	1935	Robert Z. Leonard
The Night Is Young	1935	Dudley Murphy
The King Steps Out	1936	Josef von Sternberg
Champagne Waltz	1937	A. Edward Sutherland
The Great Waltz	1938	Julien Duvivier
Hotel Imperial	1939	Robert Florey
Bitter Sweet	1940	W. S. Van Dyke II
Florian	1940	Edwin L. Marin
Spring Parade	1940	Henry Koster
New Wine	1941	Reinhold Schunzel
The Strange Death of Adolf Hitler	1943	James P. Hogan
Above Suspicion	1943	Richard Thorpe
Letter from an Unknown Woman	1948	Max Ophuls
The Emperor Waltz	1948	Billy Wilder
The Red Danube	1950	George Sidney
A Breath of Scandal	1960	Michael Curtiz
The Magnificent Rebel	1962	George Tressler
Almost Angels	1962	Steve Previn
Freud	1962	John Huston
The Waltz King	1963	Steve Previn
Miracle of the White Stallions	1963	Arthur Hiller
The Sound of Music	1965	Robert Wise
The Salzburg Connection	1972	Lee H. Katzin
The Great Waltz	1972	Andrew L. Stone
The Seven-Per-Cent Solution	1976	Herbert Ross
Amadeus	1984	Milos Forman
Immortal Beloved	1994	Bernard Rose
Before Sunrise	1995	Richard Linklater
The Illusionist	2006	Neil Burger

Table A.2. Films set in a place identified as Austria, but where place is of little or no significance

Film	Date	Director
The Marriage Circle	1924	Ernst Lubitsch
*For Wives Only**	1926	Victor Heerman
*Serenade**	1927	Harry d'Abbadie d'Arrast
*The Masks of the Devil**	1928	Victor Seastrom
Her Private Affair	1929	Paul L. Stein
General Crack	1929	Alan Crosland
The Guardsman	1931	Sidney Franklin
Alias the Doctor	1932	Michael Curtiz
Downstairs	1932	Monta Bell
Jewel Robbery	1932	William Dieterle
Beauty and the Boss	1932	Roy del Ruth
The Kiss Before the Mirror	1933	James Whale
The Firebird	1934	William Dieterle
Paradise for Three	1938	Edward Buzzell

Table A.3. Films where less than one-half of the action takes place in Austria, but where historical events in Austria in the thirties play an important role

Film	Date	Director
So Ends Our Night	1941	John Cromwell
They Dare Not Love	1941	James Whale
Once upon a Honeymoon	1942	Leo McCarey
The Cardinal	1963	Otto Preminger
Julia	1977	Fred Zinnemann

Table A.4. Additional films set partially in a recognizable Austria

Film	Date	Director
Viennese Nights	1930	Alan Crosland
The Smiling Lieutenant	1931	Ernst Lubitsch
Dodsworth	1936	Willian Wyler
The Emperor's Candlesticks	1937	George Fritzmaurice
Scorpio	1973	Michael Winner
The Living Daylights	1987	John Glen
The Peacemaker	1997	Mimi Leder
Knight and Day	2010	James Mangold
Rush	2013	Ron Howard
Mission Impossible: Rogue Nation	2015	Christopher McQuarrie
Spectre	2015	Sam Mendes
The Spy Who Dumped Me	2018	Susanna Fogel

Notes

Introduction

[1] Quoted in Hirsch, *Sound of Music*, 75.

[2] Refer to the appendix for a table of films set in a recognizable Austria and those where the backdrop is merely named.

[3] Sklar, *Movie-Made America*, 96.

[4] See Higson and Maltby's introduction to their edited volume *"Film Europe" and "Film America,"* 1–31. They note that already in 1908 Edison made efforts to "control the US market, partly by restricting foreign imports to the US market" (23). Of the twenties they write, "there were no formal barriers to the distribution of foreign pictures in the US, but the American oligopoly had constructed powerful and effective barriers to entry" (19). According to Kristin Thompson in her chapter in the same volume (56–81), only a trickle of German films made it to American markets; French films were limited largely to the "art-cinema circuit" (62) and exports from the Soviet Union faced internal censorship by the communist regime when labelled "decadent" (70).

[5] See Chase, "An American Heroine in Paris." See also "France Made in Hollywood" for an extensive on-line list compiled by a State Department employee of films set partially or completely in France.

[6] Robinson, *Russians in Hollywood, Hollywood's Russians*. An early favorite was "the tragic fate of the Russian aristocrats" (21). Films made as early as World War I reflect "American hostility toward the newly created Bolshevik regime—its stated goal was to destroy capitalism—and American fear that Lenin would take Russia out of the war against Germany" (21). Robinson relates a new ambivalence to the Soviets after the election of Roosevelt and the promise of closer official relations. After the United States was allied with the Soviet Union in World War II, screen versions of the country were decidedly positive. Perhaps the most famous film of this era is Warner Brothers' *Mission to Moscow* (1943). According to the International Movie Data Base (https://www.imdb.com) "Ambassador Joseph Davies is sent by FDR to Russia to learn about the Soviet system and returns to America as an advocate of Stalinism" (https://www.imdb.com/title/tt0036166/?ref_=nv_sr_2). Accessed June 9, 2018. This film, like other Soviet-friendly films made during World War II, stirred up quite a controversy domestically (Robinson, 126–27), providing evidence of an ongoing suspicion of Hollywood's political leanings. Hollywood's representations of the Soviet Union and Soviets changed dramatically with the end of the war and the onset of the

[7] For publications on Hollywood, Germany, and World War I and II see: Isenberg's *War on Film* and a condensed version of his book with the same title; Schneider and Wagener, eds., *"Huns" vs. "Corned Beef"*; Leab, "Goethe or Attila? The Celluloid German," "Deutschland. USA German Images in American Film," "Total War On-Screen. The Hun in U.S. Films 1914–1920"; Barta, "Film Nazis"; and Crawford and Martel, "Representations of Germans and What Germans Represent."

[8] See chapter five (especially p. 147) in Moore, *Know Your Enemy*, on the efforts of the Office of War Information.

[9] Vienna long had a reputation as the capital of gaiety and hedonistic pleasures that distinguished it from other European metropolises. For an examination of the reflection of the myth in German-language literature see Midgley, "City Mythologies." See also Frisby's chapter, "The City Compared," in *Cityscapes of Modernity*, where he focuses on discussions of the two cities in the late nineteenth and early twentieth centuries. He devotes much space to Werner Sombart's essays on Berlin and Vienna; Sombart posits the German capital as very American and the Austrian metropolis as one of high culture.

[10] L'Estrange Fawcett *Die Welt des Films*, 145. "Aus Wiener Kultur, Kunst und Literatur haben alle Filmateliers der Welt Anregungen empfangen und heute noch ist Wien als Filmmilieu überaus beliebt." The chapter entitled "Europa" appears to be an elaboration of the chapter "Germany" from L'Estrange Fawcett's *Films. Facts and Forecasts*. C. Zell and S. Walter Fischer are given credit on the title page "Unter Mitwirkung des Wiener Filmbundes für die deutsche Ausgabe frei bearbeitet und ergänzt von C. Zell und S. Walter Fischer." (In cooperation with the Vienna Film Association, freely revised and expanded for the German edition by C. Zell and S. Walter Fischer). Translations are mine unless otherwise stated.

[11] Zell and Fischer, 145. "Die alte 'Kaiserstadt' ist in Hunderten von Filmen verewigt worden, die nie versagende Lebensfreude, der Charme seiner Bewohner, die Schönheit seiner einzigartigen Umgebung fanden in aller Welt Anklang. Wien ist in der internationalen Filmwelt Mode geworden und wird es hoffentlich noch recht lange bleiben."

[12] Kracauer, *From Caligari to Hitler*, 141.

[13] Zell and Fischer, 145; Grafe, "Wiener Beiträge zu einer wahren Geschichte des Kinos," 123; Beckermann and Blümlinger, eds., *Ohne Untertitel*, 11; Elsaesser's chapter, "To be or not to be: extra-territorial in Vienna—Berlin—Hollywood," in *Weimar Cinema and After*; and Seibel, *Visions of Vienna*, 13–14.

[14] For a lexical source book on Austrians in Hollywood, see Ulrich's *Österreicher in Hollywood*.

[15] Elsaesser, "ethnicity, authenticity, and exile." Elsaesser notes that they were "film artists and cinema professionals who were attracted because of the technology, resources, and rewards that Hollywood could offer" (103).

[16] See Hake's chapter "The Annexation of an Imaginary City" in *Popular Cinema of the Third Reich*, where she discusses the ways in which the National Socialist

ideology found its way into the Vienna films made by the production company Wien-Film-AG after the Anschluss.

[17] Horak, "'We love the Viennese,'" 452. "Wo die Europäer dem Publikum eine ironische Distanzierung gönnen, die Handlung die Figuren motiviert und die Schauspieler sowohl Stärke als auch Komplexität zeigen dürfen, wollen die Amerikaner eine deutliche Ausdifferenzierung der Figuren sehen, eine schauspielerische Glanzleistung erleben, die um die Identifikation des Publikums buhlt."

[18] Horak, 459–60. "Die unterschiedlichen Grundtöne in beiden Filmen haben somit auch mit den moralischen Vorstellungen der jeweiligen Kulturen bzw. ihrer Macher zu tun. Während Forst einen romantischen Pessimismus und moralische Ambiguität pflegt, die den Zeitgeist der österreichischen Monarchie in ihren letzten Tagen reflektieren, konstruiert MGM einen Film, dem jeder Hauch des moralisch Anrüchigen fern ist, weil vor allem in der Welt des Studio-Bosses Louis B. Mayer der Held und die Heldin die puritanischen Moralvorstellungen der Amerikaner widerspiegeln mussten."

[19] Grafe, "Wiener Beiträge zu einer wahren Geschichte des Kinos," 123. "Die Filmzentren anderer Länder profitierten von der Kunstliebe, dem Leichtsinn, der Vergnügungssucht, von Wiener Lebensart. Wien war Traumreservoir. Aber es quoll auch über von Talenten."

[20] Grafe, 132. "Der Hauptdarsteller ist er selbst, weil es ihn gelüstete, hineinzuschlüpfen in die Uniformen. Der ausgestoßene, der illegitime Sohn eignet mit seinen Mitteln sich an, was ihm versagt war."

[21] Grafe, 127.

[22] Ornitz, "An Outline with Dialogue."

[23] Bacher, *Max Ophuls in the Hollywood Studios*, 132.

[24] Saffle, "'Do You Ever Dream of Vienna?'"

[25] Between 1906 and 1920 Stephen Bonsal, Roger W. Babson, Frederick Cunliffe-Owen, Charles J. Rosebault, and an unidentified author published feature articles on Emperor Franz Josef, the Archdukes Franz Ferdinand and Karl, and their royal brethren in the *New York Times*. They express both admiration and ambivalence toward Austria Hungary's aristocratic leaders and disdain toward the aristocracy in general. The 1906 article "Fifty-Eight Years on a Trembling Throne" and the article "Francis Joseph," published in the wake of the monarch's death in 1916, provide different perspectives on the monarch. Two additional examples reveal the fascination and ambivalence felt toward European monarchs. An article on Empress Elisabeth and another on her son revisit the lives of these Habsburgs in curious ways. "Empress Elisabeth—Her Tragic Death Last Summer—New Light on Her Life" is a long article based on a biography, whose author was allegedly a member of the court. Since then she has been revealed as Marguerite Cunliffe-Owen, whose husband often wrote articles for the *Times* as "A Veteran Diplomat." A second *Times* article, "Light Thrown on Austria's Royal Tragedy," supposedly told by Crown Prince Rudolf's widow, explains his death as accidental.

[26] See two *New York Times* articles by the art critic James Huneker from 1913. He differentiates between the Austrian and German mentalities and the two

capitals in "The Gayest City in Europe—Not Paris, but Vienna" and "Huneker Prowls Around Kaiser's Jubilee City." A comparison reveals that he views Vienna much more positively than Berlin. See also Rosebault's "Decline of Vienna, the City of Charm" in the *New York Times*. Rosebault, a writer and business manager for the *New York Sun*, sensed that "all the world may well mourn the decadence of Vienna," pronouncing the city "Once Europe's Gayest and Most Alluring Capital."

[27] A smattering of reviews of Schnitzler's plays performed in New York in the first two decades of the twentieth century include the following: "American and Continental Ideas in Plays and Acting"; "A Literary Night in Irving Place"; "Schnitzler's Plays at Madison Square"; "New Plays That Bid for Favor"; and "The Stage Society Offers Two Plays." See also Gerd K. Schneider's chapter on the reception of Schnitzler's *La Ronde* in the United States in *Die Rezeption von Arthur Schnitzlers REIGEN 1897–1994* and Leroy R. Shaw's "Modern Austrian Dramatists on the New York Stage."

[28] In *The Decline of Sentiment* Jacobs examines shifts in taste in the twenties—from sentimental fare to an increase in more "sophisticated" stories. She discusses the following Austria films: *The Woman Disputed*, *His Glorious Night*, and *Hotel Imperial*, set in an identifiable Austria, and *The Marriage Circle* and *Her Sister from Paris*, films in which the place is merely established by name.

[29] Ornitz, "An Outline with Dialogue."

[30] Vasey, *The World According to Hollywood*, 52. Vasey establishes that, according to Joseph Schenk, with the changes there would be nothing in the film that either Austria or Germany would object to.

[31] See Proctor's *Female Intelligence*, in which she discusses both fictional and factual women in the intelligence profession.

[32] According to a *New York Times* article from December 21, 1933, entitled "Austria Attacks Film on a Hapsburg Love; Seeks to Bar Showings Throughout World," the Austrian Chamber of Commerce threatened to boycott MGM pictures if it continued showing *Reunion in Vienna* abroad.

[33] *New Wine* was preceded in the thirties in Hollywood by James Tinling's Schubert biography *Love Time* (1934).

[34] Horak, "Schauplatz Wien," 208–10.

[35] See Robinson, *Russians in Hollywood, Hollywood's Russians*. "The ideological message of *Red Danube* leaves no room for the ambivalence concerning the Soviet system that was typical of Hollywood films made before World [War] II. In the atmosphere of the Cold War, the only good Russian as far as Hollywood was concerned was one who wanted to defect to the capitalist West" (148).

[36] Shandley, *Runaway Romances*, 9.

[37] In a draft letter in English to Leon Zelman of the Jewish Welcome Service in Vienna from February 4, 1987, Zinnemann expressed this quite clearly, when he wrote, "I deeply believe that all Jews should leave Austria for countries where they can function better and with more resonance" ("Jewish Welcome Service 1987"). A series of letters from Zinnemann to Zelman appeared in German in *Wochenpresse* from April 10, 1987, including a translation of the February 4 letter.

[38] Vienna-born director Francis Lawrence places his 2018 thriller *Red Sparrow* primarily in Eastern European countries. He includes a brief shot of and from Michaelerplatz in Vienna, lasting less than a minute. The action-comedy *The Spy Who Dumped Me*, released in August 2018, uses Vienna in similar fashion in a very short segment.

[39] Neil Burger, "Feature Audio Commentary by Writer/Director," *The Illusionist*, 1:48.

[40] Burger, 2:27.

[41] Burger, 27:49.

[42] Castelli, "Vienna, Texas. Linklater's Junior Year Abroad," 61.

[43] See my article "'Wien' als transnationaler Gedächtnisort," in which I discuss the ways in which Linklater uses sites in the film as places of memory.

[44] In his dissertation "America's Germany" Schmundt-Thomas offers a succinct overview of work by anthropologists, new critics, sociologists, and imagologists. He captures this when he writes "every description of another culture implicates and comments on one's own culture" (10).

[45] Kracauer, "National Types as Hollywood Presents Them," 56.

[46] Refer to the bibliography for articles by Horak, Dassanowsky, Riemer, and myself. See also Horwath and Omasta's *Josef von Sternberg; The Case of Lena Smith*.

[47] Important examples include Koszarski, *VON*, Lenning, *Stroheim*, and Lignon, *Erich von Stroheim*.

[48] The most recent publications that focus on international and domestic Austrian films range from the published version of a dissertation to a glossy book for a broad audience. Seibel's *Visions of Vienna* (2017), based on her dissertation from 2009, focuses on Austrian and foreign mainstream productions. Two publications that reach out to a wider audience are the exhibition catalog *Wien im Film*, edited by Dewald, Loebenstein, and Schwarz, and *World Film Locations Vienna*, edited by Dassanowsky; Conley's 2016 *Screening Vienna: The City of Dreams in English-Language Cinema and Television* offers a catalogue-like overview of this corpus. Grafl's *Imaginiertes Österreich: Erzählung und Diskurs im international Film* (2017) offers an at times confusing examination of Austria films made around the globe. An important reference work on Austrians working in the American film industry is Ulrich's *Österreicher in Hollywood*.

[49] Two books on a broad history of the film industry that I have found invaluable are Finler's *The Hollywood Story* and Gomery's *The Hollywood Studio System*. The work of film historians on specific eras and genres and historians of American and Austrian history will be referred to in the individual chapters.

[50] Hake, *Screen Nazis*, 32–33.

Chapter One

[1] Koszarski, *VON*, 118.

[2] Koszarski, 207.

[3] Lenning, *Stroheim*, 239.

[4] Grafe, "Wiener Beiträge zu einer wahren Geschichte des Kinos. "Der Hauptdarsteller ist er selbst, weil es ihn gelüstete, hineinzuschlüpfen in die Uniformen. Der ausgestoßene, der illegitime Sohn eignet mit seinen Mitteln sich an, was ihm versagt war" (132).

[5] In *The Complete Wedding March of Erich von Stroheim*, Weinberg writes, "In it [*The Wedding March*] he [Stroheim] evoked the figurative myth of the 'gay Vienna' of pre–World War I during the fading light of the Austro-Hungarian Empire" (40). In "Erich von Stroheim: Wien in Hollywood. Erinnerung, Wirklichkeit, Fiktion," Heiß argues that Stroheim's Vienna is the creation of the filmmaker and that it takes on a reality of its own. He maintains Stroheim constructed it from fragments from his childhood (255). In *Visions of Vienna* Alexandra Seibel argues, "Together with *The Wedding March*, *Merry-Go-Round* maps a topography of Vienna that subsequently came to shape the representation of the city in international filmmaking—Josef von Sternberg's *The Case of Lena Smith* being a case in point" (27). In *Ethics and Social Criticism in the Hollywood Films of Erich von Stroheim, Ernst Lubitsch, and Billy Wilder*, Henry offers another approach. "With all the speculation about Stroheim's life, it seems more sensible and fairer to look at his work and appreciate him first of all as an artist" (13). She looks at his films "with regard to themes, characters, character constellations, and relationships" and points to the influence of Austrian playwright Arthur Schnitzler (17).

[6] In *Stroheim* Lenning opens his chapter on *Merry-Go-Round* as follows: "The history of each Stroheim film is a nightmare, but *Merry-Go-Round* is perhaps the most difficult to discuss, not because of its intellectual complexity but because of its confused authorship" (156). Roughly three months into production on *Merry-Go-Round* (October 1923), Stroheim was fired in the infamous battle with the producer Irving Thalberg. Having gone way over budget, he was replaced by Rupert Julian. For more background on the conflicts over *Merry-Go-Round*, see Lenning, 157–61 and Koszarski, *VON*, 118–27. *The Wedding March* was also not without conflict. Although all the footage of *The Wedding March* is from Stroheim, he was not allowed to edit it. The length of the film he envisioned would have challenged most audiences and proved commercially untenable. For more on this see Koszarski, 220–22.

[7] Kracauer, "National Types as Hollywood Presents Them," 56.

[8] Kracauer, 56.

[9] See Parrish, *Anxious Decades*, for his discussion of public opinion toward immigrants and official efforts to slow down immigration.

[10] Lasch, *The True and Only Heaven*, 106, 107.

[11] Boym, *The Future of Nostalgia*, xiv.

[12] Rosebault, "Decline of Vienna, the City of Charm."

[13] In "Symbolic Representation and the Urban Milieu" Wohl and Strauss maintain, "The entire complex of urban life can be thought of as a person rather than as a distinctive place, and the city may be endowed with a personality—or, to use common parlance—a character of its own" (528).

[14] In *Visions of Vienna* Alexandra Seibel offers a historical explanation for Stroheim's negative connotations of the Iron Man on the city hall. She ties it to Karl Lueger, the anti-Semitic mayor who sat in the house from 1897 until 1910. She argues that the Iron Man represents von Stroheim's experience of anti-Semitic Vienna before the war. "It seems that Stroheim's Iron Man symbolizes not simply the dark eternal force of mythical evil; rather, he stands for an experience Stroheim had in Vienna before he left for America. What he calls intolerance, cruelty, and hate, is, in fact, a more general circumvention for the experience of anti-Semitism" (59–60).

[15] In "ethnicity, authenticity, and exile," Elsaesser writes, "The secret affinity that existed between Hollywood on one side and Vienna or Paris on the other was that they were societies of the spectacle, cities of make-believe and of the show" (112).

[16] It is not just the monied classes who view marriage as a social and financial arrangement rather than a union based on love. Mitzi's mother considers the crude and cruel Schani, the butcher's son, her daughter's "best chance," knowing full well that her daughter does not love him. Mitzi's father seems to be the only one who is concerned with his daughter's happiness.

[17] In "New Man and Early Twentieth-Century Emotional Culture" White notes, "As late as the 1920s, Judge Lindsey surmised that 50 percent of men in Denver had consorted with prostitutes" (336).

[18] Pat Powers, "Letter to Von." See Koszarski, *VON*, 122, for similar information on the shooting of *Merry-Go-Round*.

[19] Mutschlechner, "The Corpus Christi procession—'God's Court Ball.'" Compared to documentary pieces from the Kolm Company, founded in 1910, Seibel finds the similarity to Stroheim's re-creation "astonishing" (*Visions of Vienna*, 47). In *Die Welt des Films* Zell and Fischer write, "Die in Hollywood aufgenommenen Szenen von der Fronleichnamsprozession werden das Herz jedes alten Wieners erfreuen (215). (The scenes of the Corpus Christi Procession filmed in Vienna will warm the heart of every old Viennese.)

[20] In *Merry-Go-Round*, the emperor orders Count Hohenegg to marry Countess Gisela, a change Rupert Julian made.

[21] Cott, *Public Vows*, 151.

[22] Pressbook. *The Wedding March*, 1.

[23] Seidman, *Romantic Longings*, 73. See also D'Emilio and Freedman, *Intimate Matters*. The authors write of a shift in expectations, including "sexual satisfaction as a critical component of personal happiness and successful marriage" (241).

[24] Popular literature of the era and Hollywood film versions document America's fascination with aristocratic life. Examples include: George Barr McCutcheon's Graustark novels with film versions in the first decades of the twentieth century; Emma Orczy's *The Scarlet Pimpernel* (book 1905, film 1917); and British author Anthony Hope's *The Prisoner of Zenda* (1894, film 1913) and the sequel *Rupert of Hentzau* (1898, film 1923).

[25] After the unsuccessful revolutions of 1848 in Habsburg territories, American sentiment favored the plight of the defeated. Consequently, Emperor Franz Josef was not looked on favorably in his early years on the throne. See, for example,

Phelps *U.S.-Habsburg Relations from 1815 to the Paris Peace Conference*. She writes of Hungarian leader Kossuth's campaign for independence from the Habsburgs, during which he sought support from the Americans employing historical comparisons. "Kossuth and the '48ers cultivated the idea that their revolution was closely akin to the American Revolution" (55). She points to the place of the pro-Hungarian position in American popular opinion and among officials. However, by the first decade of the twentieth century, attitudes, at least among certain portions of the population, were differentiated. Not only was Emperor Franz Josef rehabilitated, but aristocrats in general gained a certain cachet. A series of feature articles about the emperor appeared in *The New York Times* between 1906 and his death in 1916, which went from admiration for the man who was able to keep a multi-ethnic empire together to damnation for the person who started the war. They include the following: "Fifty-Eight Years on a Trembling Throne," Stephen Bonsal, "An Intimate Study of Francis Joseph, The Man," and "Francis Joseph."

26 When the engagement of Gladys Vanderbilt to the Hungarian count Laslo Szechenyi was announced in the *New York Times* article "Romantic Wooing of Miss Gladys Vanderbilt" on October 6, 1907, her betrothal was compared with the romantic stories of Anthony Hope set in an imaginary Ruritania. Austria-Hungary was declared "a land of quaint customs, of traditional romance, and of Old World aristocracy in present-day surroundings." She would be able to move in court circles in Vienna, "one of the gayest of European cities." Compare this to A Veteran Diplomat, "Where Americans Lose Caste." While the reporter's earlier portrayal of her future sounded like a novel, the Veteran Diplomat suggests that Vanderbilt's time in Austria-Hungary was less romantic. "Although they have been married two years or more, the Countess has not yet been presented at the Court of Vienna." Before her marriage, she would have been welcomed as a "distinguished foreigner," but as an Austrian she did not have the requisite ancestors to be presented at this court with its exceedingly strict rules.

27 In the introduction to the reprint *Titled Americans*, Homberger maintains, "The *New York Times* suggested in 1893 that as much as $50 million might have accompanied the American brides as they sailed across the Atlantic for their new lives in the decayed and impoverished estates of the great aristocratic families." (Although the pages are not numbered, the quotation is on pages 3–4 from the beginning of the introduction).

28 Koszarski, *VON*, 3.

29 Two films where he played the German "Hun" include D. W. Griffith's *Hearts of the World* (June 1918) and Allen Holubar's *The Heart of Humanity* (February 1919), in which he rapes a nurse and throws a baby, who disturbs his attack, out the window. Lenning notes that Stroheim had actually only served in the military five months (14).

30 See Henry's discussion of Stroheim's attack of the decadent aristocracy: *Ethics and Social Criticism in the Hollywood Films of Erich von Stroheim, Ernst Lubitsch, and Billy Wilder*, 34–36. She does not tie her analysis to any contemporary discussions, however.

31 Stroheim was over forty years old and a year older than Maude George, who played his mother.

[32] Lasch, *The True and Only Heaven*, 82–83.
[33] Quoted in Koszarski, *VON*, 209.
[34] Stroheim, "T*he* Vienna *of* Von Stroheim," 30. Italics in title.
[35] Kracauer, "National Types as Hollywood Presents Them," 56.
[36] Stroheim, "T*he* Vienna *of* Von Stroheim," 30.
[37] Lasch, *The True and Only Heaven*, 83.
[38] Stroheim, "T*he* Vienna *of* Von Stroheim," 30.
[39] Stroheim, 30.
[40] Stroheim, 85.
[41] See Heiß, "Erich von Stroheim," for information on the Danube Maidens, 262.
[42] Stroheim, "T*he* Vienna *of* Von Stroheim," 78.
[43] Stroheim, 78.
[44] Barker, *Fictions of an Orphan State*, 8. He also notes O'Shaughnessy's anti-Semitic tone.
[45] Stroheim, "T*he* Vienna *of* Von Stroheim," 78.
[46] Roberts, *Europe's Morning After*, 72. He also speaks of "the diseased but royal breed" (65).
[47] James, "Vienna A Spectre of Departed Glory."
[48] Gruber, *Red Vienna*.
[49] Rosebault, "Fading Hopes of a Once Proud Aristocracy: How the Haughty Have Become Humble and Uncertain of Themselves in Austria—Gay Vienna Turned Into a Sad and Hungry City." *New York Times*. February 15, 1920.

Chapter Two

[1] The films I have omitted include the following films: Bobby Connolly's *Expensive Husbands* (1937, Warner Bros.), in which an American starlet marries an Austrian aristocrat for publicity; the nationality of the aristocrat appears to have originally been Italian; William Wyler's *Dodsworth* (1936, Samuel Goldwyn Company), which includes an episode where the older American married woman falls in love with an Austrian aristocrat; in Leo McCarey's *Once upon a Honeymoon* (1942, MGM) his gold digging female protagonist marries an Austrian baron, who turns out to be Hitler's right hand man (see chapter four); Otto Preminger's *The Cardinal* (1963, Otto Preminger Films) includes an episode in which a priest on a leave of absence teaching English falls in love with one of his students (see chapter five); and Lee H. Katzin's *The Salzburg Connection* (1972, Twentieth Century-Fox), a spy story in which an unsuspecting American gets involved in international intrigue and falls for an Austrian; Richard Linklater's *Before Sunrise* (1995, Castle Rock Entertainment et al) presents a twenty-four hour encounter between an American and a young French woman in Vienna.

[2] For other discussions on celluloid Americans in Europe see: Sklar, *Movie-Made America*, 95–96; Shandley, *Runaway Romances;* Smedley, *A Divided World*, 197; and Chase, "An American Heroine in Paris."

[3] *Serenade* (1927) tells the story of a Viennese composer who neglects his wife and begins an affair with an opera singer before he realizes what he has lost and pursues his wife. In *The Wedding March* (1928) and *The Case of Lena Smith* (1929), imperial officers, loyal to their class, betray their lovers. *Dishonored* (1931) features Marlene Dietrich as a spy for Austria-Hungary, who ends up facing a firing squad. The one comedy, *The Smiling Lieutenant* (1931), features a flirtatious Austrian officer who finds himself married to a neighboring princess.

[4] Dramas from other studios portraying postwar Austria, such as *The Crimson Runner*, *The Greater Glory* or *Night Life*, depict a postwar Vienna in which former "haves" deal with the challenges of societal upheaval.

[5] See Beller, *A Concise History of Austria*, 220–21. By 1932, the Credit-Anstalt, Austria's major bank, had failed, unemployment had reached over 20 percent, internecine violence was widespread, and democracy was seriously threatened.

[6] Basinger, *A Women's View*, 6.

[7] Stowe, *Going Abroad*, 54.

[8] Although not the Maxim's of *The Merry Widow*, there actually was and still is a Maxim's in Vienna. In the *New York Times* article "Vienna A Spectre of Departed Glory" from February 2, 1925, Edwin L James, writes, "A few night cafés and restaurants are left, but they are not the original article—cheap and gaudy 'Auslander' imitations, American bars and sorry copies of the famed Paris resorts. There is the Moulin Rouge, Maxim's, the Tabaria—French names, but lacking French crowds. They are dull and sad and deserted."

[9] Kennedy, *Freedom from Fear*, 86–87.

[10] Kennedy, 87.

[11] Hanson, *This Side of Despair*, 18.

[12] Compare Robinson, *Russians in Hollywood, Hollywood's Russians*, on the negative portrayal of the Russian Revolution in Hollywood films.

[13] In the article "Dr. Bach Bemoans Vienna's Lost Joy" his thoughts are recorded as follows: "'Our world renowned "Gemuetlichkeit" seems to have disappeared forever,' he said, 'and most of the Viennese have forgotten the healthy joy of laughter. We only smile ironically when we see foreign made films, picturing us as merry and carefree, and pretending that the old Vienna still exists. It only continues to exist in our memories.... Film and reality—what a paradox!'" Bach was active in the Social Democratic movement and the *Kunststelle* mentioned in the article was founded in 1919 to give workers access to cultural activities. See "David Joseph Bach."

[14] The band members are portrayed as sophomoric through the jokes they play on the hapless manager Gallagher, from putting cold cream on his sheets to Buzzy telling the hotel manager he is an Indian and therefore sleeps without a bed. They hardly appear open to discovering what another culture has to offer. They are exposed as liars and downright rude. When Herr Strauss wishes to talk to Buzzy Bellew about the volume of the jazz music, two band members knowingly lie

when they say Buzzy will be right back. Although not unsympathetic, even the US consul appears as a yokel from Texas with a co-worker who slavishly protects his stash of chewing gum. A slight criticism occurs when the male worker at the consulate rudely tells a man and woman dressed in traditional garb that they have filled out the immigration forms incorrectly.

[15] Later in the film a newspaper clipping announces that the Waltz Palace is closing after fifty years, which would make it 1917, before Austria became a Republic.

[16] In his review of *Champagne Waltz*, Idwal Jones writes that Emperor Franz Josef "complimented one lady, danced with another" ("Vienna vs. Broadway," *New York Times*). In the version I saw the emperor does not speak or dance.

[17] Rayno, *Paul Whiteman*, 132–33.

[18] Quoted in Aurich, Hutter, Jacobsen, and Krenn, *"Billie." Billy Wilders Wiener journalistische Arbeiten*, 195. From the article "Whiteman feiert in Berlin Triumphe," in *Die Stunde* (June 29, 1926). "Für Jazz? Gegen Jazz? Modernste Musik? Kitsch? Kunst?" and "Bedürfnis! Notwendige Bluterneuerung des verkalkten Europas."

[19] Billy Wilder, who arrived in the US in 1934, wrote the story "Moon over Vienna" with H. S. Kraft. In addition to Wilder, Frederick Hollander (Friedrich Holländer), a refugee from Hitler's Germany, contributed to the music in the film. He was responsible for the opening song "Paradise in Waltz Time." The earlier émigrés, Germans Hans Dreier and Ernst Fegté, who had worked in Hollywood since the twenties and established themselves as art directors at Paramount, are credited with working on *Champagne Waltz*.

In Paramount's second attempt to integrate what was perceived as "higher culture" into the popular form, other Europeans fleeing Hitler indirectly made their mark on *Champagne Waltz*. The first attempt to introduce operetta to film with opera singers in the late twenties and early thirties was not particularly financially successful. See Barrios, *A Song in the Dark*, 274–308. According to Barrios, at that time "Paramount's Continental artists were prone to overestimate American spectators' affinity for sophisticated fare" (299). While the earlier efforts of continental artists may have been out of sync with American taste, continentals fleeing Nazi Germany successfully reintroduced "light classical music" to celluloid. The Jewish-Hungarian producer Joseph Pasternak, who had been working for Universal for some time, brought a favorite German-born director of his, Henry Koster (Hermann Kosterlitz), with him to the United States where they worked together on the film *Three Smart Girls* (1936) with the then thirteen-year-old Deanna Durbin. See Taylor, *Strangers in Paradise*, 78–79. Although Universal had been wary of Europeans and their "high-brow" taste, the film with its light classical music proved a hit that launched Durbin's career. Paramount's *Champagne Waltz* not only included an opera singer to bring more "high-brow" entertainment to their audiences, but also made the integration of such music the focus of the story through the Austrian-American romance.

[20] See "Vienna is Alarmed by Inroads of Jazz," *New York Times*, April 15, 1928, for an article about the Austrian reception of the operetta.

[21] Frey, "*Unter Tränen lachen.*" *Emmerich Kálmán*, 188–90.

[22] In the play, a thirty-two year-old widow of eleven years and first lady-in-waiting to the future empress, Olympia, has fallen for a lowly Hungarian officer and at the bidding of her mother sends him away. To exact his revenge, he starts a rumor that he is an international jewel thief posing as an officer. To buy his silence, Olympia spends the night with him. When she finds out the truth and learns, too, that her father quite approves of him, she declares her love to him. Holding on to his principles as a "lowly peasant," he leaves her and the military service. When it was first adapted for the Hollywood screen in 1930 by MGM under the title *His Glorious Night*, the director Lionel Barrymore retained much of the story. As in the play, Olympia sleeps with Kovacs. However, in contrast to the play, the officer returns to the pleading Olympia to make for a happy ending. Barrymore also introduces two peripheral American characters, a mother and daughter. The mother is hoping to nab an aristocrat for her daughter, who is embarrassed by her mother and horrified by European decadence and sexual impropriety.

[23] Brackett, *"It's the Pictures That Got Small,"* 245.

[24] Brackett, 275.

[25] Brackett and Wilder, *The Emperor Waltz*, 2.

[26] Brackett and Wilder, 1–2.

[27] Wagnleitner, *Coca-Colonization and the Cold War*, 44. Ellipsis in original.

[28] Wagnleitner, 44.

[29] Finler, *The Hollywood Story*, 197.

[30] In *Coca-Colonization and the Cold War* Wagnleitner maintains that "U.S. planners were thoroughly convinced that the 'liberal' capitalistic system of the United States could, as it were, be equated with the culmination of all previous human forms of organization, superseding all other social systems not only materially but morally as well" (67).

[31] See Lundestad, "Empire by Invitation?" For example, he writes, "The United States came out of the Second World War by far the strongest power on earth" (145).

[32] Schmundt-Thomas, *America's Germany*, 123.

[33] There are conflicting reports as to whether he knew about their fates or not. In *Wilder Times*, Lally claims that he received confirmation while he was in Germany (153). By contrast, in *On Sunset Boulevard* Sikov states that Wilder did not find out anything definitive about his mother (240).

[34] See Lally, *Wilder Times*, 170; Sikov, *On Sunset Boulevard*, 269; Steffen-Fluhr, "Palimpsest," 186; Arens, "Syncope, Syncopation," 44; Lang, *Legacy of Johann Strauss*, 148; Gemünden, "Gained in Translation," 36.

[35] A sampling of the reviews include "Summer Musicals," (*Life Magazine*, June 1948); McCarten, "The Current Cinema," (*New Yorker*, June 26, 1948, 55); Bosley Crowther, "The Screen, Bing Crosby Rambles Through 'Emperor Waltz,' with Joan Fontaine, at Music Hall," (*New York Times*, June 18, 1948).

[36] Wilder received several letters that complained about the filthy picture; they were ironically filed as "Fan Letters." They are held at the Margaret Herrick Library in the Charles Brackett papers. For example Mrs. M. M. Hilliard from

Pipestone, Minnesota, wrote on July 30, 1948: "It not only is nauseating, but is dripping with filth and uncleanness. How long must we continue to have such rot thrust down the unwilling throats of our fine young people" (1). She continues in a tone typical of the complaints: "Pictures with regard to sacredness of marriage, upholding family life and helping build up moral character among our youth instead of sexy pictures (which they loathe) which drive them to commit sexal [sic] offences from over stimulated emotions" (1–2).

[37] In the script file for *A Breath of Scandal* in the Paramount Pictures scripts is a one-page document concerning the purchase of the rights of the playscript "Olympia" on July 1, 1943, for $30,000. It also lists a payment to Billy Wilder for $16,666.66 with the parenthetical note "Wrote Nothing."

[38] Reumann, *American Sexual Character*, 20.

[39] Reumann, 90.

[40] Chosen by the two as a vehicle for Ponti's wife, Sophia Loren, the film was the next to last of multiple films she made with Paramount. In *Sophia Loren*, Small notes that *A Breath of Scandal* "was an Italo-American co-production between Titanus and Paramount, supported by the usual subsidies from the Italian government" (52). She explains that Paramount's business deal with Titanus was "a pattern of funding that suggested Paramount had increasingly less confidence in Loren's earning potential as a star" (52).

[41] Girosi, "Notes of Suggested Revisions on the Screenplay of Olympia by Sam Taylor," 3–4.

[42] Girosi, 1.

[43] Girosi, 1.

[44] Girosi, 4.

[45] May, *Homeward Bound*, 14.

[46] Unless otherwise noted, the dialogue is transcribed from the film.

[47] Bernstein, "1st Preliminary Green Script," 93–94. Ellipsis in original.

[48] Lardner, "Letter to Marcello Girosi," 1.

[49] Lardner, 1.

[50] The chilling effects of the Cold War did not bypass Hollywood. The anti-communist campaign of the HUAC, beginning in September 1947, resulted in the imprisonment and blacklisting of many working in the film industry and often led to a more conservative approach to movie content. Ceplair and Englund, *Inquisition in Hollywood*, 423.

[51] May, *Homeward Bound*, 10.

[52] Compare to Rosenberg, "'Foreign Affairs' after World War II." Rosenberg explores the romantic triangles in Billy Wilder's *A Foreign Affair* and Nunnally Johnson's *The Man in the Grey Flannel Suit* (1956) among an American male, an American woman, and a foreign female, and reports that "both resolve the foreign affair by constructing a stable, happy couple in which the male protagonist embraces the role of responsible family man and the American woman projects understanding and submissiveness" (60).

Chapter Three

[53] Reumann, *American Sexual Character*, 104.

[54] Reumann, 107. Italics in original.

[1] Moore, *Know Your Enemy*, 8. See also Leab's "Total War On-Screen." Leab writes of British propaganda and its American reception, pointing out the undocumented charges of the Bryce Report: "According to the Bryce Report [by British Viscount James Bryce] which was serialized in many American newspapers, German policy in Belgium and Northern France (areas it occupied) called for the deportation of men and women, the indiscriminate execution of civilians, the destruction of historic buildings, forced confiscations, the abuse of women" (162). He notes, "although the Germans never behaved as viciously as the Bryce Report claimed, one recent history records they 'executed a number of Belgian priests [. . .] for encouraging resistance to the invasion,' and rounded up 'villagers—men, women, and in some cases children—[. . .] shooting groups of them'" (163–64). Ellipsis with brackets in original.

[2] Moore, *Know Your Enemy*, 8. Journalists who sought to inform, politicize, and ultimately mobilize the American public about and against the German threat faced similar challenges. Foreign correspondents, who had spent time in Germany after 1933, were quick to see and report on the dangers the new Germany posed for European and world peace. See particularly Moore's Chapter 2, "News from Germany."

[3] Moore, 72. See also Dinnerstein, *Anti-Semitism in America*, for a long-term overview of anti-Semitism in the United States; Breitman and Lichtman, *FDR and the Jews*, for a connection between government policies and anti-Semitism in the State Department; Wyman, *Paper Walls*, for a discussion of American anti-Semitism and immigration policies; and Doherty's chapter "'Our Semitic Brethren'" in *Hollywood's Censor*. He offers a nuanced view of Breen and his relationship to Jews and Jewish persecution in Europe.

[4] Moore, *Know Your Enemy*. "Even the German documents testify to the heterogeneous composition of the anti-interventionist camp: pacifist women's organizations, Republican and Socialist politicians and congressmen, native fascists, Catholic anti-Semites, and right-wing radical Protestants" (95).

[5] Birdwell, *Celluloid Soldiers*. To insure that US neutrality was not violated, the industry and the government monitored the industry. "Restrictions imposed by the MPPDA [Motion Picture Producers and Distributors Association], the PCA [Production Code Administration], and the state department made it difficult to produce anti-Nazi films before 1939" (34).

[6] Breitman and Lichtman, *FDR and the Jews*, 105. The authors reference the article "Austria Seizure Not US Affair, Borah Asserts" in the *Washington Post*, March 29, 1938. Borah is quoted as saying, "It is nothing less than a flimsy piece of transparent acting for those nations who joined in committing that first crime [the Treaty of Versailles] to seek to make a great world tragedy of the fact that the nation thus outraged has come under a new master."

[7] Members of the Hollywood Anti-Nazi League (HANL), founded in 1936, brought together a coalition of left, right, and center opposed to Hitler. See Doherty, *Hollywood and Hitler*, 99. There Doherty writes, "Blending high-society diversions, educational outreach, and street-level activism, the group aspired to be what it eventually became—the hectoring conscience of the motion picture industry on all matters pertaining to Nazism." This included rallies, conferences, and radio shows. See particularly his chapter on the HANL, 96–121. Although the coalition fell apart after the Hitler-Stalin Pact in 1939, it points to the concern and engagement of those involved in the industry.

[8] Doherty, *Hollywood and Hitler*, 316–17.

[9] Doherty, 202. Although *Variety* had reported in 1933 that long-time émigrés in Hollywood were none too pleased with the arrival of the refugees, many European émigrés jumped into the breach to help their colleagues. The European Film Fund (EFF), which émigrés founded in November 1938, provided affidavits for refugees and financial aid for new arrivals by tithing their income. The Los Angeles area was not without its anti-Semitic factions, but Hollywood was more welcoming of refugees than the general American public. Indeed, the German American Bund was active in Los Angeles. See Bernstein's *Swastika Nation*, 107–13.

[10] Gmünden, *Continental Strangers*, 49. See his chapter "Tales of Urgency and Authenticity."

[11] With the shrinking world market in mind, the idea of producing Viennese confections for both domestic consumption and export may have been particularly appealing to studio executives. According to the International Movie Data Base (https://www.imdb.com), *The Great Waltz* was marketed in Finland, Hungary, France, Denmark, and Sweden in 1939; *Florian* in Sweden in 1940, and Portugal in 1941; and *New Wine* was shown in Sweden and Portugal in 1941.

[12] Horak, "*Spring Parade* (1940)," 82. Horak considers how the 1940 remake of the German-language film *Frühlingsparade* (1934) can be read "against the grain as a political critique of a Nazified Austria" (74). I have not included *Spring Parade*, because Austria-Hungary is portrayed as a stable monarchy, and I look at those films that show the empire in crisis. However, I am indebted to Horak for his insights. Universal presented *Spring Parade*, directed and produced by émigrés, Henry Koster (Hermann Kosterlitz) and Joseph Pasternak respectively, who were responsible for the earlier German-language version *Frühlingsparade* (1934). Set in Franz Josef's Austria, when it was gay and far removed from any strife, the film is a vehicle for Deanna Durbin and relates the adventures of a young Hungarian peasant who ends up far from home in Vienna after falling asleep on a haystack exhausted from a czardas competition.

[13] Traubner, *Operetta*, 426–27.

[14] MGM also released a film version of Noel Coward's musical *Bitter Sweet*. However, as the Viennese atmosphere is already mediated through Anglo-Saxon eyes and there is little émigré participation, it is not included here. By contrast, *Florian* outstrips it in contemporary messages and is even included in Shull and Wilt's *Hollywood War Films, 1937–1945*, 113. They write, "There are several scenes in the film that would directly relate to 1940 audiences. At the beginning of *Florian*

there are pro-democracy comments made during a discussion in a tavern. Later, there is a scene portraying Austria's revered Emperor in which it is implied Germany is forcing Austria into a world war." They also mention its anti-Soviet tenor. Parts of the discussion of *Florian* in this chapter appeared in my article "Political and Humanitarian Messages in a Horse's Tale."

15 *Das Dreimäderlhaus* was in turn based on the 1912 novel *Schwammerl* by the Austrian writer Rudolf Hans Bartsch. In addition to the successful stage productions, numerous Schubert films preceded *New Wine*. They include the following: Willi Forst's *Leise flehen meine Lieder* (1933), his English-language remake *Unfinished Symphony* (1934), and Paul L. Stein's *Blossom Time* (1934), a second British-made version of the Schubert story. Fox Film Corporation produced James Tinling's Schubert film *Love Time* (1934). For an overview of various stage and film versions of the Berté pastiche see Traubner, *Operetta*, 424–26.

16 Gloria Pictures Corp. was a William Szekely-Alexander Korda operation. The film was released by United Artists. German-Jewish actor/director Reinhold Schunzel (Schünzel), who left Germany in 1937, was chosen to direct the film.

17 Hake, *Popular Cinema of the Third Reich*, 156.

18 Hake, 157.

19 Hake, 157.

20 A brief segment of newsreel footage features the Anschluss in Warner Bros.'s *Confessions of a Nazi Spy* (1939).

21 Fielding, *March of Time*, 238.

22 See Traubner, *Operetta*, 299–300, for background on the Austrian roots of the film in Fritz Kreisler's operetta *Sissy* (1932).

23 Compare with Horak, "*Spring Parade* (1940)." He argues that "Austria was remembered as a constitutional monarchy, as if the post-World-War-I Socialist Republic, the Austro-Fascist period, and the Anschluss had never happened" (82). The imperial Austria of *Spring Parade*, Horak argues, was also "a mirror image of an idealized American democracy, a point the filmmakers certainly wanted to communicate" (83). He compares the emperor to Roosevelt: "Like Roosevelt and his famous 'Fireside Chats,' this Emperor Franz Joseph I enjoys communicating with the people" (83). The multi-ethnic state with its Polish baker and Hungarian girl from the country is at peace with itself, a far cry from either historical reality or the make-believe Austria seen in the original film, which Horak notes, is much more ethnically homogenous. In contrast to the positive comparisons, Horak points to events in the film that could serve as reminders of Viennese reality. When the friendly baker is unjustly arrested, his property confiscated and himself carted off in a wagon, Horak likens this to the brutality of the Gestapo and "the Nazi 'aryanization' of Jewish property" (84).

24 Beller, *Concise History of Austria*, 124.

25 Beller, 129.

26 See Stelzer, *Constitution of the Republic of Austria*, 2–5, for a concise summary of the fate of the constitution during and after the revolution of 1848.

27 Baum and Reinhardt, "Outline," 19.

²⁸ Reports on Johann Strauss Jr.'s actual involvement in the revolution vary. However, scholars generally agree that he and his father were on opposing sides, and he played the Marseillaise and composed some marches for the rebelling students. In *Johann Strauss* Egon Gartenberg writes that Strauss fled the barricades after the first bullet whizzed by him (88). See also Crittenden, *Johann Strauss and Vienna*, 87.

²⁹ In reality Strauss would have been sixty-three and Franz Josef fifty-eight in 1888.

³⁰ Géza Herczeg, who moved to Hollywood after the Anschluss, is given major credit for the screenplay in the pressbook for the film. Other central Europeans involved in the creation of Austria-Hungary in *Florian* were the cinematographer Karl Freund, the technical advisor William von Wymetal, and George Richlavie, a technical advisor who received no credit for his work. S. Z. Sakall played a jovial but silent innkeeper. Felix Bernstein, who had run MGM's office in Vienna up until the Anschluss, served as a technical advisor, and Jewish-German Franz Waxman (Wachsmann) arranged and composed music for the film. See Ulrich, *Österreicher in Hollywood* and Horak, *Fluchtpunkt Hollywood*.

³¹ The soprano was born Marie Jedličková in Brno on 6 October 1887.

³² Gyory, "Florian," 1. I have not been able to find any biographical information on Nicholas Gyory. Barbara Hall, formerly a Research Archivist at the Margaret Herrick Library, noted that Nicholas Gyory was listed as translator of scripts and stories at MGM. E-mail to author, August 4, 2010. He also worked on *New Wine*.

³³ Gyory, 1.

³⁴ Zernatto, *Die Wahrheit über Österreich*, 9, "die Ereignisse in Österreich objektiv darzustellen" and "Ich schrieb dieses Buch—so viele Mängel es auch haben mag—mit blutendem Herzen, erfüllt von einer unbändigen Liebe zu meinem Vaterland, aus dem man mich vertrieben konnte, das ich aber nie aufhören werde zu lieben, zu lieben, zu lieben."

³⁵ Gyory, "Florian," 2. Compare with Zernatto, *Die Wahrheit über Österreich*, 37.

³⁶ Gyory, 3. Compare with Zernatto, 40–41.

³⁷ Gyory, 2. Compare with Zernatto, 38.

³⁸ Gyory, "Florian," 2. Compare with Zernatto, 15–16.

³⁹ Gyory, "Florian," 4.

⁴⁰ The lack of an Umlaut in Glucksberg is another example of Hollywood adjusting for an American audience.

⁴¹ Inexact and inaccurate nomenclature is not unusual for Hollywood. Here is just one example of an incorrect usage of Austrian, which included all residents of Cisleithania. Moreover, while Islam was a recognized religion in Bosnia Herzegovina, after the annexation in 1908, it was not a recognized ethnic group.

⁴² Wall, *Inventing the "American Way,"* 7.

⁴³ Austria and Germany were, of course, Allies in World War I, and Austria was not a victim in World War I, nor was its declaration of war inevitable. See Tunstall's chapter "Austria-Hungary" in *The Origins of World War I*, 112–49.

⁴⁴ Moore, *Know Your Enemy*, 41–77.

⁴⁵ Botz, *Gewalt in der Politik*, 35–36. Botz relates the unsuccessful attempts of the Communists to take over the government in Austria. Two incidents appear reminiscent of scenes portrayed in *Florian*. On November 11, 1918, the *Rote Garde* had planned to occupy Schönbrunn and take Emperor Karl captive, fearing a monarchist putsch. The Socialist politician Julius Deutsch was able to talk them out of it. However, the next day, when the republic was proclaimed, the *Rote Garde* could not be dissuaded from action. Working together with the Communists, they set out to take over parliament. Despite the loss of life in the wake of the monumental changes in postwar Austria, the Habsburgs appeared to suffer less bodily harm than the general population.

⁴⁶ See Healy, *Vienna and the Fall of the Habsburg Empire*, for an in-depth study of the domestic situation in Vienna during the war.

⁴⁷ Boyer, "Silent War and Bitter Peace." Boyer states, "The revolution was in fact two revolutions—a high political revolution, wrought by and against ex-imperial elites . . . and a cascading series of popular upheavals reflecting actually existing social conditions in the city" (12).

⁴⁸ Robinson, *Russians in Hollywood, Hollywood's Russians*, 21–24.

⁴⁹ Ellipsis in original.

⁵⁰ Romani, *Neapolitan Revolution of 1820–1821*. In actuality, Metternich and the Austrian army were involved in putting down the Neapolitan revolution and restoring King Ferdinand to power, who had to agree to terms Metternich dictated.

⁵¹ Corson, *Loiterings in Europe*, 225.

⁵² Corson, 225–26.

⁵³ Corson, 226.

⁵⁴ Corson, 226.

⁵⁵ Gedye, "Old Vienna is Dead." To compare with the post-Anschluss framing of Strauss, see Crittenden, *Johann Strauss and Vienna*: "Strauss's works also proved to be astonishingly durable in the newly installed Nazi regime," so much so that Strauss's Jewish ancestry was whitewashed. She reports that "Strauss's stage works were among those officially supported by the new regime" (106). See also Lang, *Legacy of Johann Strauss*, 74–75.

⁵⁶ See Nußbaumer, *Musikstadt Wien*, who follows the cultivation of music as a part of Austrian identity and how it has been used to promote different political agendas within Austria.

⁵⁷ George, "Hollywood on the Danube?" 153. The most often filmed musical personalities in the twenties were Carl Michael Ziehrer, Franz Lehár, Franz Schubert, and Johann Strauss Jr.

⁵⁸ Those at MGM preparing the publicity for *Florian* saw an opportunity to underscore the differences between Germany and Austria. In an article from the pressbook on the film's music entitled "Making a Musical Score Take Place of Dialogue" the film's composer Franz Waxman is quoted: "'We took only Austrian and Hungarian themes,' states Waxman, 'avoiding the Germanic, as the spirit is

entirely different, just as the spirit of American music differs from Italian. Historically, Austria for centuries was separated from the Prussians, hence the wide difference in the spirit of the music in the two countries, which has continued down to today. Musically they have nothing in common'" (6). By means of such references, the opposition between the two German-speaking countries suggested in the film was "pre-enforced." Moreover, by maintaining that Germany and Austria shared nothing musically, Waxman implied the illegitimacy of the country's union with Germany.

[59] See Lang's discussion of "The Emperor Waltz" and "The Blue Danube Waltz" in *Legacy of Johann Strauss*, 147–48. She writes about their place as part of the New Year's Concert. Begun in 1939, "The Emperor Waltz" was heard during the years of the *Ostmark*, with the exception of 1941 and 1945. By contrast, "The Blue Danube Waltz," which is so tied to an Austrian identity separate from Germany, did not appear on the program until 1945.

[60] In his introduction to *The Cambridge Companion to Schubert*, the editor and Schubert biographer Christopher H. Gibbs comments on the politicization of Franz Schubert's life by different regimes before and after Hitler (18).

[61] For a discussion on history in biopics, see Custen, *Bio/Pics*.

[62] See Gibbs, *The Life of Schubert*. Among the many untruths, Schubert did not work as a sheep shearer or bookkeeper in Hungary. However, he did work there on numerous occasions as a music teacher for the daughters of Count Johann Carl Esterházy.

[63] Lipizza was no longer a part of Austria after 1918, nor is it near enough to Vienna for the quick trip implied in the film. Yet, the visit plays an important function. Not only do Anton and Dr. Hofer find out that Diana thinks Anton is dead, but the brutality of the new regime and the loss it has brought about are underscored. Moreover, Anton realizes his dream is dead, and he must move on.

[64] Certainly, adapting to the United States was not as easy as Hofer suggests. For example, see Wolman, *Crossing Over*.

[65] Higham, *Strangers in the Land*, 198. He discusses how in the wake of World War I the "hyphenated American" was viewed as "the immigrant of divided loyalty."

[66] Kennedy, *Freedom From Fear*, 410.

[67] Kennedy, 417. Ellipsis in original.

[68] Herczeg, "Temporary Complete Screenplay by Geza Herczeg," 9.

[69] Sheehan, "Florian Change," C.

[70] Wyman, *Paper Walls*, 3. Here Wyman writes, "Three major factors in American life in the late 1930's tended to generate public resistance to immigration of refugees: unemployment, nativistic nationalism, and anti-Semitism."

[71] Wyman, 5.

[72] Nugent, "Screen in Review"; Crowther, "'Florian,' a Tale of a Noble Horse in Old Vienna"; and T.S., "The Screen."

Chapter Four

[1] Spieker, *Hollywood unterm Hakenkreuz*. See also Hake, *Popular Cinema of the Third Reich* and her chapter "The Foreign and the Familiar."

[2] Dick, *Star-Spangled Screen*, 67–68.

[3] "Detroit Spending 'Boom' Goes Boom," *Variety*, May 21, 1941, 10.

[4] "Propaganda in Motion Pictures," *Hearings Before a Subcommittee of the Committee on Interstate Commerce United States Senate, Seventy-Seventh Congress First Session on S. Res. 152*, 1.

[5] "Propaganda in Motion Pictures," *Hearings Before a Subcommittee of the Committee on Interstate Commerce United States Senate, Seventy-Seventh Congress First Session on S. Res. 152*, 172–74 and 182–83. Although not the main target of the attack, both *So Ends Our Night* and *They Dare Not Love* where brought up on September 15 as films the Senate Subcommittee was considering as propaganda. The witness, Mr. Fidler, was asked if he considered them propaganda. *They Dare Not Love* he had not seen, but he definitely viewed *So Ends Our Night* as propaganda (171–72 of the report). There are also summaries of the films taken from the *Harrison Reports* (*They Dare Not Love*, 173–74; *So Ends Our Night*, 182–83).

[6] See Birdwell, "Hollywood under the Gun" for a detailed account of the hearings; and Moser, "'Gigantic Engines of Propaganda.'"

[7] There are basically three post–December 1941 films in which Austria plays an important role. *Once upon a Honeymoon* (November 1942) presents the Anschluss as a prelude to Nazi aggrandizement of territory. "Occupied" Austria or the *Ostmark*, as it was known, appeared as a major backdrop in only two Hollywood films made during the war both in 1943—MGM's *Above Suspicion* and Universal's *The Strange Death of Adolf Hitler*. In *Above Suspicion* (May 1943), the British foreign service enlists an American couple on their honeymoon to do some spying, which takes them to Salzburg and Innsbruck. *The Strange Death of Adolf Hitler* (September 1943) has a truly bizarre plot, in which a prisoner talented at imitating voices undergoes plastic surgery and becomes an unwilling stand-in for Hitler. His wife, having been told he is dead, and heartbroken at what the party has done to her children, assassinates her husband, thinking he is Hitler.

[8] Certainly, the complex situation in Austria did not lend itself to simple portrayals. Although the Austrian Social Democrats and the ethnic-German majority saw Austria's salvation in the union with Germany after World War I, the Allies had forbidden this in the Treaty of St. Germain in 1919. Consequently, Austria, the predominantly ethnic German leftover from the Habsburg Empire, faced multiple challenges. The country was wracked with economic problems and marred by political strife, which often played out in violent confrontations. As the economic situation deteriorated in the thirties and unemployment rose, internecine violence increased and democracy hung by a thread. The dominance and innovations of the anti-capitalist Socialist Party in the early years of the First Republic and then the death of democracy under the leadership of the Catholic Christian Socials in 1933 hardly seemed suitable fare for the Hollywood screen. The struggle to create and instill a sense of national identity in Austrian citizens as an antidote

to the wish for the Anschluss did not invite screenplays that would draw a wider American public.

[9] See Keyserlingk's discussion of the "occupationist" position versus the "annexationist" school in the United States in *Austria in World War II*.

[10] "Austria Seizure Not U.S. Affair, Borah Asserts," *Washington Post*, March 29, 1938.

[11] Breitman and Lichtman, *FDR and the Jews*, 102.

[12] Breitman and Lichtman, 102.

[13] Thompson, "Introduction," ix.

[14] Thompson, xxv.

[15] Thompson, xxv. Ellipsis in original.

[16] Horak, "Schauplatz Wien," 200: "Auftakt zum Zweiten Weltkrieg, die Österreicher als erste Opfer des Naziterrors, Wien als belagerte Stadt unterm Joch des Faschismus."

[17] Horak, 200: "So kommt in den Anti-Nazi-Filmen immer wieder ein gewisses Unbehagen zum Ausdruck—als ob man den Österreichern ihre 'Unschuld' nicht ganz glaubte."

[18] Horak, 201: "Von eben dieser Unsicherheit mag es auch herrühren, daß Österreich als Thema im Anti-Nazi-Film Hollywoods, vor allem dem der deutschsprachigen Emigration, nur selten in Erscheinung tritt—und dann meistens am Rande des Geschehens."

[19] Finler, *Hollywood Story*, 238.

[20] See Rostron, "'No War, No Hate, No Propaganda.'" See also Horak, "Wunderliche Schicksalsfügung," where he reminds readers that anti-Nazi films are not just propaganda, but commercial products: "Die Anti-Nazi Filme sind aber nicht nur in einem propagandistischen Kontext zu sehen, sondern auch in einem kommerziellen: sie verstehen sich als Ware im massenmedialen Angebot der amerikanischen Filmkonzerne" (263). "The anti-Nazi films are not only to be understood in the context of propaganda, but also in a commercial one. They are products in the mass-media offering of American film concerns."

[21] Ellipsis, unconventional punctuation, and misuse of the apostrophe in "'its'" in original.

[22] In "The 'Hated Hun'—Then and Now," Stroheim wrote about his villain role in the film in the *New York Times*, February 9, 1941.

[23] In Weaver's *Attack of the Monster Makers*, Charles Bennett, who was one of the screenplay writers of *They Dare Not Love*, claims it was directed by Charles Vidor, even though it was credited to James Whale, known for his horror films (21).

[24] Vajda's Hollywood Austria movies include *Serenade*, *The Smiling Lieutenant*, *The Guardsman*, and *Reunion in Vienna*.

[25] "Text of Schuschnigg's Speech of his Resignation," *L. A. Times*, March 12, 1938.

26 Pieter Judson, *Habsburg Empire*. See pages 95–96 for a short discussion of Andreas Hofer, who led a rebellion against the Bavarian "occupiers" and Tyrol's reputation as extremely Catholic and loyal to the Habsburgs.

27 The film includes reenactments of Max Jordan's live report from Europe for CBS announcing the Anschluss, an actor playing a German officer announcing in German the institution of German law in Austria, and commentary on Austrian history coupled with newsreel footage. In *March of Time* Fielding writes briefly about this coverage on page 229.

28 Fielding, *March of Time*, 175.

29 *The March of Time* produced a seven-minute feature on Otto von Habsburg in 1936 and one of the clips from that film appears in the featurette on the Anschluss. See also *Hitler and Hollywood*, where Doherty writes, "In June 1936, in a segment on the former glory of the Austro-Hungarian Empire, Van Voorhis speculated that the territorial greed of Hitler and Mussolini was the main impediment to a restoration of the royal line of the Hapsburgs" (243–44).

30 Hitler justified his actions by arguing that the conditions outlined in the February meeting with Schuschnigg had not been fulfilled. Schuschnigg resigned on March 11; Austria's official end as an independent state was proclaimed on March 13, and Hitler celebrated with a triumphant entrance into Vienna on March 15 with much media fanfare.

31 The official transcript of this episode of *March of Time* erroneously has "his spouse," when it should be "of Strauss."

32 See Anthony Burke Smith's discussion of the protagonists' Irish-American ethnic-national identity in *The Look of Catholics*. See particularly pages 172–73, where he discusses the film in terms of a cultural conversion.

33 Gehring, *Leo McCarey*, 174–81. See also Doherty, *Projections of War*, 128–30, in which he discusses *Once upon a Honeymoon* alongside *To Be or Not to Be* as "the other famous, though not as long-lived, marker of the initial confusion over how to play the Nazis for comedy" (128).

34 See Hake, *Screen Nazis*, for her discussion of the links between World War II movies and the fight for democracy.

35 See Hosley, *As Good as Any*, who writes of the increased importance of the foreign correspondent after the Anschluss. He also describes the creation of the first live radio broadcasts in the wake of the Anschluss. See particularly pp. 43–47 and 49–52.

36 In *Austria in World War II*, Keyserlingk writes, "In President Roosevelt's radio message to the nation on 9 December 1941, explaining why the United States had entered the war, Austria was included in the list of countries forcibly occupied by Hitler" (22).

Chapter Five

1 Archer, "Moviemaker Clarifies the 'Cardinal' Issues."

2 Barthel, "Biggest Money-Making Movie of All Time."

3 For a more detailed description of the film's background, see Wilk, *Making of The Sound of Music* and Flinn, *Sound of Music*. Two books for a more popular audience include Hirsch, *Sound of Music* and Santopietro, *Sound of Music Story*.

4 See Izod's chapter "New Order" in *Hollywood and the Box Office, 1895–1986*.

5 See Shandley, *Runaway Romances*.

6 See Dulles's chapter "The Postwar Scene" in *Americans Abroad*.

7 Articles from the *New York Times* in the fifties and sixties that highlight Austria's Alpine beauty and describe the range of tourist attractions that Vienna and environs include the following: Fithian, "Exploring Austria's Mountain Villages" (June 22, 1952); MacCormac, "Alpine Tours and Music in Austria" (March 3, 1957); Handler, "Austria Set to Take Tourist Influx in Stride" (November 28, 1960); and Horkan's articles "Exploring Austria's Land of Castles" (April 10, 1960), "Stream of History, Blue Danube" (May 8, 1960), "There's Nostalgia in Vienna's Baroque Beauty" (September 11, 1960) and "In Old Austria's 'Salt Crown Lands'" (February 19, 1961).

8 Izod, *Hollywood and the Box Office*, 138.

9 See Lytle, *America's Uncivil Wars*, 2006.

10 Shandler, *While America Watches*. See especially 81 and 85.

11 Preminger, *Preminger*, 182.

12 Preminger, *Preminger*, 23, 25.

13 Hirsch, *Otto Preminger*, 46.

14 Hirsch, 46.

15 See Horak, *Saul Bass*, 276–78, where he analyzes Bass's credit sequence.

16 For the full German text of the letter see Reimann, *Innitzer*, 114.

17 Quoted in Reimann, 114. "Wir sind auch der Überzeugung, daß durch das Wirken der nationalsozialistischen Bewegung die Gefahr des alles zerstörenden gottlosen Bolschewismus abgewehrt wurde."

18 "Nazi Group in Austria Linked to Ku Klux Klan," *New York Times*, February 22, 1960.

19 Hirsch, *Otto Preminger*, 390. See also an unidentified critic, "A Priest's Story," *Time*, December 13, 1963, 97–98.

20 "Vienna Mob Storms Cardinal Innitzer's Home; He Is Reported Injured," *New York Times*, October 9, 1938. This article reported that the cardinal "issued a pastoral letter on Sept. 4 challenging the Nazi party particularly on the secularization of marriage and the dismissal of priests from teaching posts and of nuns from hospitals in which they had served as nurses."

21 Reimann, *Innitzer*, writes that over 9000 were there (188). On October 9, 1938, the *New York Times* reported that the cathedral was packed, with another 10,000 outside.

22 Reimann, *Innitzer*, 188–89.

23 Quoted in Reimann, *Innitzer*. "Wir grüßen unseren Bischof" and "Wir wollen unseren Bischof sehen" (190).

24 A flurry of articles in *The New York Times* in October recount the attacks on the cardinal and the official Nazi response. In addition to "Vienna Mob Storms Cardinal Innitzer's Home," (cited above), see "Cardinal Innitzer Put Under Guard" and "New Innitzer Step Infuriates Nazis." In Reimann, *Innitzer*, 191–93, an eyewitness, Dr. Weinbacher, recalls the events. Another eyewitness, Hermann Lein recounts his experiences on the website of the Dokumentationsarchiv des österreichischen Widerstands: https://www.doew.at/erinnern/biographien/erzaehlte-geschichte/widerstand-1938-1945/hermann-lein-rosenkranzfeier-1938.

25 Micewski, *Cardinal Wyszyński*.

26 Alpers, *Dictators, Democracy, and American Public Culture*, 277.

27 Indeed, the connection between the Church and democracy appears a very American one, and certainly not one shared by the Vatican in the thirties. In registering his growing concern with Italian fascism, Pope Pius XI argued, "'If there is a totalitarian regime, totalitarianism in fact and by right—it is the regime of the Church, because man belongs totally to the Church.'" Quoted in Kertzer, *The Pope and Mussolini*, 328.

28 In his autobiography Preminger ties together Hollywood, the repression of the McCarthy Era, and totalitarianism. "Freedom of expression is the most powerful defense of democracy. No totalitarian government, right or left, can exist without censorship" (*Preminger*, 115).

29 Parts of this section were taken from my article "Robert Wise's *The Sound of Music* and the 'Denazification' of Austria in American Cinema."

30 Compare Flinn, *Sound of Music*, 22.

31 Wilk, *Making of The Sound of Music*, explains the process by which Wise was hired and how the changes are largely thanks to Ernest Lehman's work as scriptwriter (66).

32 Lehman, "*The Sound of Music*. Cameraman's script," 4.

33 Lehman, 1.

34 The combination of the skillful camera work and the stunning landscape, and the weaving in of locales in and around Salzburg garnered Ted D. McCord an Oscar nomination for Best Cinematography (https://www.imdb.com/name/nm0005792/?ref_=nv_sr_1). See Thomas, *So Long Until Tomorrow* for his discussion on technological advances that had an impact on the photography in travelogues and consequently feature films.

35 Compare to Dyer, *Only Entertainment*, 48. Although Dyer views music and nature as inextricably bound, he does not connect them at all to the construction of an Austrian identity.

36 Hoffmann, "Im Zeichen von Festspielgründung, allgemeinem Wahlrecht und Wirtschaftskrise," 60.

37 Kreisky, *Zwischen den Zeiten*, 179. "Massenarbeitslosigkeit, Dauerelend und Hungerlöhne prägten das Leben in Österreich und beeinflussten auch das politische Geschehen."

[38] Compare with Dassanowsky's interpretation in "An Unclaimed Country," 41. He argues, "The film is quite clearly an allegory for the Austrian *Ständestaat*, and casts an approving light on the era's very general atmosphere." Although there may be symbols attached to the Austro-fascist regime, there is no indication in the screenplay or in its realization that Wise or Lehman were making any connections to that regime. I would argue that they come closest to suggesting that Austria was a monarchy.

[39] The depiction of the Anschluss in the German film also offers a surprising twist. In *Die Trapp-Familie*, Ruth Leuwerik, the film's Maria, is from Cologne and her German accent lends a "neutral" tone to the Austrian accents in the film. The other actors are Austrian but speak in High German. The Anschluss is announced on the radio with Austrians wildly greeting the Germans. This in itself is not surprising. But when a National Socialist shows up to demand that the baron fly the Nazi flag, the actor playing the Nazi is a rather uncultured oaf who speaks with a decidedly Austrian accent bordering on dialect. Through the use of the radio coverage and language, it almost appears as if the Austrians are the villains rather than the Germans. For an examination of the German films in light of their commentary on the fifties, see Moltke, "Trapped in America."

[40] Lehman, "*The Sound of Music*. Cameraman's script," 114.

[41] Lehman, 114.

[42] Zanuck, "Letter to Mr. Richard Zanuck from Darryl Zanuck on 30 January 1964."

[43] Hirsch, *Sound of Music*, 181–82.

[44] Dyer, *Only Entertainment*. See particularly 57–58.

[45] Hirsch, *Sound of Music*, 146.

[46] Quoted in Hirsch, *Sound of Music*, 146. Compare with Preminger's comments on filming in Vienna: "Former Nazis held high positions of power and influence in Austria, and they made it as difficult as possible for me to work in Vienna" (*Preminger*, 182).

[47] Quoted in Hirsch, *Sound of Music*, 146.

[48] See Wilk, *Making of The Sound of Music*, 62–65, for an extended discussion on Wyler's machinations.

[49] Madsen, *William Wyler*, 367.

[50] See Barthel, "Biggest Money-Making Movie Of All Time." Barthel links the film's popularity to the players.

[51] See Flinn's discussion of "Edelweiss" in his *Sound of Music*, 76–78.

[52] Dyer, *Only Entertainment*, 56.

[53] Strasser, *Sound of Klein-Hollywood*, 291.

[54] "The Sound of Music Tour," https://www.salzburg.info/en/hotels-offers/guided-tours/the-sound-of-music-tour.

[55] See Graml's "'The Hills Are Alive . . .,'" and his "(Re)mapping the nation."

[56] Villa Trapp: The Original Sound of Music Family Home, http://www.villa-trapp.com/.

⁵⁷ "Die Trapp Familie—Realität und 'Sound of Music,'" Salzburg Musuem. http://www.salzburgmuseum.at/index.php?id=trappfamilie.

⁵⁸ "The Sound of Music World eröffnet ihre Ausstellung," http://www.villa-trapp.com/aktuelles-detail/?tx_ttnews%5Btt_news%5D=13&cHash=ee7332126038bb37be4da7dbc134a731.

⁵⁹ See Flinn's chapter "Afterlife and Influence," in *Sound of Music*.

⁶⁰ The site https://en.wikipedia.org/wiki/The_Cardinal references the website "The Numbers" https://www.the-numbers.com/movie/Cardinal-The#tab=summary. See also "Big Rental Pictures of 1964," *Variety*, January 6, 1965, 39.

⁶¹ Hirsch, *Sound of Music*, 176.

Conclusion

¹ Kracauer, "National Types as Hollywood Presents Them," 61.

² Kracauer, 66.

³ See Robinson, *Russians in Hollywood, Hollywood's Russians*; Strada and Troper, *Friend or Foe?*; and Glancy, *When Hollywood Loved Britain*.

⁴ See Phelps, *U.S.-Habsburg Relations from 1815 to the Paris Peace Conference*.

⁵ Spaulding, *Quiet Invaders*, 3–4.

⁶ Spaulding, 1.

⁷ See *2011 U.S. Residents Travel to Europe* for a sample of travel statistics and *2015 United States Resident Travel Abroad* http://travel.trade.gov/outreachpages/download_data_table/2015_US_Travel_Abroad.pdf.

⁸ See "France Made in Hollywood" for an extensive list of films set partially or completely in France compiled by a State Department employee.

⁹ As Todd Herzog pointed out in a talk given at the Modern Language Association Annual Conference in Vancouver, Canada, on January 9, 2015, this is Cohen's second film set in Vienna. While he maintains that this is "the closest Cohen has come to the principles of Classical Hollywood Cinema," he argues "that it is also perhaps his most explicit meditation on the experimental documentary process of most of his films, blurring the boundaries between fiction, documentary, and essay filmmaking and between art and everyday life."

¹⁰ Information on the exhibition is on the website for die Neue Galerie. Accessed on July 10, 2018. http://neuegalerie.org/content/gustav-klimt-and-adele-bloch-bauer-woman-gold.

¹¹ "Vienna Unveiled: A City in Cinema." Accessed on June 24, 2018. http://www.moma.org/visit/calendar/films/1460.

¹² In his remarks on the image of Austria in the United States in 2000, Waldemar Zacharasiewicz maintained, "The popular image of Austria over the last decades ... has been defined by Hollywood" ("The Image of Austria in the United States," 39).

Bibliography

Filmography

360. Dir. Fernando Meirelles. BBC et al. 2011.
Above Suspicion. Dir. Richard Thorpe. MGM, 1943.
Almost Angels. Dir. Steve Previn. Buena Vista Distribution Co., 1962.
Amadeus. Dir. Milos Forman. Orion Pictures, 1984.
Before Sunrise. Dir. Richard Linklater. Columbia and Sony Pictures, 1995.
Bitter Sweet. Dir. W. S. Van Syke II. MGM, 1940.
Blind Husbands. Dir. Erich von Stroheim. Universal Film Manufacturing Company, 1919.
The Blue Danube. Dir. Paul Sloane. DeMille Pictures Corporation, 1928.
A Breath of Scandal. Dir. Michael Curtiz. Paramount Pictures, 1960.
The Cardinal. Dir. Otto Preminger. Columbia Pictures, 1963.
The Case of Lena Smith. Dir. Josef von Sternberg. Paramount Pictures, 1928.
Champagne Waltz. Dir. A. Edward Sutherland. Paramount Pictures, 1937.
Come Live with Me. Dir. Clarence Brown. MGM, 1941.
The Crimson Runner. Dir. Tom Forman. Hunt Stromberg Productions, 1925.
Daybreak. Dir. Jacques Feyder. MGM, 1931.
Dishonored. Dir. Josef von Sternberg. Paramount Pictures, 1931.
The Emperor Waltz. Dir. Billy Wilder. Paramount Pictures, 1948.
The Enemy. Dir. Fred Niblo. MGM, 1928.
Escapade. Dir. Robert Z. Leonard. MGM, 1935.
Evenings for Sale. Dir. Stuart Walker. Paramount Pictures, 1932.
Eyes Wide Shut. Dir. Stanley Kubrick. Warner Bros., 1999.
The Firebird. Dir. William Dieterle. Warner Bros., 1934.
Florian. Dir. Edwin L. Marin. MGM, 1940.
Freud. Dir. John Huston. Universal International Pictures, 1962.
Fugitive Road. Dir. Frank R. Strayer. Chesterfield Motion Pictures Corp., 1934.
Gigi. Dir. Vincente Minnelli. MGM, 1958.
The Grand Budapest Hotel. Dir. Wes Anderson. Fox Searchlight Pictures, 2014.
The Great Waltz. Dir. Julien Duvivier. MGM, 1938.
The Great Waltz. Dir. Andrew L. Stone. MGM, 1972.
The Greater Glory. Dir. Curt Rehfeld. First National Pictures, 1926.
The Guardsman. Dir. Sidney Franklin. MGM, 1931.
Her Private Affair. Dir. Paul L. Stein. Pathé Exchange, 1929.
Her Sister from Paris. Dir. Sidney Franklin. Joseph Schenck Productions, 1925.

His Glorious Night. Dir. Lionel Barrymore. MGM, 1929.
Hopscotch. Dir. Ronald Neame. Edie & Ely Landau, Inc., 1980.
Hotel Imperial. Dir. Mauritz Stiller. Paramount Pictures, 1927.
Hotel Imperial. Dir. Robert Florey. Paramount Pictures, 1939.
The Illusionist. Dir. Neil Burger. Freesyle Releasing and Yari Film Group Releasing, 2006.
Immortal Beloved. Dir. Bernard Rose. Columbia Pictures, 1994.
Jewel Robbery. Dir. William Dieterle. Warner Bros., 1932.
Julia. Dir. Fred Zinnemann. Twentieth Century-Fox, 1977.
The King Steps Out. Dir. Josef von Sternberg. Columbia Pictures, 1936.
Letter from an Unknown Woman. Dir. Max Ophuls, Universal Pictures, 1948.
The Living Daylights. Dir. John Glen. Eon Productions, 1987.
Love Me and the World Is Mine. Dir. E. A. Dupont. MGM, 1928.
Love Time. Dir. James Tinling. Fox Film Corporation, 1934.
The Magnificent Rebel. Dir. George Tressler. Walt Disney Productions, 1962.
The Marriage Circle. Dir. Ernst Lubitsch. Warner Bros., 1924.
Maskarade. Dir. Willi Forst. Sascha-Verleih, 1934.
Mata Hari. Dir. George Fitzmaurice. MGM, 1931.
Merry-Go-Round. Dir. Erich von Stoheim/Rupert Julian. Universal, 1923.
Miracle of the White Stallions. Dir. Arthur Hiller. Buena Vista Distribution Co., 1963.
Mission Impossible: Rogue Nation. Dir. Christopher McQuarrie. Paramount Pictures, Skydance Productions, 2015.
Museum Hours. Dir. Jem Cohen. The Cinema Guild, 2012.
"Nazi Conquest Nr. 1." *The March of Time.* Volume 4, Episode 9. New York, NY: Home Box Office, 1938, 11 mins. Accessed on June 23, 2018 through *The March of Time*, a part of Alexander Street Databases.
New Wine. Dir. Reinhold Schunzel. United Artists, 1942.
The Night Is Young. Dir. Dudley Murphy. MGM, 1935.
Night Life. Dir. George Archainbaud. Tiffany Productions, 1927.
Once upon a Honeymoon. Dir. Leo McCarey. RKO, 1942.
"Otto von Habsburg." *The March of Time* Volume 2, Episode 6. New York, NY: Home Box Office, 1936, 7 mins. Accessed on June 23, 2018 through *The March of Time*, a part of Alexander Street Databases.
Paradise for Three. Dir. Edward Buzzell. MGM, 1938.
The Peacemaker. Dir. Mimi Leder. DreamWorks, 1997.
The Red Danube. Dir. George Sidney. MGM, 1949.
The Republic Pictures Story. Dir. Len Morris. Made for TV, 1991.
Reunion in Vienna. Dir. Sidney Franklin. MGM, 1933.
The Salzburg Connection. Dir. Lee H. Katzin. Twentieth Century-Fox, 1972.
Scorpio. Dir. Michael Winner. United Artists, 1973.
Serenade. Dir. Harry d'Abbadie d'Arrast. Paramount Famous Lasky Corporation, 1927.
The Seven-Per-Cent Solution. Dir. Herbert Ross. Universal Pictures, 1976.
The Smiling Lieutenant. Dir. Ernst Lubitsch. Paramount Pictures, 1931.
So Ends Our Night. Dir. James Cromwell. United Artists, 1941.

The Sound of Music. Dir. Robert Wise. Twentieth Century-Fox, 1965.
Spectre. Dir. Sam Mendes. Eon Productions, 2015.
Spring Parade. Dir. Henry Koster. Universal, 1940.
The Strange Death of Adolf Hitler. Dir. James P. Hogan. Universal Pictures, 1943.
They Dare Not Love. Dir. James Whale. Columbia, 1941.
The Third Man. Dir. Carol Reed. London Film Productions & David O. Selznick, 1949.
Three Faces West. Dir. Bernhard Vorhaus. Republic Pictures, 1940.
The Waltz King. Dir. Steve Previn. Walt Disney Productions, 1963.
Ein Walzertraum. Dir. Ludwig Berger. Universum Film, 1925.
The Wedding March. Dir. Erich von Stroheim. Paramount Pictures, 1928.
The Woman Disputed. Dir. Henry King/Sam Taylor. Joseph M. Schenck Productions, 1928.
Woman in Gold. Dir. Simon Curtis. Origin Pictures/BBC Films, 2015.
A Woman of Experience. Dir. Harry Joe Brown. RKO-Pathé Distributing Corp., 1931.

Archival Material

The materials below are from: Harry Ransom Humanities Research Center (HRC) at the University of Texas-Austin, Margaret Herrick Library (MHL) in Beverly Hills, CA, and the USC Cinematic Arts Library (USC) at the University of Southern California.

Allan, Allida. "Synopsis of Screenplay by Samuel Taylor, 'Lady in Waiting.'" September 17, 1958. *A Breath of Scandal.* Paramount Pictures scripts. MHL.
Audrey Chamberlain Scrapbooks. MHL. The scrapbooks contain clippings on many of the early films.
Baum, Vicki, and Gottfried Reinhardt. "Outline." *The Great Waltz.* Oct. 9, 1934. Turner/MGM scripts. MHL.
Bernstein, Walter. "1st Preliminary Green Script." *A Breath of Scandal.* May 15, 1959. Paramount Pictures scripts. MHL.
Brackett, Charles, and Billy Wilder. *The Emperor Waltz.* May 31, 1946. Paramount Pictures scripts. MHL.
"The Enemy." Fred Niblo. 1927. Turner/MGM scripts. MHL.
"Fan Letters." *The Emperor Waltz.* Charles Brackett papers. MHL.
Girosi, Marcello. "Notes of Suggested Revisions on the Screenplay of Olympia by Sam Taylor." *A Breath of Scandal.* March 3, 1959. Paramount Pictures scripts. MHL.
Gyory, Nicholas. "Florian. To Winfield Sheehan," September, 14, 1939. MGM Collection (Series 2), USC.
Herczeg, Geza. "Temporary Complete Screenplay by Geza Herczeg." *Florian.* September 1, 1938. Turner/MGM scripts. MHL.
Lardner, Jr., Ring. *A Breath of Scandal.* Ring Lardner Jr. Papers, MHL.

———. "Letter to Marcello Girosi." May 31, 1959. Ring Lardner Jr. papers, MHL.
Lehman, Ernest. "*The Sound of Music*. Cameraman's script." Box 39a #8. 1963. HRC.
"Masks of the Devil." Victor Seastrom. 1927. Turner/MGM scripts. MHL.
Motion Picture Association of American. Production Code Administration (MPAA) records: *Bitter Sweet, The Blue Danube, A Breath of Scandal, The Cardinal, The Emperor Waltz, Evenings for Sale, The Great Waltz, Florian, His Glorious Night, Love Me and the World Is Mine, New Wine, Reunion in Vienna, So Ends Our Night, They Dare Not Love*. MHL.
Ornitz, Samuel. "An Outline with Dialogue." *The Case of Lena Smith*. July 18, 1928. Paramount Pictures scripts. MHL.
Powers, Pat. "Letter to Von." September 3, 1926. Erich von Stroheim papers. *The Wedding March*. MHL.
Pressbooks for *The Emperor Waltz, Florian, Once upon a Honeymoon, So Ends Our Night, The Case of Lena Smith, They Dare Not Love,* and *The Wedding March*. MHL.
Selznick, David O. "Memo to Carol Reed and Graham Greene." October 1948. Box 2733.7. HRC.
"Serenade." Harry D'Abbadie D'Arrast. 1927. Paramount Pictures scripts. MHL.
Sheehan, Winfield. "Florian Change." October 3, 1938. MGM Collection (Series 2), USC.
Siff, Philipp, and Claudine West. "Synopsis of *Daybreak*." *Daybreak*. October 24, 1927. Turner/MGM scripts. MHL.
Sigman, S. "Communications from S. Sigman to Mr. Haskell Masters." Re: Fox short-playing time. April 25, 1941. MHL.
———. "Communications from S. Sigman to Mr. Haskell Masters." Re: *So Ends Our Night*. May 13, 1941. MHL.
Taylor, Samuel. "Lady In Waiting." *A Breath of Scandal*. March 17, 1958. Paramount Pictures scripts. MHL.
West, Claudine. "Synopsis of *Daybreak*." *Daybreak* 1927–1928. Turner/MGM scripts. MHL.
Wilder, Billy, and Hy Kraft, "Moon over Vienna." *Champagne Waltz*, May 11, 1936. Paramount Pictures scripts. MHL.
Zanuck, Darryl. "Letter to Mr. Richard Zanuck from Darryl Zanuck on 30 January 1964," with a handwritten note from Lehman dated March, 31 1986. Box 114e #9. HRC.
Zinnemann, Fred. "Jewish Welcome Service 1987." Fred Zinnemann papers. MHL.

Published Works

Aaronson, Charles S. "*So Ends Our Night*." *Motion Picture Daily*, January 27, 1941.

"Accents Cut." *Variety*, December 9, 1942.
Agee, James. "*The Emperor Waltz.*" *The Nation*, July 24, 1948.
Alpers, Benjamin L. *Dictators, Democracy, and American Public Culture: Envisioning the Totalitarian Enemy, 1920s–1950s*. Chapel Hill: University of North Carolina Press, 2003.
"American and Continental Ideas in Plays and Acting." *New York Times*, February 17, 1907.
Archer, Eugene. "Moviemaker Clarifies the 'Cardinal' Issues." *New York Times*, December 8, 1963.
Arens, Katherine. "Syncope, Syncopation: Musical Homages to Europe." In *Billy Wilder: Movie-Maker: Critical Essays on the Films*, edited by Karen McNally, 41–55. Jefferson, NC: McFarland, 2011.
Asper, Helmut G. "Making a Living: Dupont und Hollywood." In *Ewald André Dupont: Autor und Regisseur*, edited by Hans-Michael Bock, Wolfgang Jacobsen, and Jörg Schöning, 101–10. Munich: edition text & kritik, 1992.
Aurich, Rolf, Andreas Hutter, Wolfgang Jacobsen, and Günter Krenn, eds. "*Billie.*" *Billy Wilders Wiener journalistische Arbeiten*. Vienna: verlag filmarchiv austria, 2006.
"Austria Attacks Film on a Hapsburg Love; Seeks to Bar Showings Throughout World." *New York Times*, December 21, 1933.
"Austria on Display at the Chicago's Columbian Exposition, 1893: A Collection of Sources." *Journal of Austrian-American History* 1, no. 2 (2017): 117–27.
"Austria Seizure Not US Affair, Borah Asserts." *Washington Post*, March 29, 1938.
"Austrian Press Bans Innitzer Retraction." *New York Times*, April 8, 1938.
Babson, Roger W. "'Watch Austria-Hungary' Says Roger W. Babson." *New York Times*, January 19, 1913.
Bacher, Lutz. *Max Ophuls in the Hollywood Studios*. New Brunswick: Rutgers University Press, 1996.
Bahr, Eberhard. *Weimar on the Pacific: German Exile Culture in Los Angeles and the Crisis of Modernism*. Oakland: University of California Press, 2007.
Barker, Andrew. *Fictions from an Orphan State: Literary Reflections of Austria between Habsburg and Hitler*. Rochester, NY: Camden House, 2012.
Barrios, Richard. *A Song in the Dark: The Birth of the Musical Film*. New York: Oxford University Press, 1995.
Barta, Tony. "Film Nazis: The Great Escape." In *Screening the Past. Film and the Representation of History*, edited by Tony Barta, 127–48. Westport, CT: Praeger, 1998.
Barthel, Joan. "Biggest Money-Making Movie of All Time–How Come?" *New York Times*, November 20, 1966.
Basinger, Jeanine. *A Women's View: How Hollywood Spoke to Women, 1930–1960*. New York: Alfred A. Knopf, 1993.
Baxter, John. *Von Sternberg*. Lexington: University Press of Kentucky, 2010.

Beckermann, Ruth, and Christa Blüminger, eds. *Ohne Untertitel: Fragmente einer Geschichte des österreichischen Kinos*. Vienna: Sonderzahl, 1996.
Beller, Steven. *A Concise History of Austria*. Cambridge: Cambridge University Press, 2006.
Belton, John, ed. *Movies and Mass Culture*. New Brunswick, NJ: Rutgers University Press, 1996.
Berghahn, Volker R. "Philanthropy and Diplomacy in the 'American Century.'" *Diplomatic History* 23, no. 3 (Summer 1999): 393–419.
Bernstein, Arnie. *Swastika National: Fritz Kuhn and the Rise and Fall of the German-American Bund*. New York: St. Martin's Press, 2013.
Bernstein, Walter. *Inside Out: A Memoir of the Blacklist*. New York: Alfred A. Knopf, 1996.
"Big Rental Pictures of 1964." *Variety*. January 6, 1965.
Birdwell, Michael E. *Celluloid Soldiers: Warner Bros.'s Campaign against Nazism*. New York: New York University Press, 1999.
Bonsal, Stephen. "An Intimate Study of Francis Joseph, The Man." *New York Times*, October 20, 1907.
Bordman, Gerald. *American Musical Theater: A Chronicle*. New York: Oxford University Press, 2001.
Botz, Gerhard. *Gewalt in der Politik: Attentate, Zusammenstösse, Putschversuche, Unruhen in Österreich 1918 bis 1934*. Munich: Wilhelm Fink Verlag, 1976.
Bowser, Eileen. *The Transformation of Cinema, 1907–1915*. Oakland: University of California Press, 1990.
Boyer, John W. "Silent War and Bitter Peace: The Revolution of 1918 in Austria." *Austrian History Yearbook* 34 (2003): 1–56.
Boym, Svetlana. *The Future of Nostalgia*. New York: Basic Books, 2001.
Brackett, Charles. *"It's the Pictures That Got Small": Charles Brackett on Billy Wilder and Hollywood's Golden Age*, edited by Anthony Slide. New York: Columbia University Press, 2015.
"*A Breath of Scandal*." *Limelight*, October 27, 1960.
"*A Breath of Scandal*." *Playboy*, February 1961.
Breitman, Richard, and Allan J. Lichtman. *FDR and the Jews*. Cambridge: Belknap Press of Harvard University Press, 2013.
Brill, Lesley. *John Huston's Filmmaking*. Cambridge: Cambridge University Press, 1997.
Brown, John Mason. *The Worlds of Robert E. Sherwood: Mirror to His Times 1896–1939*. Westport, CT: Greenwood Press, 1965.
Bruckmüller, Ernst. *The Austrian Nation: Cultural Consciousness and Socio-Political Processes*. Translated by Lowell A. Bangerter. Riverside, CA: Ariadne Press, 2003.
Buhle, Paul, and Dave Wagner. *Radical Hollywood: The Untold Story behind America's Favorite Movies*. New York: The New Press, 2002.
Callenbach, Ernest. "Freud." In *Perspectives on John Huston*, edited by Stephen Cooper, 161–63. New York: G. K. Hall & Co., 1994.
"Cardinal Innitzer Put under Guard." *New York Times*, October 9, 1938.

Castelli, Jean-Christophe. "Vienna, Texas: Linklater's Junior Year Abroad." *Filmmaker* (Winter 1995): 59–62.
Ceplair, Larry, and Steven Englund. *The Inquisition in Hollywood: Politics in the Film Community, 1930–1960.* Garden City, NY: Anchor Press/Doubleday, 1980.
Chase, Alicia Grace. "An American Heroine in Paris: Hollywood and Women in the City of Light in the 1950s." PhD diss., University of Minnesota, 2002.
Cohan, Steven. *Masked Men: Masculinity and the Movies in the Fifties.* Bloomington: Indiana University Press, 1997.
Conley, Timothy K. *Screening Vienna: The City of Dreams in English-Language Cinema and Television.* Amherst, NY: Cambria Press, 2016.
Corson, John W., MD. *Loiterings in Europe; or, Sketches of Travel in France, Belgium, Switzerland, Italy, Austria, Prussia, Great Britain, and Ireland.* New York: Harper & Brothers, 1848.
Cortesi, Arnaldo. "Innitzer Retreats on Nazi-Appeal After 2-Hour Talk with the Pope." *New York Times*, April 7, 1938.
Cott, Nancy F. *Public Vows: A History of Marriage and the Nation.* Cambridge, MA: Harvard University Press, 2000.
"Count Geza von Mattachich Tells How He Loved and Lost the Princess Louise of Saxe-Coburg: A Remarkable Confession of One of the Principals in a Royal Idly that Ended in Tragedy." *New York Times*, September 11, 1904.
Coward, Noël. *The Autobiography of Noël Coward.* London: Methuen, 1986.
———. *Bitter Sweet and Other Plays by Noël Coward.* Garden City, NY: Doubleday, Doran & Company, 1929.
Craig, Steve. *Out of the Dark: A History of Radio and Rural America.* Tuscaloosa: University of Alabama Press, 2009.
Crawford, Beverly, and James Martel. "Representations of Germans and What Germans Represent: American Film Images and Public Perceptions in the Postwar Era." In *Transatlantic Images and Perceptions: Germany and America since 1776*, edited by David E. Barclay and Elisabeth Glaser-Schmidt, 285–308. Cambridge: Cambridge University Press, 1997.
Creelman, Eileen. "An Emotional Melodrama of Refugees in Europe, 'So Ends Our Night.'" *New York Sun*, February 28, 1941.
Crittenden, Camille. *Johann Strauss and Vienna: Operetta and the Politics of Popular Culture.* Cambridge: Cambridge University Press, 2000.
Crowther, Bosley. "The Screen." *New York Times*, November 28, 1942.
———. "The Screen: Bing Crosby Rambles Through 'Emperor Waltz,' with Joan Fontaine, at Music Hall." *New York Times*, June 18, 1948.
———. "Screen: Episodes of a Man of the Cloth." *New York Times*, December 13, 1963.
———. "The Screen in Review: 'Florian,' a Tale of a Noble Horse in Old Vienna. . . ." *New York Times*, June 6, 1940.
———. "The Screen: 'So Ends Our Night,' a Tragic Story of Refugees, at the Music Hall. . . ." *New York Times*, February 28, 1941.

———. "Sophie Loren Starred with John Gavin." *New York Times*, December 17, 1960.
Culbert, David Holbrook. *News for Everyman: Radio and Foreign Affairs in Thirties America*. Westport, CT: Greenwood Press, 1976.
Cunliffe-Owen, Frederick. "What Will New Emperor Do: Charles Francis of Austria: Hungary Thought by Some to be Likely to Listen to Separate Peace Overtures." *New York Times*, November 26, 1916.
[Cunliffe-Owen, Marguerite]. *The Martyrdom of an Empress*. New York: Harper & Brothers, 1899.
Custen, George F. *Bio/Pics: How Hollywood Constructed Public History*. New Brunswick, NJ: Rutgers University Press, 1992.
Dassanowsky, Robert. "An Unclaimed Country: The Austrian Image in American Film and the Sociopolitics of *The Sound of Music*." *Bright Lights Film Journal* 41 (2003). Accessed on June 26, 2018. http://brightlightsfilm.com/41/soundofmusic.php.
———, ed. *World Film Locations Vienna*. Chicago: University of Chicago Press, 2012.
"David Joseph Bach." psyalpha: Wissensplattform für Psychoanalyse. Accessed on June 21, 2018. http://www.psyalpha.net/biografien/david-josef-bach.
Davie, Maurice R., *Refugees in America: Report of the Committee for the Study of Recent Immigration from Europe*. New York: Harper & Brothers, 1947.
D'Emilio, John and Estelle B. Freedman. *Intimate Matters: A History of Sexuality in America*. New York: Harper & Row, 1988.
"Detroit Spending 'Boom' Goes Boom." *Variety*, May 21, 1941.
Dewald, Christian, Michael Loebenstein, and Werner Michael Schwarz, eds. *Wien im Film: Stadtbilder aus 100 Jahren*. Vienna: Czernin Verlag, 2010.
Dick, Bernard F. *The Star-Spangled Screen: The American World War II Film*. Lexington: University Press of Kentucky, 1985.
Dinnerstein, Leonard. *Anti-Semitism in America*. New York: Oxford University Press, 1994.
Doherty, Thomas. *Hitler and Hollywood, 1933–1939*. New York: Columbia University Press, 2013.
———. *Hollywood's Censor: Joseph I. Breen and the Production Code Administration*. New York: Columbia University Press, 2007.
———. *Pre-Code Hollywood*. New York: Columbia University Press, 1999.
———. *Projections of War: Hollywood, American Culture, and World War II*. New York: Columbia University Press, 1993.
"Dr. Bach Bemoans Vienna's Lost Joy." *New York Times*, February 3, 1935.
Dulles, Foster Rhea. *Americans Abroad: Two Centuries of European Travel*. Ann Arbor: University of Michigan Press, 1964.
Dunning, John. *Tune in Yesterday: The Ultimate Encyclopedia of Old-Time Radio, 1925–1976*. Englewood Cliffs, NJ: Prentice-Hall, 1976.
Dyer, Richard. *Only Entertainment*. New York: Routledge, 1992.

Ellwood, David W. *The Shock of America: Europe and the Challenge of the Century.* Oxford: Oxford University Press, 2012.
Elsaesser, Thomas. "ethnicity, authenticity, and exile: a counterfeit trade? german filmmakers and hollywood." In *Home, Exile, Homeland, Film, Media, and the Politics of Place*, edited by Hamid Naficy, 97–123. New York: Routledge, 1999.
———. *Weimar Cinema and After. Germany's Historical Imaginary.* London: Routledge, 2000.
"Empress Elisabeth: Her Tragic Death Last Summer—New Light on Her Life." *New York Times*, March 18, 1899.
Feldman, Egal. "Prostitution, the Alien Woman and the Progressive Imagination, 1910–1915." *American Quarterly* 19, no. 2, pt. 1 (Summer 1967): 192–206.
Fernett, Gene. *American Film Studios: An Historical Encyclopedia.* Jefferson, NC: McFarland, 1988.
Fielding, Raymond. *The March of Time, 1935–1951.* New York: Oxford University Press, 1978.
"Fifty-Eight Years on a Trembling Throne." *New York Times*, December 2, 1906.
Filene, Peter G. *Him/Her/Self: Gender Identities in Modern America.* Baltimore: Johns Hopkins University Press, 1998.
Finler, Joel W. *The Hollywood Story.* London: Wallflower Press, 2003. Originally published with Octopus Books Limited, 1988.
Fithian, Theodore. "Exploring Austria's Mountain Villages." *New York Times*, June 22, 1952.
Flinn, Caryl. *The Sound of Music.* London: BFI Palgrave, 2015.
"France Made in Hollywood." Accessed June 21, 2018. http://photos.state.gov/libraries/france/45994/irc/films.pdf.
"Francis Joseph." *New York Times*, November 23, 1916.
Frey, Stefan. *"Unter Tränen lachen." Emmerich Kálmán: Eine Operettenbiographie.* Berlin: Henschel, 2003.
Frisby, David. *Cityscapes of Modernity: Critical Explorations.* Cambridge: Polity, 2001.
Fujiwara, Chris. *The World and its Double: The Life and Work of Otto Preminger.* New York: Faber and Faber, 2008.
Gartenberg, Egon. *Johann Strauss: The End of an Era.* New York: Da Capo Paperback, 1979. Hardback edition, University Park: The Pennsylvania University Press, 1974.
Gedye, G. E. R. *Betrayal in Central Europe: Austria and Czechoslovakia: The Fallen Bastions.* New York: Harper & Brothers, 1939.
———. *Heirs to the Habsburgs.* Bristol: Arrowsmith, 1932.
———. "Old Vienna is Dead: A Nazi Vienna is Born." *New York Times*, March 20, 1938.
Gehring, Wes D. *Leo McCarey: From Marx to McCarthy.* Lanham, MD: Scarecrow Press, 2005.

Gemünden, Gerd. *Continental Strangers: German Exile Cinema 1933–1951.* New York: Columbia University Press, 2014.

———. *A Foreign Affair: Billy Wilder's American Films.* New York: Berghahn, 2008.

———. "Gained in Translation. Exile Cinema and the Case of Billy Wilder." In *The Cosmopolitan Screen: German Cinema and the Global Imaginary, 1945 to the Present,* edited by Stephan K. Schindler and Lutz Koepnick, 25–38. Ann Arbor: University of Michigan Press, 2007.

George, Alys X. "Hollywood on the Danube? Vienna and Austrian Silent Film of the 1920s." In *Interwar Vienna: Culture between Tradition and Modernity,* edited by Deborah Holmes and Lisa Silverman, 143–60. Rochester, NY: Camden House, 2009.

Gibbs, Christopher H., ed. *The Cambridge Companion to Schubert.* Cambridge: Cambridge University Press, 1997.

———. *The Life of Schubert.* Cambridge: Cambridge University Press, 2000.

Gilbert, James. *Men in the Middle: Searching for Masculinity in the 1950s.* Chicago: University of Chicago Press, 2005.

Glancy, H. Mark. *When Hollywood Loved Britain: The Hollywood "British" Film 1939–45.* Manchester: Manchester University Press, 1999.

Gomery, Douglas. *The Hollywood Studio System: A History.* London: British Film Institute, 2005.

———. *Shared Pleasures: A History of Movie Presentation in the United States.* Madison: University of Wisconsin Press, 1992.

Görtschacher, Wolfgang, and Holger Klein, ed. *Austria and Austrians: Images in World Literature.* Tübingen: Stauffenburg Verlag, 2003.

Grafe, Frieda. "Wiener Beiträge zu einer wahren Geschichte des Kinos." In *Film/Geschichte: Wie Film Geschichte anders schreibt.* Berlin: Verlag Brinkmann & Bose, 2004, 122–40. Originally published in *Aufbruch ins Ungewisse,* edited by Christian Cargnelli and Michael Omasta. Vienna: Wespennest, 1993.

Grafl, Franz. *Imaginiertes Österreich: Erzählung und Diskurs im internationalen Film.* Vienna: Böhlau Verlag, 2017.

Graml, Gudolf. "'The Hills Are Alive . . .': *Sound of Music* Tourism and the Performative Construction of Places." *Women in German Yearbook* 21 (2005):192–215.

———. "(Re)mapping the nation: Sound of Music tourism and national identity in Austria, ca 2000 CE." *Tourist Studies* 4, no. 2 (August 2004): 137–59.

Grande, Julian. "Bishop Sees Vienna Near Revolution." *New York Times,* December 25, 1918.

Gruber, Helmut. *Red Vienna: Experiment in Working-Class Culture, 1919–1934.* New York: Oxford University Press, 1991.

Hake, Sabine. *Popular Cinema of the Third Reich.* Austin: University of Texas Press, 2001.

———. *Screen Nazis: Cinema, History, and Democracy.* Madison: University of Wisconsin Press, 2012.

Halle, Randall, and Margaret McCarthey. *Light Motives: German Popular Film in Perspective*. Detroit, MI: Wayne State University Press, 2003.
Handler, Helen. "Austria Set to Take Tourist Influx in Stride." *New York Times*, February 28, 1960.
Handler, M. S. "Jews in Austria Set Plea to Big 4." *New York Times*, November 20, 1960.
Hanson, Philip. *This Side of Despair: How the Movies and American Life Intersected during the Great Depression*. Madison, NJ: Fairleigh Dickinson University Press, 2008.
Healy, Maureen. *Vienna and the Fall of the Habsburg Empire: Total War and Everyday Life in World War I*. Cambridge: Cambridge University Press, 2004.
Heisner, Beverly. *Hollywood Art: Art Direction in the Days of the Great Studios*. Jefferson, NC: McFarland, 1999.
Heiß, Gernot. "Erich von Stroheim: Wien in Hollywood. Erinnerung, Wirklichkeit, Fiktion." In *Glücklich ist, wer vergißt . . .? Das andere Wien um 1900*, edited by Hubert, Ch. Ehalt, Gernot Heiß, and Hannes Stekl, 247–84. Vienna: Hermann Böhlaus Nachf, 1986.
Henry, Nora. *Ethics and Social Criticism in the Hollywood Films of Erich von Stroheim, Ernst Lubitsch, and Billy Wilder*. Westport, CT: Praeger, 2001.
"Herz-Jesu-Bundeslied und Messe für Tirol." Accessed on June 21, 2018. http://tiroler-schuetzen.at/uploads/6.11_herz_jesu_lied.pdf.
Herzog, Todd. "Jem Cohen's Vienna." Annual Meeting of the Modern Language Association. Vancouver, Canada, January 9, 2015.
Higham, John. *Strangers in the Land: Patterns of American Nativism, 1860–1925*. 2nd ed., New Brunswick, NJ: Rutgers University Press, 1988.
Higson, Andrew, and Richard Maltby, eds. *"Film Europe" and "Film America": Cinema, Commerce and Cultural Exchange 1920–1939*. Exeter: University of Exeter Press, 1999.
Hirsch, Foster. *Otto Preminger: The Man Who Would Be King*. New York: Alfred A. Knopf, 2007.
Hirsch, Julia Antopol. *The Sound of Music: The Making of America's Favorite Movie*. Chicago: Contemporary Books, 1993.
Hoffmann, Robert. "Im Zeichen von Festspielgründung, allgemeinem Wahlrecht und Wirtschaftskrise: Die Stadt Salzburg in der Zwischenkriegszeit." In *Hoffnungen und Verzweiflung in der Stadt Salzburg 1938/39: Vorgeschichte—Fakten—Folgen*, edited by Peter F. Kramml and Ernst Hanish, 32–74. Salzburg: Schriftreihe des Archivs der Stadt Salzburg, 2010.
Holland, Norman N. "How to See Huston's *Freud*." In *Perspectives on John Huston*, edited by Stephen Cooper. 164–83. New York: G. K. Hall, 1994.
Homberger, Eric. "Introduction." *Titled Americans: The Real Heiresses' Guide to Marrying an Aristocrat*. Great Britain: Old House Books, 2013. Reprint of *Titled Americans, A List of American Ladies Who Have Married Foreigners or Rank*. New York: Street & Smith, 1890.

Horak, Jan-Christopher. *Anti-Nazi-Filme der deutschsprachigen Emigration von Hollywood 1939–1945*. Münster: MAKS Publikationen, 1985. 2 Auflage.

———. "Ewig auf der Flucht: Die Romanverfilmung *So Ends Our Night*." In *Erich Maria Remarque: Leben, Werk und weltweite Wirkung*, edited by Thomas Schneider, 235–49. Osnabrück: Universitätsverlag Rasch, 1998.

———. *Fluchtpunkt Hollywood: Eine Dokumentation zur Filmemigration nach 1933*. Muenster: MAKS Publikationen, 1984.

———. "Sauerkraut and Sausages with a Little Goulash: Germans in Hollywood, 1927." *Film History* 17, no. 2 (2005): 241–60.

———. *Saul Bass: Anatomy of Film Design*. Lexington: University Press of Kentucky, 2015.

———. "Schauplatz Wien: Österreich im Anti-Nazi-Film Hollywoods." In *Aufbruch ins Ungewisse: Österreichische Filmschaffende in der Emigration vor 1945*, edited by Christian Cargnelli and Michael Omasta, 198–211. Vienna: Wespennest, 1993.

———. "*Spring Parade* (1940): Imperial Austria Lives Again (at Universal)." *Modern Austrian Literature* 32, no. 4 (1999): 74–86.

———. "'We Love the Viennese': Willi Forst nach Hollywood-Art." In *Willi Forst: Ein Filmstil aus Wien*, edited by Armin Loacker, 440–77. Vienna: Filmarchiv Austria, 2003.

———. "Wunderliche Schicksalsfügung: Emigranten in Hollywoods Anti-Nazi-Film." *Exilforschung, Erinnerungen ans Exil—kritische Lektüre der Autobiographien nach 1933 und andere Themen* 2 (1984): 257–70.

Horkan, Kay. "Exploring Austria's Land of Castles." *New York Times*, April 10, 1960.

———. "In Old Austria's 'Salt Crown Lands.'" *New York Times*, February 19, 1961.

———. "Stream of History: Blue Danube." *New York Times*, May 8, 1960.

———. "There's Nostalgia in Vienna's Baroque Beauty." *New York Times*, September 11, 1960.

Horwath, Alexander, and Michael Omasta, eds. *Josef von Sternberg: The Case of Lena Smith*. Vienna: Österreichisches Filmmuseum/SYNEMA, 2007.

Hosley, David H. *As Good As Any: Foreign Correspondence on American Radio, 1930–1940*. Westport, CT: Greenwood Press, 1984.

Huneker, James. "The Gayest City in Europe—Not Paris, but Vienna." *New York Times*, April 13, 1913.

———. "Huneker Prowls around Kaiser's Jubilee City." *New York Times*, June 22, 1913.

Isenberg, Michael T. *War on Film: The American Cinema and World War I, 1914–1941*. Rutherford: Fairleigh Dickinson University Press, 1981.

———. "War on Film: The American Cinema and World War I, 1914–1941." In *Hollywood and War: The Film Reader*, edited by J. David Slocum, 123–36. New York: Routledge, 2006. A condensed version of his book.

Isserman, Maurice, and Michael Kazin. *America Divided: The Civil War of the 1960s*. New York: Oxford University Press, 2000.

Izod, John. *Hollywood and the Box Office, 1895–1986*. London: Macmillan Press, 1988.
Jacobs, Lea. *The Decline of Sentiment: American Film in the 1920s*. Oakland: University of California Press, 2008.
James, Edwin L. "Allies See Danger in Vienna Outbreak." *New York Times*, July 20, 1927.
———. "Austria Staggering on the Brink of Chaos." *New York Times*, February 1, 1925.
———. "Vienna A Spectre of Departed Glory." *New York Times*, February 2, 1925.
Jarka, Horst and Lois, eds. *The Others' Austria: Impressions of American and British Travelers*. Riverside, CA: Ariadne Press, 2006 and 2012. Volume one covers 1814–1914 and volume two 1919–2007.
John, Michael. "From Vienna to Hollywood: Erich von Stroheim and Josef von Sternberg." In *Jews and Film/Juden und Film: Vienna Prague Hollywood*, edited by Eleonore Lappin, 2–13. Vienna: Mandelbaum, 2004.
Johnson, David T. *Richard Linklater*. Urbana, IL: University of Illinois Press, 2012.
Jones, Idwal. "Vienna vs. Broadway." *New York Times*, January 31, 1937.
Judson, Pieter. *The Habsburg Empire: A New History*. Cambridge, MA: Belknap Press of Harvard University Press, 2016.
Katz, Michael B. *In the Shadow of the Poorhouse: A Social History of Welfare in America*. New York: Basic Books, 1986. Revised and Updated 1996.
Kennedy, David M. *Freedom from Fear: The American People in Depression and War, 1929–1945*. New York: Oxford University Press, 1999.
Kertzer, David I. *The Pope and Mussolini: The Secret History of Pius XI and the Rise of Fascism in Europe*. New York: Random House, 2014.
Keyserlingk, Robert H. *Austria in World War II. An Anglo-America Dilemma*. Kingston/Montreal: McGill-Queen's University Press, 1988.
Koppes, Clayton R., and Gregory D. Black. *Hollywood Goes to War: How Politics, Profits and Propaganda Shaped World War II Movies*. Oakland: University of California Press, 1987.
Koszarski, Richard. *VON: The Life and Films of Erich von Stroheim*. New York: Lightlime Editions, 2001. Original edition published by Oxford University Press under the title *The Man You Love to Hate*, 1983.
Kracauer, Siegfried. *From Caligari to Hitler: A Psychological History of German Film*. Princeton: Princeton University Press, 1947, 2004.
———. "National Types as Hollywood Presents Them." *The Public Opinion Quarterly* 13 (Spring 1949): 53–72.
Kreisky, Bruno. *Zwischen den Zeiten: Erinnerungen aus fünf Jahrzehnten*. Berlin: Siedler, 1986.
Lally, Kevin. *Wilder Times: The Life of Billy Wilder*. New York: Henry Holt, 1996.
Lang, Zoë Alexis. *The Legacy of Johann Strauss: Political Influence and Twentieth-Century Identity*. Cambridge: Cambridge University Press, 2014.

Lardner Jr., Ring. *I'd Hate Myself in the Morning*. New York: Thunder Mouth Press, 2000.
Lasch, Christopher. *The True and Only Heaven: Progress and Its Critics*. New York: W. W. Norton, 1991.
Leab, David J. "Deutschland, USA: German Images in American Film." In *The Kaleidoscopic Lens: How Hollywood Views Ethnic Groups*, edited by Randall Miller, 156–81. New Jersey: Jerome S. Ozer, 1980.
———. "Goethe or Attila? The Celluloid German." In *Ethnic Images in American Film and Television*, edited by Randall M. Miller, 63–68. Philadelphia: Balch Institute, 1978.
———. "Total War On-Screen: The Hun in U.S. Films 1914–1920." In: *"Huns" vs. "Corned Beef": Representations of the Other in American and German Literature and Film on World War I*, edited by Thomas F. Schneider and Hans Wagener, 153–84. Göttingen: V&R unipress Universitätsverlag Osnabrück, 2007.
Lein, Hermann. "Hermann Lein. Rosenkranzfeier 1938." Dokumentionsarchiv des österreichischen Widerstands. Accessed on June 21, 2018. http://www.doew.at/erinnern/biographien/erzaehlte-geschichte/widerstand-1938-1945/hermann-lein-rosenkranzfeier-1938.
Lenning, Arthur. *Stroheim*. Lexington: University Press of Kentucky, 2000.
L'Estrange Fawcett [Arthur Wellesley]. *Films: Facts and Forecasts*. London: Geoffrey Bles, 1927.
———. *Die Welt des Films*. Zurich: Amalthea Verlag, n.d. [around 1930]. Unter Mitwirkung des Wiener Filmbundes für die deutsche Ausgabe frei bearbeitet und ergänzt von C. Zell and S. Walter Fischer. (In cooperation with the Vienna Film Association, freely revised and expanded for the German edition by C. Zell and S. Walter Fischer).
"Light Thrown on Austria's Royal Tragedy." *New York Times*, January 19, 1908.
Lignon, Fanny. *Erich von Stroheim: Du Ghetto au Gotha*. Paris: Éditions L'Harmattan, 1999.
"A Literary Night in Irving Place." *New York Times*, October 30, 1907.
Lundestad, Geir. "Empire by Invitation? The United States and Western Europe, 1945–1952." In *The Cold War in Europe*, edited by Charles S. Maier, 143–65. New York: Markus Wiener, 1991.
Lytle, Mark Hamilton. *America's Uncivil Wars: The Sixties Era from Elvis to the Fall of Richard Nixon*. New York: Oxford University Press, 2006.
MacCormac, John. "Alpine Tours and Music in Austria." *New York Times*, March 3, 1957.
Maderthaner, Wolfgang, and Lutz Musner. *Die Anarchie der Vorstadt: Das andere Wien um 1900*. Frankfurt: Campus Verlag, 1999.
Madsen, Axel. *William Wyler*. New York: Thomas Y. Crowell, 1973.
Marksteiner, Franz, "Schubert heiß ich. Bin ich Schubert? Der Komponist ohne Heimat. Zu den Filmen 'Leise flehen meine Lieder' (Ö 1933) und 'Blossom Time'(GB 1934)." In *Aufbruch ins Ungewisse: Österreichische*

Filmschaffende in der Emigration vor 1945, edited by Christian Cargnelli and Michael Omasta, 75–86. Vienna: Wespennest, 1993.
Martyn, T. J. C. "Austria Still Divided By Postwar Questions." *New York Times*, October 14, 1928.
May, Elaine Tyler. "Commentary: Ideology and Foreign Policy: Culture and Gender in Diplomatic History." *Diplomatic History* 18, no. 1 (Winter 1994): 71–78.
———. *Homeward Bound: American Families in the Cold War Era*. New York: Basic Books, 1988.
May, Lary. *The Big Tomorrow: Hollywood and the Politics of the American Way*. Chicago. University of Chicago Press, 2000.
———. *Screening Out the Past: The Birth of Mass Culture and the Motion Picture Industry*. Chicago: University of Chicago Press, 1980.
McCarten, John. "The Current Cinema." *New Yorker*, June 26, 1948.
McCormick, Anne O'Hare. "Lesser and Happier Austria." *New York Times*, August 12, 1923.
Meyers, Jeffrey. *John Huston: Courage and Art*. New York: Crown Archetype, 2011.
Micewski, Andrzej. *Cardinal Wyszyński: A Biography*. Translated by William R. Brand and Katarzyna Mroczkowska-Brand. San Diego, CA: Harcourt Brace Jovanowich, 1984.
Midgley, David. "City Mythologies: Berlin and Vienna." In *Vienna Meets Berlin: Cultural Interaction 1918–1933*, edited by John Warren and Ulrike Zitzlsperger, 169–82. Bern: Peter Lang, 2005.
Minnigerode, F. L. "Preparing Austria's Comeback." *New York Times*, October 15, 1922.
"Miscellany." *Cue*, December 24, 1960. (Review of *A Breath of Scandal*.)
Molnár, Ferenc. "Olympia." In *The Plays of Ferenc Molnár*, 784–823. New York: Vanguard Press, 1929.
Moltke, Johannes von. "Trapped in America: The Americanization of the *Trapp-Familie*, or 'Papas Kino' Revisited." *German Studies Review* 19, no. 3 (October 1996): 455–78.
Moore, Michaela Hoenicke. *Know Your Enemy: The American Debate on Nazism, 1933–1945*. Cambridge: Cambridge University Press, 2010.
Moser, John E. "'Gigantic Engines of Propaganda': The 1941 Senate Investigation of Hollywood." *The Historian* 63, no. 4 (Summer 2001): 731–51.
Mutschlechner, Martin. "The Corpus Christi procession—'God's Court Ball.'" In *The World of the Habsburgs*. Accessed on June 15, 2018. http://www.habsburger.net/en/chapter/corpus-christi-procession-gods-court-ball.
"Nazi Group in Austria Linked to Ku Klux Klan." *New York Times*, February 22, 1960.
Negra, Diane. "Immigrant Stardom in Imperial America: Pola Negri and the Problem of Typology." In *A Feminist Reader in Early Cinema*, edited by Jennifer M. Bean and Diane Negra, 374–403. Durham, NC: Duke University Press, 2002.

"New Heir is Popular. Charles Francis Joseph a Young Man of Good Impulses." *New York Times*, June 29, 1914.
"New Innitzer Step Infuriates Nazis." *New York Times*, October 12, 1938.
"New Picture, 'So Ends Our Night.'" *Time Magazine*, February 10, 1941.
"The New Pictures." *Time Magazine*, July 19, 1948.
"New Plays that Bid for Favor." *New York Times*, October 13, 1912.
Nugent, Frank. "The Paramount Brings in its Silver Jubilee Pictures, 'Champagne Waltz,' With Gladys Swarthout." *New York Times*, February 4, 1937.
———. "The Screen in Review." *New York Times*, November 25, 1938.
Nußbaumer, Martina. *Musikstadt Wien: Die Konstruktion eines Images*. Freiburg i. Br: Rombach Verlag, 2007.
Oakes, George W. "Walking Tour in Old Vienna. The Ancient Imperial Capital beside the Danube Offers Rich Panorama of History, Architecture, and Art." *New York Times*, November 17, 1963.
Oberhauser, Franz Friedrich. "People of Austria Adopt Many Customs from America." *New York Times*, June 23, 1929.
"The Official Academy Awards Database." Accessed on June 21, 2018. http://awardsdatabase.oscars.org/.
"Once upon a Honeymoon." *The Hollywood Reporter*, November 2, 1942.
O'Shaughnessy, Edith. *Viennese Medley*. New York: B. W. Huebsch. 1924.
Palmier, Jean-Michel. *Weimar in Exile: The Antifascist Emigration in Europe and America*. Translated by David Fernbach. London: Verso, 2006.
"Panorama: The Foreign Scene." *New York Times*, January 10, 1937.
Parrish, Michael E. *Anxious Decades: America in Prosperity and Depression 1920–1941*. New York: W. W. Norton, 1992.
Pasternak, Joe. *Easy the Hard Way* as told to David Chandler. New York: G. P. Putnam's Sons, 1956.
Phelps, Nicole M. *U.S.-Habsburg Relations from 1815 to the Paris Peace Conference: Sovereignty Transformed*. Cambridge: Cambridge University Press, 2013.
Pollock, Channing. *The Enemy*. New York: Longmans, Green, 1927.
———. *Harvest of My Years*. Indianapolis: Bobbs-Merrell, 1943.
Preminger, Otto. *Preminger. An Autobiography*. Garden City, NY: Doubleday, 1977.
Price, Clair. "Austria's Hands Tied by Two Armed Parties." *New York Times*, December 2, 1928.
"A Priest's Story." *Time Magazine*, December 13, 1963.
Proctor, Tammy M. *Female Intelligence: Women and Espionage in the First World War*. New York: New York University Press, 2003.
"Propaganda in Motion Pictures." *Hearings Before a Subcommittee of the Committee on Interstate Commerce United States Senate, Seventy-Seventh Congress First Session on S. Res. 152: A Resolution Authorizing an Investigation of War Propaganda Disseminated by the Motion-Picture Industry and of any Monopoly in the Production, Distribution, or Exhibition of Motion Pictures. September 9 to 26, 1941*. Washington, DC: United States Government Printing Office, 1942.

Rabel, Roberto, ed. *The American Century: In Retrospect and Prospect.* Westport, CT Praeger, 2002.
Rathkolb, Oliver, Otto M. Maschke, and Stefan August Lütgenau, eds. *Mit anderen Augen gesehen: Internationale Perzeptionen Österreichs 1955–1990.* Vienna: Böhlau Verlag, 2002.
Rayno, Dan. *Paul Whiteman: Pioneer in American Music: Vol. I, 1890–1930.* Lanham, MD: Scarecrow Press, 2003.
Reimann, Viktor. *Innitzer: Kardinal zwischen Hitler und Rom.* Vienna: Verlag Fritz Molden, 1967.
Reumann, Miriam G. *American Sexual Character: Sex, Gender, and National Identity in the Kinsey Reports.* Oakland: University of California Press, 2005.
Riemer, Willy. "Composers, Celebrities and Cultural Memory: Walter Reisch's Musical Biopics." In *Walter Reisch: Film schreiben*, edited by Günter Krenn, 301–40. Vienna: Filmarchiv Austria, 2004.
Roberts, Kenneth L. *Europe's Morning After.* New York: Harper & Brothers, 1921.
Robinson, Harlow. *Russians in Hollywood, Hollywood's Russians: Biography of an Image.* Boston: Northeastern University Press, 2007.
Robinson, Henry Morton. *The Cardinal.* New York: Simon and Schuster, 1950.
Romani, George T. *The Neapolitan Revolution of 1820–1821.* Evanston, IL: Northwestern University Press, 1950.
"Romantic Wooing of Miss Gladys Vanderbilt." *New York Times*, October 6, 1907.
"Roosevelt Speech Hits Popular Key." *New York Times*, September 29, 1937.
Rosebault, Charles J. "Decline of Vienna, the City of Charm." *New York Times*, August 31, 1919.
———. "Fading Hopes of a Once Proud Aristocracy: How the Haughty Have Become Humble and Uncertain of Themselves in Austria—Gay Vienna Turned Into a Sad and Hungry City." *New York Times*, February 15, 1920.
Rosenberg, Emily S. "Consuming Women: Images of Americanization in the 'American Century.'" *Diplomatic History* 23, no. 3 (Summer 1999): 479–97.
———. "'Foreign Affairs' after World War II: Connecting Sexual and International Politics." *Diplomatic History.* 18, no. 1 (Winter 1994): 59–70.
"Rosenkranzfest 1938: 'Euer Führer ist Christus.'" Accessed June 21, 2018. https://www.erzdioezese-wien.at/site/glaubenfeiern/christ/unser glaube/gottesmuttermaria/marienfeste/rosenkranzmonat/article/39140.html.
Rostron, Allen. "'No War, No Hate, No Propaganda': Promoting Films about European War and Fascism during the Period of American Isolationism." *Journal of Popular Film and Television* 30, no. 2 (Summer 2002): 85–96.

Saffle, Michael. "'Do You Ever Dream of Vienna?' America's Glorification of Musical Central Europe, 1865–1965." In *Identität, Kultur, Raum. Kulturelle Pratiken und die Ausbildung von Imagined Communities in Nordamerika und Zentraleuropa*, edited by Susan Ingram, Markus Reisenleitner, and Cornelia Szabó-Knotik, 59–75. Vienna, Turia & Kant. 2001.

———. "Family Values: The Trapp Family Singers in North America, 1938–1956." *Canadian University Music Review: Revue de Musique des Universités Canadiennes* 24, no. 2 (Sommaire 2004): 62–79.

———. "From *Schlagobers* to Schoenberg: Cultural Transfer, Identity and Otherness, and Depictions of Musical Vienna in the *New York Times*, 1918–1938." In *Reverberations: Representations of Modernity, Tradition and Cultural Value in-between Central Europe and North America*, edited by Susan Ingram, Markus Reisenleitner, and Cornelia Szabó-Knotik, 63–89. Bern: Peter Lang, 2002.

———. "Traveling Tales: The Trapp Family Singers and Maria von Trapp's Post–World War II Immigration Narratives." In *Ports of Call: Central European and North American Culture/s in Motion*, edited by Susan Ingram, Markus Reisenleitner, and Cornelia Szabó-Knotik, 67–100. Bern: Peter Lang, 2003.

Santopietro, Tom. *The Sound of Music Story*. London: Bantam Press, 2015.

Schallert, Erwin. "'Once upon a Honeymoon' Ekes Fun Out of Tragedy." *Los Angeles Times*, December 26, 1942.

Schmundt-Thomas, Georg. "America's Germany: National Self and Cultural Other after World War II." PhD diss., Northwestern University, 1992.

Schneider, Gerd K. *Die Rezeption von Arthur Schnitzlers REIGEN 1897–1994: Pressespiegel und andere zeitgenössische Kommentare*. Riverside, CA: Ariadne Press, 1995.

Schneider, Thomas, and Hans Wagener, eds. *"Huns" vs. "Corned Beef": Representations of the Other in American and German Literature and Film on World War I*. Göttingen: V&R unipress Universitätsverlag Osnabrück, 2007.

Schnitzler, Arthur. *Spiel im Morgengrauen*. First published in *Berliner Illustrierte Zeitung* in 1926 and in book form: Frankfurt am Main: S. Fischer Verlag, 1927.

"Schnitzler's Plays at Madison Square." *New York Times*, January 14, 1908.

"The Screen." *New York Times*, July 2, 1923.

"The Screen in Review." *New York Times*, May 16, 1941.

Seibel, Alexandra. "Vienna, Girls, and Jewish Authorship: Topographies of a Cinematic City, 1920–1940." PhD diss., New York University, 2009.

———. *Visions of Vienna: Narrating the City in 1920s and 1930s Cinema*. Amsterdam: Amsterdam University Press, 2017.

Seidman, Steven. *Romantic Longings: Love in America, 1830–1980*. New York: Routledge, 1991.

"Senate Seizing Film Bally: Ads on 17 Pix to Be Probed." *Variety*, September 5, 1941.

Shandler, Jeffrey. *While America Watches: Televising the Holocaust.* New York: Oxford University Press, 1999.
Shandley, Robert R. *Runaway Romances: Hollywood's Postwar Tour of Europe.* Philadelphia: Temple University Press, 2009.
Shaw, Leroy R. "Modern Austrian Dramatists on the New York Stage." In *Österreich und die angelsächische Welt: Kulturbegegnungen und Vergleiche,* edited by Otto Hietsch, 547–63. Vienna: Wilhelm Braunmüller, 1968.
Sherwood, Robert Emmet. *Reunion in Vienna: A Play in Three Acts.* New York: Charles Scribner's Sons, 1932.
Shull, Michael S., and David Edward Wilt. *Hollywood War Films, 1937–1945: An Exhaustive Filmography of American Feature-Length Motion Pictures Relating to World War II.* Jefferson, NC: McFarland, 1996.
Sikov, Ed. *On Sunset Boulevard: The Life and Times of Billy Wilder.* New York: Hyperion, 1998.
Sklar, Robert. *Movie-Made America: A Social History of American Movies.* New York: Random House, 1975.
Small, Pauline. *Sophie Loren: Moulding the Star.* Bristol, UK: Intellect, 2009.
Smedley, Nick. *A Divided World: Hollywood Cinema and Émigré Directors in the Era of Roosevelt and Hitler, 1933–1948.* Bristol, UK: Intellect, 2011.
Smith, Anthony Burke. *The Look of Catholics: Portrayals in Popular Culture from the Great Depression to the Cold War.* Lawrence: University Press of Kansas, 2010.
Smith, Dina. "Sabrina, Hollywood and Postwar Internationalism." In *Billy Wilder, Movie-Maker,* edited by Karen McNally, 193–208. Jefferson, NC: McFarland, 2011.
"So Ends Our Night." *The Hollywood Reporter,* January 22, 1941.
"So Ends Our Night." *Variety,* January 22, 1941.
"The Sound of Music Tour." Accessed on June 21, 2018. https://www.salzburg.info/en/hotels-offers/guided-tours/the-sound-of-music-tour.
Spaulding, E. Wilder. *The Quiet Invaders: The Story of the Austrian Impact upon America.* Vienna: Österreichischer Bundesverlag für Unterricht, Wissenschaft und Kunst, 1968.
Spieker, Markus. *Hollywood unterm Hakenkreuz: Der amerikanische Spielfilm im Dritten Reich.* Trier: Wissenschaftlicher Verlag Trier, 1999.
Stadler, Karl R. *Austria.* New York: Praeger, 1971.
"The Stage Show: A Review of the New Pictures." *Photoplay Magazine* 24 (September 1923): 64.
"The Stage Society Offers Two Plays." *New York Times,* November 10, 1913.
Starr, Jimmy. "'So Ends our Night' Another Drama of Nazi Terror." *Los Angeles Evening Herald and Express,* January 22, 1941.
Steffen-Fluhr, Nancy. "Palimpsest: The Double Vision of Exile." In *Billy Wilder, Movie-Maker: Critical Essays on the Films,* edited by Karen McNally, 178–92. Jefferson, NC: McFarland, 2011.
Steininger, Rolf, Günter Bischof, and Michael Geyer, eds. *Austria in the Twentieth Century.* New Brunswick, NJ: Transaction Publishers, 2002.

Stelzer, Manfred. *The Constitution of the Republic of Austria: A Contextual Analysis.* Oxford: Hart Publishing, 2011.
Stevens, Laura. "Christoph Waltz's Oscar Spurs Debate: Austrian or German?" *Wall Street Journal Blog.* Accessed on June 30, 2018. https://blogs.wsj.com/speakeasy/2013/02/25/christoph-waltzs-oscar-spurs-debate-austrian-or-german/.
Stowe, William W. *Going Abroad: European Travel in Nineteenth-Century American Culture.* Princeton: Princeton University Press, 1994.
Strada, Michael J., and Harold R. Troper. *Friend or Foe? Russians in American Film and Foreign Policy, 1933–1991.* Lanham, MD: Scarecrow Press, 1997.
Strasser, Christian. *The Sound of Klein-Hollywood: Filmproduktion in Salzburg—Salzburg im Film.* Vienna: Österreichischer Kunst- und Kulturverlag, 1993.
Stroheim, Erich von. "The 'Hated Hun'—Then and Now." *New York Times,* February 9, 1941.
———. "*The* Vienna *of* von Stroheim. It Was—It Is Not Now—A City of Romance and Pageantry and Waltzing." As told by Eric [*sic*] Von [*sic*] Stroheim to Dorothy Calhoun. *Motion Picture Classic,* April 1930.
"Summer Musicals." *Life Magazine,* June 12, 1948.
T.S. "The Screen." *New York Times,* February 2, 1942.
Tatar, Maria. "'We Meet Again, Fräulein': Hollywood's Fascination with Fascism." *German Politics and Society* 13, no. 3 (1995): 190–98.
Taylor, John Russell. *Strangers in Paradise. The Hollywood Émigrés, 1933–1950.* New York: Holt, Rinehart, and Winston, 1983.
"Text of Schuschnigg's Speech of his Resignation." *Los Angeles Times,* March 12, 1938.
"'They Dare Not Love' Only Fair War Refugee Story: Roles Unworthy of Scott and Brent." *The Hollywood Reporter,* April 29, 1941.
Thomas, Lowell. *So Long Until Tomorrow. From Quaker Hill to Kathmandu.* New York: William Morrow, 1977.
Thompson, Dorothy. "Introduction." In *My Austria* by Kurt Schuschnigg, v–xxv. New York: Alfred A. Knopf, 1938.
Thompson, Kristin. "The Rise and Fall of Film Europe." In: *"Film Europe" and "Film America,"* edited by Andrew Higson and Richard Maltby, 56–81. Chicago: University of Chicago Press, 1999.
Tibbetts, John C. *Composers in the Movies: Studies in Musical Biography.* New Haven: Yale University Press, 2005.
———. "'An Unruly Completeness': Fritz Lehner's *Mit meinen heißen Tränen.*" In *Floodgates. Technologies, Cultural (Ex)Change and the Persistence of Place,* edited by Susan Ingram, Markus Reisenleitner, and Cornelia Szabó-Knotik, 77–106. Bern: Peter Lang, 2006.
Torpey, John. *The Invention of the Passport: Surveillance, Citizenship and the State.* Cambridge: Cambridge University Press, 2000.
"Die Trapp Familie—Realität und 'Sound of Music.'" Salzburg Museum. Accessed on June 30, 2018. http:/www.salzburgmuseum.at/index.php?id=trappfamilie.

Traubner, Richard. *Operetta: A Theatrical History*. London: Routledge, 2003.
Tunstall, Jr., Graydon A. "Austria-Hungary." In *The Origins of World War I*, edited by Richard F. Hamilton and Holger H. Herwig, 112–49. Cambridge: Cambridge University Press, 2003.
Ulrich, Rudolf. *Österreicher in Hollywood*. Vienna: Verlag Film Archiv Austria, 2004.
U.S. Residents Travel to Europe. Washington, DC: US Department of Commerce, International Trade Administration. For a sample of travel statistics refer to these yearly reports:
2011 U.S. Residents Travel to Europe. Accessed on June 26, 2018. http://tinet.ita.doc.gov/outreachpages/download_data_table/2011_US_Travel_Abroad.pdf.
2013 U.S. Residents Travel to Europe. Accessed on June 26, 2018. https://travel.trade.gov/outreachpages/download_data_table/2013-US-to-Europe.pdf.
2014 U.S. Residents Travel to Europe. Accessed on June 26, 2018. https://travel.trade.gov/outreachpages/download_data_table/2014-US-to-Europe.pdf.
2015 U.S. Resident Travel Abroad. Accessed on June 26, 2018. https://travel.trade.gov/outreachpages/download_data_table/2015_US_Travel_Abroad.pdf.
Urwand, Ben. *The Collaboration: Hollywood's Pact with Hitler*. Cambridge, MA: Belknap Press of Harvard University, 2013.
Vansant, Jacqueline. "Austria and Dustbowl Refugees Unite in *Three Faces West* (1940)." *Journal of Austrian-American History* 1 (2017): 98–116.
———. "'Harry Lime und Maria von Trapp treffen sich am Stammtisch': Die Entnazifizierung Österreichs in amerikanischen Filmen." In *The Sound of Austria*, edited by John Bunzl, 169–84. Vienna: Braumüller, 1995.
———. "Hollywoods 'Wien' als transnationaler Gedächtnisort." In *Jenseits von Grenzen. Transnationales, translokales Gedächtnis*, edited by Moritz Csáky and Elisabeth Großegger, 183–96. Vienna: Präsens Verlag, 2007.
———. "Österreichbilder im amerikanischen Film nach 1945." In *Das ist Österreich: Innen- und Außensichten*, edited by Ursula Prutsch and Manfred Lechner, 287–310. Vienna: Döcker Verlag, 1997.
———. "Political and Humanitarian Messages in a Horse's Tale: MGM's *Florian*." *Austrian History Yearbook* 42 (2011): 164–84.
———. "Robert Wise's *The Sound of Music* and the 'Denazification' of Austria in American Cinema." In *From World War to Waldheim: Politics and Culture in Austria and the United States*, edited by David Good and Ruth Wodak, 165–86. New York: Berghahn, 1999.
Vasey, Ruth. *The World According to Hollywood, 1918–1939*. Madison: University of Wisconsin Press: 1997.
A Veteran Diplomat [Frederick Cunliffe-Owen]. "What Austria's Change Will Mean to Europe." *New York Times*, June 28, 1908.
———. "Where Americans Lose Caste." *New York Times*, July 18, 1909.

"Vienna Is Alarmed by Inroads of Jazz." *New York Times*, April 15, 1928.
"Vienna Lives Again." *New York Times*, February 5, 1928.
"Vienna Makes Director Unhappy." *New York Times*, October 12, 1930.
"Vienna Mob Storms Cardinal Innitzer's Home: He Is Reported Injured." *New York Times*, October 9, 1938.
"Vienna Welcomes Paul Whiteman." *New York Times*, June 12, 1926.
"Vienna's Catholics Urged to Show Faith." *New York Times*, October 8, 1938.
"Vienna's Milder Socialists." *New York Times*, November 3, 1926.
"Von Stroheim tells of Making *The Wedding March*." *Hollywood Filmograph*, April 7, 1928.
Wagnleitner, Reinhold. *Coca-Colonization and the Cold War: The Cultural Mission of the United States in Austria after the Second World War*. Translated by Diana M. Wolf. Chapel Hill: University of North Carolina Press, 1994.
———. "The Empire of the Fun, or Talkin' Soviet Union Blues: The Sound of Freedom and U.S. Cultural Hegemony in Europe." *Diplomatic History* 23, no. 2 (Summer 1999): 499–524.
Waldman, Harry. *Nazi Films in America, 1933–1942*. Jefferson, NC: McFarland, 2008.
Wall, Wendy L. *Inventing the "American Way": The Politics of Consensus from the New Deal to the Civil Rights Movement*. Oxford: Oxford University Press, 2008.
Walton, William. "Foreign News: Austria." *Time Magazine*, August 13, 1945.
Weaver, Tom. *Attack of the Monster Movie Makers: Interviews with 20 Genre Giants*. Jefferson, NC: McFarland, 1994.
Weaver, William R. "*So Ends Our Night*: Plight of the Refugees." *Motion Picture Herald*, January 25, 1941.
Wechsberg, Joseph. *The Waltz Emperors: The Life and Times and Music of the Strauss Family*. London: Weidenfeld & Nicholson, 1973.
Weinberg, Herman G. *The Complete Wedding March of Erich von Stroheim*. Boston: Little, Brown, 1974.
Welky, David. *The Moguls and the Dictators: Hollywood and the Coming of World War II*. Baltimore: Johns Hopkins University Press, 2008.
White, Kevin. "The New Man and Early Twentieth-Century Emotional Culture in the United States." In *An Emotional History of the United States*, edited by Peter N. Stearns and Jan Lewis, 333–56. New York: New York University Press, 1998.
Wilk, Max. *The Making of The Sound of Music*. New York: Routledge, 2007.
Williams, Wythe. "10,000 Troops Hold Socialists and Foes in Check in Austria." *New York Times*, October 8, 1928.
Winterer, Matthias Paul. "Das Österreichbild im US-amerikanischen Anti-Nazi-Film bis 1945." MA thesis, University of Vienna, 2013.
Withey, Lynne. *Grand Tours and Cook's Tours: A History of Leisure Travel, 1750–1915*. New York: William Morrow. 1997.

Wohl, R. Richard, and Anselm L. Strauss. "Symbolic Representations and the Urban Milieu." *The American Journal of Sociology* 63, no. 5 (March 1958): 523–32.

Wolman, Ruth E. *Crossing Over: An Oral History of Refugees from Hitler's Reich*. New York: Twayne Publishers, 1996.

Wood, Robin. *Sexual Politics and Narration: Hollywood and Beyond*. New York: Columbia University Press, 1998.

Wylie, I. A. R. "Widow's Evening." *The Delineator*, June 1931.

Wyman, David S. *Paper Walls: America and the Refugee Crisis 1938–1941*. Amherst: University of Massachusetts Press, 1968.

Ybarra, T. R. "Ancient Vienna Lives in a New World." *New York Times*, October 23, 1927.

———. "Old Hapsburg Tragedy Explained by Diplomat." *New York Times*, November 25, 1928.

———. "Vienna Riot Dead Buried in One Grave." *New York Times*, July 21, 1927.

Zacharasiewicz, Waldemar. "The Image of Austria in the United States." In *Austria's Image in the United States*, 35–49. Vienna: Diplomatische Akademie, 2000.

Zahn, Alf-Tobias. "*Image Austria*—Die Darstellung Österreichs in US-amerikanischen Filmproduktion nach 1945." MA thesis, University of Vienna, 2009.

Zernatto, Guido. *Die Wahrheit über Österreich*. New York: Longmans, Green and Co., 1939.

Index

Above Suspicion (Thorpe), 14, 17, 160n7
Almost Angels (Previn), 16
Alpers, Benjamin L., 122
Amadeus (Forman), 17
Andrews, Julie, 123
Anschluss, 21–22, 69–71; in films, 94, 95–112, 113–30, 162n27
anti-Semitism, 3, 5, 16, 22, 69, 92, 115, 118; Stroheim's experience of, 147n14
Arthur, Jean, 58
Asther, Nils, 84
Austria: American ideas of, 7–8, 12, 16, 18–19, 27, 31–32, 39, 59, 70, 131, 147n25, 166n12; American vs. Austrian mores, 6, 28, 40, 42, 63–65; anti-American attitudes in, 40, 55, 57–58; aristocracy of, 4, 7–8, 10, 12–13, 20, 23–38, 45–46, 143n25; during Nazi era, 1, 4, 14, 16, 21–22, 47–48, 60 (*see also* Anschluss); gender of, 47, 54; musical heritage of, 84–89, 127–28, 131, 158n58; political and cultural history of, 3–4, 21, 36–37, 39, 77–80, 106–7, 160n8; recent scholarship on, 145n48; as spy haven, 17; as travel destination, 7, 113, 129, 132–33; victim status of, 4, 13, 97, 99, 101–3, 108, 111–12, 114, 123–24, 126

Bach, David Joseph, 47, 150n13
Barnova, Irina, 92
Basinger, Jeanine, 40
Baum, Vicki, 73, 75
Beethoven, Ludwig van, 16, 17, 26, 49
Before Sunrise (Linklater), 18, 149n1

Berger, Ludwig, 4, 13
Bernstein, Felix, 69–70, 157n30
Bernstein, Walter, 63, 65
Bing, Herman, 48
Bitter Sweet (Van Dyke), 14, 155n14
blacklisting, 65, 122, 153n50
Blind Husbands (Stroheim), 19, 32
Blossom Time (Stein), 156n15
Blue Danube, The (Sloane), 8
"Blue Danube Waltz, The." *See* Strauss, Johann, II
Boland, Mary, 40, 43
Bolshevism, 3, 73, 81, 117, 141n6
Borah, William E., 69, 96, 154n6
Bowman, Lee, 92
Boym, Sventlana, 24
Brackett, Charles, 55–59
Breath of Scandal, A (Curtiz), 15–16, 20–21, 39–40, 54, 61–67, 153n37 153n40
Brecher, Egon, 100
Brent, George, 100
Bryce Report, 154n1
Burger, Neil, 17–18

Calhoun, Dorothy, 34, 35
Cardinal, The (Preminger), 15, 22, 113–23, 127, 129–30, 149n1
Carroll, John, 122
Case of Lena Smith, The (Sternberg), 6–7, 10–11, 150n3
Castelli, Jean-Christoph, 18
Chamberlain, Neville, 80
Champagne Waltz (Sutherland), 20–21, 39–40, 47–54, 67, 84, 90, 150n14, 151n16, 151n19
Chevalier, Maurice, 66, 84
Clark, Bennett Champ, 95
Coburn, Charles, 92

Cold War, 17, 21, 39–40, 61–62, 65, 67, 114, 144n35, 153n50
Confessions of a Nazi Spy (Litvak), 156n20
Corson, John W., 84
Coward, Noel, 14
Crimson Runner, The (Forman), 12, 36, 150n4
Crosby, Bing, 55, 56, 58
Crowther, Bosley, 94, 119
Curtiz, Michael, 5, 15

Dassanowsky, Robert, 165n38
Daybreak (Feyder), 12
De Mille, Cecil B., 2, 23
Dee, Frances, 98
Dickens, Charles, 82
Dieterle, William, 5
Dietrich, Marlene, 58, 150n3
Dishonored (Sternberg), 12, 150n3
Dodsworth (Wyler), 149n1
Dollfuss, Engelbert, 106
Dozier, William, 7
Dreier, Hans, 151n19
Dreimäderlhaus, Das (pastiche operetta), 71, 156n15
Dupont, E. A., 5
Durbin, Deanna, 14, 151n19, 155n12
Dyer, Richard, 126, 164n35

Elsaesser, Thomas, 142n15, 147n15
Emperor Waltz, The (Wilder), 14, 20–21, 39–40, 54–61, 67, 152n36
Enemy, The (Niblo), 11
Escapade (Leonard), 5–6
European stereotypes, 2, 6, 13, 34, 39, 131, 134
Evenings for Sale (Walker), 13, 20–21, 38, 39–47, 67
Expensive Husbands (Connolly), 149n1
Eyes Wide Shut (Kubrick), 133

Fegté, Ernst, 151n19
Ferdinand I (of Austria), 73
Ferdinand I (Naples and Sicily), 83, 158n50
Fielding, Raymond, 105, 162n27
Firebird, The (Dieterle), 20, 131

Florian (Marin), 14, 21, 38, 70, 71, 75–82, 83, 89–94, 155n11, 155n14; music in, 158n58
Fontaine, Joan, 7, 55, 56
Ford, Glenn, 98
Foreign Affair, A (Wilder), 58, 66, 153n52
Forst, Willi, 5–6
Franz I, 82–83
Franz Ferdinand, 79–80, 143n25
Franz Josef I, 3, 4, 6, 7, 13, 14, 18, 31, 72–74, 143n25, 147n25, 156n23; in *A Breath of Scandal*, 55, 62–63; in *Champagne Waltz*, 50, 151n16; in *The Emperor Waltz*, 55, 58; in *Florian*, 72, 77–80; in *The Great Waltz*, 70, 72–75; in *Merry-Go-Round*, 32; Stroheim and, 23, 33, 36; in *They Dare Not Love*, 105
Freud (Huston), 15
Freud, Sigmund, 15, 16
Freund, Karl, 157n30
Frey, Stefan, 54
Frisby, David, 142n9

Gavin, John, 62
Gedye, G. E. R., 84
George, Maude, 148n31
Gigi (Minnelli), 16
Gilbert, Helen, 92
Girosi, Marcello, 62–63, 65
Grafe, Frieda, 6–7, 23
Grand Budapest Hotel, The (Anderson), 133
Grant, Cary, 108
Great Depression, 12–13, 39–40, 44–46
Great Waltz, The (Duvivier), 13, 21, 70–76, 83, 84–87, 88, 94, 104, 155n11
Great Waltz, The (Stone), 16
Greater Glory, The (Rehfeld), 12, 36, 150n4
Griffith, D. W., 23
Gruenberg, Louis, 99
Guardsman, The (Franklin), 20

Gyory, Nicholas, 75, 77–78, 79, 157n32

Hake, Sabine, 71
Hammerstein, Oscar, II, 13
Hanson, Philip, 44
Haydn, Joseph, 26, 60
Haydn, Richard, 55
Her Private Affair (Stein), 20
Her Sister from Paris (Franklin), 19–20, 144n28
Herczeg, Géza, 157n30
Herzog, Todd, 166n9
Herzogin von Chicago, Die (operetta), 53–54
Higson, Andrew, and Richard Maltby, 141n4
Hirsch, Foster, 116, 119
His Glorious Night (Barrymore), 8, 10, 55, 144n28, 152n22
Hitler, Adolf, 4, 5, 21, 69–70, 72, 73, 75–76, 78, 95, 97, 105–7, 162nn29–30; in *The Cardinal*, 116–21; music and, 84; in *Once upon a Honeymoon*, 109–11; in *The Sound of Music*, 126; in *The Strange Death of Adolf Hitler*, 14
Hofer, Andreas, 104, 162n26
Hoffenstein, Samuel, 73
Hoffmann, Robert, 124
Hollander, Frederick, 151n19
Hollywood Anti-Nazi League, 75, 155n7
Holocaust, 60–61, 114
Hope, Anthony, 147n24, 148n26
Hopscotch (Neame), 17
Horak, Jan-Christopher, 5–6, 70, 96–97, 155n12, 156n23, 161n20
Hotel Imperial (Flory), 13
Hotel Imperial (Stiller), 11
HUAC (House Un-American Activities Committee), 15, 153n50
Huneker, James, 143n26

Illusionist, The (Burger), 17–18
immigration issues, 22, 39, 47, 71, 79, 92–93, 96–97, 132, 155n9, 155n70

Immortal Beloved (Rose), 17
Innitzer, Theodor, 115, 116–21, 129, 163n20

Jacobs, Lea, 144n28
James, Edwin L., 37, 150n8
jazz, 39, 47–54, 67, 150n14
Jeritza, Maria, 75
Jewel Robbery (Dieterle), 20
Julia (Zinnemann), 16

Kálmán, Emmerich, 53–54
Karl I, 106, 143n25
Kästner, Erich, 20, 132
Kaus, Gina, 15
Kennedy, David H., 92
Kennedy, John F., 114
Kerry, Norman, 27
King Steps Out, The (Sternberg), 13, 38, 72
Kinsey Report, 62, 65
Kiss in the Mirror, The (Whale), 20
Klimt, Gustav, and Adele Bloch-Bauer, 133–34
Koretz, Paul, 70
Koster, Henry, 151n19, 155n12
Koszarski, Richard, 23, 31
Kracauer, Siegfried, 3, 4, 18, 24, 34, 132
Kreisky, Bruno, 124

Lansbury, Angela, 64
Lardner, Ring, Jr., 65
Lasch, Christopher, 24, 33, 34
Lavery, Emmett, 115–16
Leab, David J., 154n1
Lehman, Ernest, 123–27, 164n31
Lenning, Arthur, 23, 146n6, 148n29
Letter from an Unknown Woman (Ophuls), 7, 15
Liebelei (Ophuls), 7
Linaker, Kay, 104
Lipp, Wilma, 120
Living Daylights, The (Glen), 17
Loren, Sophia, 16, 62, 153n40
Love Me and the World Is Mine (Dupont), 8, 10, 24–25
Love Time (Tinling), 84, 156n15

Lubitsch, Ernst, 5, 101
Lukas, Paul, 104
Lund, John, 58

MacInnes, Helen, 14, 17
MacMurray, Fred, 47
Magnificent Rebel, The (Tressler), 16
March, Fredric, 98
March of Time featurettes, 71–72, 162n29; on the Anschluss, 101, 105–7, 162n29
Maritza, Sari, 44
Marriage Circle, The (Lubitsch), 19, 131, 144n28
Marshall, Bruce, 15
Marshall, Herbert, 40, 43
Maskarade (Forst), 5–6
Mata Hari (Fitzmaurice), 12
May, Elaine Tyler, 63, 65
Mayer, Louis B., 6
McCormick, Anne O'Hare, 36
McCord, Ted, 123, 164n34
Meinrad, Josef, 117
Merry Widow, The (operetta), 40, 150n28
Merry-Go-Round (Stroheim and Julian), 1, 8, 19, 23, 25–27, 30, 32–33, 72, 146nn5–6
Metro-Goldwyn-Mayer (MGM), 5, 6, 15, 55, 69–70, 72–73, 92, 95
Metternich, Klemens von, 72, 74, 83, 158n50
Millhauser, Steven, 17
Miracle of the White Stallions (Hiller), 16
Mission Impossible: Rogue Nation (McQuarrie), 17
Mission to Moscow (Curtiz), 141n6
Molnár, Ferenc, 10, 54
Moore, Michaela Hoenicke, 69
Motion Picture Production Code, 12, 62, 154n5
Mozart, Wolfgang Amadeus, 17, 26, 49, 71, 120
Murrow, Edward, 95
Museum Hours (Cohen), 133, 166n9
Mussolini, Benito, 106, 116, 162n29

National Socialism (Nazism), 1, 4, 13, 14, 16, 21–22, 39–40, 55, 57, 60–61, 113; anti-individualism of, 77; Hollywood reluctance to produce anti-Nazi films, 69–70, 95, 96–97, 155n7; in newsreels, 71–72. *See also* Anschluss
Navarro, Ramon, 84
New Wine (Schunzel), 14, 21, 70–71, 82–83, 84, 87–89, 94, 155n11
newsreels, 95, 97, 99, 102, 109, 111, 116–17; in *The Sound of Music*, 126–27. *See also March of Time* featurettes
Night Is Young, The (Murphy), 13, 38, 72, 84
Night Life (Archainbaud), 12, 36, 150n4
nostalgia, 12–13, 20, 24–27, 33–35, 37, 78, 94
Nugent, Frank, 53, 94
Nye, Gerald, 95

Oakie, Jack, 48
Olympia (play), 54–55, 61, 152n22, 153n37
Once upon a Honeymoon (McCarey), 14, 21, 97, 108–12, 113, 149n1, 160n7
Ophuls, Max, 5, 7, 14–15, 134
Ornitz, Samuel, 7
O'Shaughnessy, Edith, 12, 36
Otto von Habsburg, 97, 101, 106, 107–8, 162n29
Owen, Reginald, 92

Paradise for Three (Buzzell), 19, 20, 132
Paramount Decision, 15
Paramount Pictures, 39, 53, 55, 66, 95, 151n19
Pasternak, Joseph, 151n19, 155n12
Peacemaker, The (Leder), 17
Phelps, Nicole M., 148n25
Pius XI, 164n27
Podhajsky, Alois, 16
Pollock, Channing, 11
Ponti, Carlo, 62

Powers, Pat, 28
Preminger, Otto, 22, 113–16, 129; on filming in Vienna, 165n46; on totalitarianism, 121–23, 164n28

Rainer, Luise, 5–6
Red Danube, The (Sidney), 15, 144n35
Red Sparrow (Lawrence), 145n38
Reinhardt, Gottfried, 73, 75
Reisch, Walter, 5, 73
Remarque, Erich Maria, 98
Reumann, Miriam G., 62, 66
Reunion in Vienna (Franklin), 13, 72, 144n32
Richlavie, George, 157n30
Richter, Hannes, 134
Roberts, Kenneth L., 36
Robinson, Harlow, 141n6, 144n35
Robinson, Henry Morton, 113, 115
Rogers, Ginger, 108
Romberg, Sigmund, 13
Ronde, La (Ophuls), 7
Roosevelt, Franklin D., 96, 141n6, 156n23, 162n36
Rosebault, Charles J., 24, 31–32, 37, 143n25, 144n26
Rosenberg, Emily S., 153n52

Sakall, S. Z. (Szakáll, Szöke), 92, 157n30
Salten, Felix, 70, 75
Salzburg, 1, 17, 124, 126–27, 129
Salzburg Connection, The (Katzin), 17, 149n1
Satori, William, 69
Schmundt-Thomas, Georg, 58, 145n44
Schneider, Romy, 115
Schnitzler, Arthur, 7–8, 12, 32, 133, 144n27
Schubert, Franz, 4, 14, 26, 49, 84–85, 156n15; in *New Wine*, 70–71, 82–83, 87–89, 94
Schuschnigg, Kurt, 77, 96, 102–4, 106–7, 124, 162n30
Schwarzenegger, Arnold, 134
Scorpio (Winner), 17
Scott, Martha, 100

Seastrom, Victor, 5
Seibel, Alexandra, 145n48, 146n5, 147n14, 147n19
Selznick, David O., 19
Serenade (d'Abbadie d'Arrast), 20, 150n3
Seven-Per-Cent Solution, The (Ross), 16
Seyss-Inquart, Arthur, 107, 110
Shandley, Robert R., 15
Sheehan, Winfield, 75, 78, 93
Shull, Michael S., and David Edward Wilt, 155n14
Sissy (operetta), 13, 156n22
Sklar, Robert, 2
Slezak, Walter, 108
Smiling Lieutenant, The (Lubitsch), 13, 84, 150n3
So Ends Our Night (Cromwell), 14, 21, 94, 95, 97–100, 109, 111–12, 113, 160n5
Sound of Music, The (Wise), 1, 16, 17, 22, 108, 113–15, 123–30, 165n38; Broadway musical version of, 113, 124; German version of, 126, 165n39; persistent popularity of, 134
Soviet Union, Hollywood representations of, 3, 132 141n6, 144n35
Spaulding, E. Wilder, 132
Spectre (Mendes), 17
Spring Parade (Koster), 13–14, 155n12, 156n23
Spy Who Dumped Me, The (Fogel), 145n38
Stein, Paul L., 5
Sternberg, Josef von, 5, 6–7
Stiller, Mauritz, 5
Stowe, William W., 40
Strange Death of Adolf Hitler, The (Hogan), 14, 160n7
Straus, Oscar, 4
Strauss, Johann, 4, 48, 84, 85, 157n28
Strauss, Johann, II, 13, 48, 84, 104, 157n28, 158n55, 159n59; "The Blue Danube Waltz," 41, 50, 74, 84, 86–87, 159n59; in *The Great Waltz*, 16, 70–75, 88–89

Stroheim, Erich von, 5, 6, 20, 23–38, 46, 148n29; in *So Ends Our Night*, 99
Sullavan, Margaret, 98
Swarthout, Gladys, 47, 84
Szekely, William, 70

Thalberg, Irving, 146n6
They Dare Not Love (Whale and Fleming), 14, 21, 38, 94, 95, 97, 100–108, 109, 111–12, 113, 124, 160n5; director question over, 161n23
Third Man, The (Reed), 15, 19
Thompson, Dorothy, 96
Thompson, Kristin, 141n4
360 (Meirelles), 133
Titled Americans (book), 31, 148n27
To Be or Not to Be (Lubitsch), 162n33
Trapp, Maria von, and family, 1, 22, 114–15, 123, 129–30
Tryon, Tom, 115
Twentieth Century-Fox, 16, 69–70, 95, 126

Unfinished Symphony (Forst), 156n15
United Artists, 98

Vajda, Ernst, 101, 161n24
Vanderbilt, Gladys, 148n26
Vienna: American notions of, 7, 84, 142n9, 143n26; Filmfond Wien, 18; musical reputation of, 7, 84; popularity in films, 4, 6, 15, 19–20; recent celebrations of, 133–34; talent pool in, 6; von Stroheim and, 23–38; Wien-Film, 71
Vienna Boys Choir, 16

Wagnleitner, Reinhold, 152n30

Walt Disney Pictures, 16
Waltz, Christoph, 17, 135
Waltz King, The (Previn), 16
Walzer aus Wein (operetta), 70
Warner Brothers, 70
Waxman, Franz, 157n30, 158n58
Wedding March, The (Stroheim), 8, 23, 25–30, 32–33, 72, 146nn5–6, 150n3; Corpus Christi procession in, 28–29, 43, 147n19; Iron Man in, 26, 35–36, 147n14
Whiteman, Paul, 53
Wilder, Billy, 5, 14, 53, 55–61, 151n19, 152n33
Wise, Robert, 22, 113–14, 123–24, 127, 129–30
Woman Disputed, The (King and Taylor), 11, 144n28
Woman in Gold (Curtis), 133
Woman of Experience, A (Brown), 12
woman's film genre, 40
Wray, Fay, 26
Wyler, William, 127
Wylie, I. A. R., 45
Wymetal, William von, 157n30
Wyszyński, Stefan, 116, 121

Young, Robert, 92

Zacharasiewicz, Waldemar, 166n12
Zanuck, Darryl, 126
Zanuck, Richard, 126
Zell, Carl, and S. Walter Fischer, 4, 142n10, 147n19
Zernatto, Guido, 77–78, 103
Ziehrer, Carl Michael, 7, 158n57
Zinnemann, Fred, 16, 144n37
Zuberano, Maurice, 126–27
Zweig, Stefan, 14–15, 133

www.ingramcontent.com/pod-product-compliance
Lightning Source LLC
Chambersburg PA
CBHW070805230426
43665CB00017B/2496